"WHAT'S YOUR BEST PRICE?"

Henry Purnie

Cover and Illustrations
by
Edward Graystone

Pur-Plex Press
25 N. Ocean Blvd.
Pompano Beach, Florida 33062

Catalog Card Number 97-092340

ISBN 0-9659762-0-3

©1997 Henry Purnie

ACKNOWLEDGMENTS

The wonder of it all is that those who have assisted me with this book have endured and are still with me. To them I am truly thankful and that our relationships, threatened at times, are still as strong.

During those four, long hot summers I worked on my project, they stood by me, making it all worthwhile. Would I have done the same for them?

Most of all, I am indebted to my sister, Edith Quave, an artist and writer, who prevailed during long spells of editing and agonizing over my thoughts and words as fast as I could dump the rudiments of each chapter into her lap. But she is family and blood triumphed!

Despite the task's intrusion into our leisure time, my best and dearest friend of many years, Jane Hyatt, initially urged and prompted me ever forward. However, during the last few weeks of its completion in the boondocks of upstate New York, time fell heavily upon us and things became testy as I selfishly kept busy. However, we survived this nicely.

From my life-time friend Ted Graystone I appreciate most his artistic interpretation of my story. By his exceptional talents at the drawing board for the book's cover and chapter illustrations, he masterfully rendered his skills on ideas I had only roughly sketched. As a successful artist whose life-long career had enhanced innumerable commercial projects, I was extremely fortunate to gain his expertise and enthusiasm in a work I found informative and humorous as it took me on a light journey into the world of antiques and to all those individuals associated with us.

Many thanks to Arlene Caire, who with me had opened my antique shop in Florida, and endured thousands of requests for "What's your best price?", including all the antics that go into making up the antique profession. We both learned a lot as we tangoed with the dealers and the public these many years.

I wish to express a special note of gratitude to my nephew, Michael Tiss, who, for the first time, visited my antique shop at Christmas for a well-deserved vacation. Instead, he left town with a copy of my manuscript, rendering it a last minute input. He didn't know what he was getting into!

Finally, I wish to thank all my friends and acquaintances— dealers and private individuals—who by their presence made my work days more adventurous. Some names are real, others fictitious, and I will consider this book a success if any of them can identify or associate themselves with the characters and episodes that are presented in this narration.

The Making Of An
Antique Dealer

CONTENTS

PART TWO: Bric-A-Brac

PART THREE:
Walking Canes And Hurricanes

PROLOGUE

Antique dealers have one thing in common—they have unique stories to tell. Their most impressive tales usually involve the acquisition—or loss—of something they can never forget. Recalling this, their eyes either shine brilliantly or their hearts sink in despair. Some will eagerly spill out their adventures at the slightest opportunity, while others reveal little or nothing.

One thing is certain—since exhibiting at my first antique show in New York City in 1946, through my years of canvassing from door-to-door buying old gold and jewelry all over the country right up to the Miami Beach Convention Center Antiques Show in 1997, I've experienced just about all the action the antique business has to offer. Its most obvious feature is its immense popularity and expansion through the years. There are more antique dealers, shops, galleries and shows than ever.

From my antique shop in Pompano Beach, Florida, where we have been located for ten years, we have become daily spectators and perpetrators of this increased interest between the antique dealers and the general public. To us, more fascinating than the endless tales we dealers can tell individually, are the many characters behind the events.

The constant antics, shenanigans, dealings and colorful encounters that exist between the buyers and the sellers can be intriguing, amusing, economically rewarding, disastrous or delightful, but seldom dull in their pursuit of the trivial or the treasured.

An antique shop or gallery leaves its doors open to a public that seemingly never runs out of questions, remarks or opinions, often with surprising variations. However, there are inquiries that the antique shop owner hears every day that dulls anyone's senses, yet they are a part of what comes with the territory. A few of them:

First customer: "How old does something have to be . . . to be an antique?"

Dealer's reply: "At least 100 years old."

Customer: "Oh! I'm 86. How much am I worth?" (Chuckling happily.)

Dealer: "You're very valuable, I'm sure, but not quite old enough. Come back later!"

Second customer, young and effervescent: "Wow! Where do you get all this stuff? Estates and that?"

Dealer: "Yes!"

Young customer: "Imagine! If only some of these things could talk. All those dead people!"

Third customer, walking about the shop in awe: "My grandmother had so much of this. I don't know where it all went. Imagine!"

Dealer: Rolling his eyes: "Really?"

Customer: "Heavens! I can't believe I have a cut glass pitcher just like that. How much is it?"

Dealer: "$150."

Customer: "No kidding! That much? I'd better start using mine."

Much of our business is done with dealers. A pretty female dealer enters and asks: "Anything in Art-Deco?"

Shop owner: "At the moment, only me!"

Another well-known antique dealer enters and after intense haggling over the price of several items, asks: "Now, if I buy all of these, what's your very best price?"

Shop owner: "Add 10 per-cent for D.A.!"

Dealer, looking up instantly: "What's that?"

Shop owner: "Dealer aggravation!"

Another regular dealer enters the store, back from exhibiting at an antique show the previous week, walks about the shop slowly.

Shop owner: "How was the show?"

Dealer, grimacing and shrugging his shoulders: "So-so—a lot of the dealers were complaining. The guy next to me said he didn't make his booth rent. I did OK, I guess." He saunters about, peering into cases, asks: "Anything in Tiffany or Cartier?"

Games? Nonsense? Why not? The antique business is a game, from the highest levels—museums included—to the most prestigious cosmopolitan Antique Fair—to the Saturday morning Flea Market. The antiques remain the same, but the people, the buyers and the sellers, are the forces which create all the fables, legends and fascination that revolves about them.

Most antique dealers love the business! They can all remember how they got started. And what kept them going. Myself included!

The characters involved here are a mosaic of dealers and the public; the reader may identify his or herself with any of them and the events depicted.

This is also an attempt to answer some of the many varied inquiries—logical or zany—from all who enter an antique shop.

Others may open new doors and explore the crazy and marvelous world of antiques—not the merchandise—but the people involved.

Part I

The Making
of an
Antique Dealer

Casket Case

CHAPTER 1

Many years ago, one of my best friends married into a family of antique dealers. They were pioneers in the post World War II boom in antiques. In the early 1950's, when they opened their antique shop, it was quite a novelty. They were among an elite group who had long perceived the value of artistic objects that were made during the 19th century and earlier.

Because many Americans were eager to update their homes after the Depression, and following that war, they were in an excellent position to purchase things that were now considered "too old-fashioned." Lamps, furniture, rugs, silver, paintings, china, jewelry, crystal, etc., were often bought cheaply and transformed into "antiques." The dealers had fun and made a profit in buying what someone else no longer wanted. They then sold these items to others who had an eye to the future and appreciated them for their age and beauty.

The couple became extremely knowledgeable and were foremost in their pursuit and sale of antiques in their area. Thirty years later, they sat back and enjoyed their large and well-stocked shop and smiled complacently as new dealers rushed into the business.

They had a head start, so to speak, and were well established in their community. They were remarkably adept at buying antiques. Even when prices soared in the coming decades, they stuck to their most sacred principle: If you buy something right—that is—as cheaply as possible,—it's half-sold.

They thrived on that adage, and very often when other dealers found themselves trying to sell them some antiques, they came away mumbling something like: "How cheap can you get?" When the word of this got around, they considered it a compliment and substituted the word "shrewd" for "cheap" and lived happily ever after. Besides, they were among the early dealers and looked at their richly-stocked enterprise with pride.

It was not too long ago that my friend and his wife were visiting us and told me that his brother-in-law had died recently. The wife had asked them to go along with her to make the funeral arrangements. Pausing, then taking a long breath and smiling, he continued, "First, Henry, we went to a casket warehouse, where we looked over a large selection of coffins." Glancing at his wife, he affirmed the look on her face and said, "Marge just hated to go, but you know how it is. Her sister-in-law is something else! Anyway, she was very fussy and kept repeating words like 'only the best for Will' and 'that one looks nice and comfortable.' The salesman was very polite and agreed that a man of his apparent stature no doubt deserved nothing less than what she had in mind. After spending a lot of time and comparing closely all the models and designs, she narrowed it down to just two. Finally, she pointed a finger and said, 'that one,' much to the salesman's relief."

"This one appears to be the finest we've looked at, and I think my relatives here will agree," said the very composed widow as she turned towards her companions. "Now," she said firmly to the smiling salesman, whose family had been selling tombstones, coffins and other memorial necessities for generations, "What's your best price?"

"I beg your pardon!" the funerary representative replied, leaning towards her, as if he did not hear her words.

Bringing her eyes directly to his, she again rigidly inquired, "What would be your very best price on this casket? We're antique dealers and we always give discounts to other merchants. In other words, what will be the dealer's price on this coffin?"

His face blanched, his eyelids closed in final recognition of her words and his entire body stiffened. At that moment, he could have been laid out in one of his own products and been a credit to his profession. Regaining composure, his eyes opening ever slowly, he icily replied, "Mrs. Haggle, we render a quality service here and our business is to provide our clients with the very best, according to what they wish to spend. If you require a casket of lesser-cost, we can go back to the other room and look over some of those you have already viewed."

Without waiting for her to reply, he hastily excused himself saying, "Pardon me! I have an important phone call scheduled. I'll be back in a few minutes."

"Henry," my friend said, "she was deathly serious about getting what she called a dealer's discount. It was becoming embarrassing and when the man came back, she had her business card out and proceeded to tell him how long they had been in business. She told him how well-known they were in the antique profession (if only he knew!) and that she would send other customers to him if he treated her right. 'May we talk about this privately?' the widow asked, nodding towards his office."

"Well," my friend continued, "they were in there for nearly an hour. When she came out, there was a slight smile on her face, but she quickly masked this with a black handkerchief. She muttered to us, firmly, 'Well! That's been taken care of. He should have known my Will when he was alive. Then he would have seen some real bargaining! We weren't in this business this long for nothing.'"

"On the way out," my friend concluded, "there were a few people clustered near the office door, looking our way. As we passed, I heard one of them say, 'Well, no wonder! They're antique dealers. What else could you expect?'"

After we got through chuckling about this, I said, "Ted, that can only surprise someone who is not in the antique business. Most dealers would have asked the casket salesman to throw in a headstone and free engraving as a package deal. The first four words antique dealers learn are: What's your best price? They live and die by them, and literally carry them to the grave, as you saw. As a matter-of-fact, the widow would have been pleased if they inscribed those four words on Will's headstone, but only at a dealer's discount, of course."

Guess What Came
To Dinner?

CHAPTER 2

Several months ago, my lady friend and I were invited out to dinner. There were eight of us in the upper-age group and except for the host and his wife, the other two couples were strangers. It was soon revealed that the other two men were retired and the fruits of their labors were amply demonstrated as the waiter poured the vintage wines. I knew that my friend Jane and I would sooner or later be the object of some of the evening's conversation. We were the only ones not married, she recently widowed, and I being divorced.

In Florida, where we live, it is not uncommon for widows and widowers to remarry just a few days after a deceased loved one's ashes have been blown out to sea or the body lowered into the earth. Time is of the essence and long frozen casseroles are hastily thawed and rushed over to the mourner's home immediately after the eulogy. Quite often, marriages are kept within a social group. Golf companions, bridge players or social club members intermingle and keep an eye out "in case something happens."

Frequently, a spouse will point out a certain acquaintance that he or she will select in such words, "If I die first, Harry, marry Muriel, she will take care of you properly." In the case of the women, who statistically realize they are more apt to outlive their husbands, there is probably a mental list of the men available to take Harry's place, should he go first. It is not unusual for a couple of mattresses to be shuffled from one condominium to another, following a speedy marriage after a sudden demise. Usually the older the survivors, the sooner they remarry. Many are avid collectors of spouses, which seems good for their health.

Consequently, when the conversation drifted towards Jane and myself, I was surprised when the usual question, "Are you two planning on getting married?" was not asked. In this haven for retirees, personal questions of every nature are asked of strangers as rapidly as stunning private affairs are revealed or gossiped about. There is even a sense of urgency in getting overly inquisitive.

Instead, the gentleman next to me, a retired automobile executive from Detroit, turned to me and said, "Al tells me you're an antique dealer." Glancing up quickly, I noticed the raised eyebrows on the other man's face, which I expected.

"That's right, over 40 years in the game," I hastily added.

My turn had come and I could see the retired auto executive was going to warm up to the subject. This was apt to be as juicy as the prime rib that was about to be served, I thought. His name was Milton, but he quickly told me to call him Milt.

His manner appeared informal and his cheerful expression and robust build suggested the same. Having a jolly, handsome face with an infectious laugh, he could easily make the ideal Santa Claus. Better yet, his cherubic look resembled a little boy Hummel figurine—the "Umbrella Boy"—only all grown up.

Turning his full, ample body towards me, with an incredulous look on his friendly face, and drawing everyone's attention, he started firing questions, not waiting for answers. "I didn't think there would be a market for such as that down here," he said. "Is it like auctions, garage sales and all that old stuff?"

I drew in my breath and said to myself, here we go again!

Looking at his wife Myrtle, he continued, "That's incredible, isn't it honey? We had a house full of old things, didn't we? Antiques and that, but we got rid of them before we came down here, except for our Hummel collection. The kids want that. We had a garage sale. Too bad we didn't know you then."

With that, he gave me a look of remorse; it was unfortunate that I missed out on "things we just got rid of."

If only he knew how many times I heard that before. I replied, "I'm sure you had a lot of beautiful "old things." Smiling inwardly, I didn't tell him it was good for the antique business that there were so many people like him, who knew or cared so little about it. Such people were a good source for the hovering antique dealer, always willing to help someone dispose of their "old stuff."

Feeling a slight need to be on the offense, I perked up and continued, "You'd be surprised how many antique dealers there are in this area, Milt. Sometimes it seems that everyone who retires in Florida, and has some antiques to sell, decides to become a dealer." I was laying it on a little thick, but not too far-fetched. If one were to ask the many local dealers, they would squawk that "everybody's getting into the antique business."

With this bit of news, he stretched his body towards me, eyeing me intently, like he couldn't comprehend this, and let out a loud, "No kidding!"

It was a typical situation in this locality, where a majority of the older residents are retirees. Many have little vision beyond their former professions, businesses or jobs. To them it was a curiosity that one, like myself, in their age bracket, should still be working. And an antique dealer, yet! Many of these people, men and women, had important positions in their younger years, and it would have been unusual if they and their peers were not chasing golf balls around or devoting most of their spare time to other types of leisure.

As the meal was being served, I glanced at Milt and detected an appearance of complacency spreading across his face. I could imagine that he was feeling happy that he wasn't involved in "old things." That he had a healthy pension and investments and was totally retired and enjoying life to the hilt. (Why did I suddenly feel like Rodney Dangerfield?)

Now everyone's attention was directed towards me. I was fair game. The other stranger, whose name was Fred, looked like he was eager to enter the conversation. Earlier, riding out to dinner, our host's wife had whispered to me, "Fred was an extremely successful lawyer in Chicago before he retired down here." My face didn't register any awe or surprise since I didn't know any lawyers who were not doing well.

Laughing a little, but in a friendly manner, however, Fred began, "Pardon me, Henry, but I guess my wife and I are a lot like other people who thought you had to be a bit of an oddball or something to be an antique dealer. I suppose my own profession kept me totally absorbed and not too aware."

Ah ha! Squeezing Jane's hand under the table and kicking her leg slightly, I supplied him with further ammunition. With a quizzical look, I replied, "Oh, you mean, like in the movies, how the antique dealer is always a man, flitting around the shop with his hands on his hips, voice high-pitched, fluttering eyelashes and a sophisticated accent? Maybe I should put on my act?"

This brought some chuckles around the table and I now relished the next part. "As a matter-of-fact, Fred," I continued, everyone now listening intently, "I have one lawyer friend who would love to chuck his profession so that he can become a full-time antique dealer. He is so good at his part-time specialty of dealing in antique silver that he and his wife are seriously thinking of devoting themselves entirely to this endeavor. I know of another lawyer who has become so skilled and adept at settling estates, that he knows more about antiques than many dealers, and a lot more tricks of the trade."

Looking him straight in the eyes, I added, with a full smile, "Fred, you don't have to roll your eyes or nudge your partner when someone mentions the words "antique dealer." What I've been noticing lately is that people are just as likely to raise their eyebrows when someone mentions the word "lawyer" or even "doctor." These professions are really getting a lot of attention and comments these days, aren't they?" This brought some laughter and I detected a sense of relaxation.

Now that the subject seemed open for discussion, next came the inevitable question, "How did you get into the antique business, Henry?" I then explained I had a brother who was 14 years older than me, who taught me the business after World War II.

Milt looked at me unbelievingly and asked, "Do you mean you've been working at antiques all these years and are still in business?" What's wrong with this guy, was probably his thought.

"Yes," I replied, "with the exception of four or five years when I took a fling at totally different adventures, I've been at this game over 40 years." Did I hear someone moan, whistle or groan? Was I being admired or pitied?

"You see, in this racket, folks," I continued, "we don't ever really have to retire, except for health reasons. Worry about getting old? Forget it! The older we get, the better we're at it. We tend to blend in with our merchandise. Wrinkles and antiques—they compliment each other. I even know several dealers who are older than their antiques."

Next came the usual barrage of inquiries. "I have an antique sofa. It's got to be at least 100 years old. What's it worth? I know it's hard for you to tell without seeing it." That's right, I thought, and true of most antiques.

"We deal in very little furniture," was my reply.

Then came another inquiry. "I have an old garnet necklace and earrings, way back from my father's side of the family. From Germany. What are they worth?" Still another: "Who appraises antique silver around here?" Then this, "How do you know whom to trust when you're selling antiques?" And so on.

I answered as briefly and patiently as I could, trying not to reveal by my expression that these questions are heard by dealers day after day, endlessly. People believe they are doing the antique dealer a favor by discussing any antique they might possess.

Trying to end the inquiries, I advised them, "Go to a bookstore, an antique shop or show. Browse! Ask questions. Dealers will be happy to discuss your items. They're ready to buy or sell anytime. As a matter-of-fact" I continued, "you have no idea what a jolly time you can have discussing what your grandmother had."

Dinner was over. Everyone agreed we had a delightful time, probably got to find out something unexpected about each other. I yelled out to one of the couples entering their car, "Go to the library and see if they have a book about antique dealers."

Before bidding each other good night, Milt hailed us to his car and enthusiastically said, "Henry, now that we know you're an antique dealer, Myrtle and I were thinking we might just sell our collection of Hummels if we got the right price."

After a long silence, I finally came up with, "That's probably not a bad idea."

Before Milt could latch onto that, A1 and Alice joined the group, caught the rift of the conversation and Alice said, "We have an old picture with Abraham Lincoln's signature on it. Where can we find out the value of something like that?"

Before I could mumble my answer, Fred the lawyer and his wife joined us, exclaiming, "Henry! We've collected some antiques along the way. If you want to, drop by some time and give us an idea about them."

Once we were in the car heading home, Jane looked at me, genuinely puzzled, and said, "Henry, you seemed to ignore Milt's questions about his Hummels and you didn't seem anxious to see the other couple's antiques. You even seemed a little impolite. You're always telling me that buying could be more important than selling."

"You're right, Jane," I replied, "you could say that buying is more important than selling . . . buying right, that is."

"Well," she asked, "didn't you think you could make them a fair offer and make some money on their antiques?"

"Oh, sure," I answered. "It's just that I've always avoided doing any business with friends, neighbors, relatives and acquaintances."

"That sounds strange to me," Jane said, "what's the reason for that?"

"First of all," I said, "your friends often think they're pleasing you by telling you what they and their family has or had. It's hard to act surprised all the time, when someone mentions their antiques."

"Secondly," I continued, "when I buy from neighbors, it's hard to treat them as strangers. We all make mistakes as dealers. Once I offered one of my neighbors a price on their antiques. Shortly after, another dealer offered them considerably more. This happens all the time in business. We all have different markets. And, for some time thereafter, when I'd bump into that person on the elevator, I'd always imagine him to think: There's that cheap antique buyer."

"Thereafter," I continued, "there were times when I'd done the reverse. I paid my neighbors or friends more than I really wanted to, or more than other dealers might, just to keep a good name, or so I imagined. I prefer to deal with strangers, Jane."

Before she could reply, I added, "And your worst customers can be your relatives. If you sell them something at cost, they think you're a wonderful guy. But, they sometimes implore me to charge them the same as regular customers, saying 'Just because we're blood, Henry, doesn't mean you should lose money.' However, occasionally I may sell them a piece of jewelry that comes back to haunt me. For instance, one relative visiting here last year said, 'Henry, do you remember that ring I bought from you when Michael was born? (he's 35 now) Well, a few of the garnets fell out. I don't know how, but if it's no trouble, can I send it to you?'"

"See what I mean, Jane?" I asked. There was no answer, but a long silence.

That night I did not fall asleep immediately, thinking of an unfavorable impression I might have left on my dinner companions in my role as an antique dealer. I might have portrayed myself as unfriendly, snobbish, or superior—faults I often found in my fellow antique dealers.

My mind drifted back to the many dealers I had known or come in contact with all these years. Not great dealers, perhaps, but some who were highly respected and noteworthy. Others made their mark in some fashion—for better or worse.

There are many dealers who find it hard to separate business from their private lives, since their pleasures are so often interwoven with their trade. On my part, I did not take business too seriously in my youthful years, enjoying other things more. I might say that I took time to smell the roses before the harvest was in. But, in the years of my seniority, the opposite became true: The joy of my work with antiques gave me reason not to retire.

Antique dealers differ as much in personality and method of operation as antique objects differ from one another. From the gentleman wearing a three-piece suit and assisted by the attractive woman in an elegant metropolitan "Antique Gallery," to the husband and wife, dressed in jeans and T-shirts, selling authentic antiques from the back of their station wagon at some soggy or sun-baked "Antique Flea Market," several hundred miles away from home. Such are all antique dealers.

In their operational methods, there are full-time dealers and part-time dealers, antique shop and gallery owners, antique show exhibitors and bedroom dealers. There are itinerant peddlers, auctioneers, flea-market merchants and dealers' dealers. There are pickers and pluckers too, all enjoying the trade in their special ways. There are college graduates, retired Army Generals and high-school drop-outs, all able to imbibe and feast in the knowledge and artistry gleaned from the past.

They are there for the excitement, waiting for the unexpected to appear, loving the freedom of travel that it affords and the chance to unearth some old treasure—trifling or terrific—at any time or place.

In everyday ventures, there may be the satisfaction of a small profit or the soaring exhilaration of making a "killing" on something. Above all, there's the feeling that they are some kind of show people. Amidst their merchandise and stock in trade, they reflect their specific tastes, whatever direction that takes.

Antique dealers, as a group, assuredly feel the least need for a face lift or cosmetic resurrection. They can easily assimilate the compliments heaped upon their lovely wares. Although one might be the most personally unattractive soul on earth and have the most beautiful collection of antiques, his joy arises when a total stranger enters his (or her) booth or shop and exclaims: "Absolutely beautiful!"

They are a formidable lot. I know antique dealers in their 80's and even a couple in their 90's who are still in business, the "Vladimir Horowitzes" of the business, playing their skillful melodies to the last breath.

When I was much younger and walked through the antique shows for the first time, I noticed the vibrant vitality of dealers who were well into their 70th years. That was astounding to me then. I wondered what magical ingredients flowed through their blood, what serum pulsated through their veins that compelled them, year after year, decade after decade, to appear before the public with their wares of yesteryear. What marvelous and mysterious components might enable so many of them to surpass their mid-wives in mortality, attend their doctors' funerals, outlive their heirs, and even becoming older than many of their antiques.

Now, surviving all the vagaries of the business myself after 40 years—which I would have never dreamed possible when I started—the answers have unfolded before me.

Antiques have become big business today, not merely a fanciful art of collecting for the few, as when I first entered the field. Durable as we old-timers seem to be, fortunately we are constantly being replaced by an influx of intelligent, younger, more aggressive and ambitious people.

Another phenomenon of the antique dealer is one that comes at his demise. It might not be noticed for a long time. Being around for so long—seemingly forever—we've become fixtures. It's as if a person had been walking into the same bedroom for over 40 years and suddenly exclaiming, "Wasn't there an old rocking-chair on that side of the room?" We wander off and disappear, like old elephants. Nonetheless, it's not easy to relinquish one's hold on the trifles and treasures of the past. We are the root canals of the trade.

To know and conduct his business properly, the antique dealer can become a wise and hopefully fair person, who above all, can come to love the business. The majority of them will not be lacking in ego, particularly if they specialize in select fields, and professional jealousy is an outstanding and pervasive characteristic of the entire field.

There is often a reticence when one dealer confronts another, hidden or obvious. What is he or she trying to find out from me, or what can I find out from them today, be it personal or business? There is frequently a veiled look in their eyes—inquisitive, probing and protecting, ready to defend or launch into an offense. Two antique dealers can be in the same shop looking around and without even trying, leave the impression that the other doesn't even exist, yet they are ever alert, ever eavesdropping upon the other dealer.

The dealers are only part of the business. The other necessary ingredients are the general public, which includes the collectors, and the private buyers and sellers. Needing each other, yet sometimes seeming to be pulling in opposite directions, their getting together is what the business is all about.

Unbelievable as it may seem to a casual observer, all the human emotions—joy, heartbreak, anger, zeal, love, hatred, jealousy, despair, ecstasy (one could go on and on) can accompany the mere buying of a single antique, somewhere in the path of its ownership.

This blend of possession and the possessed presents many diverse situations, and for those people who have ever bought or sold an antique, if they haven't already looked beyond the merchandise, getting a closer look at the dealers themselves might add more fun and interest to the encounter.

I Didn't Meet My Mother
Until I Was 7 Years Old

CHAPTER 3

The first twenty years of my life I had no interest, awareness or association with antiques. It was not until the end of World War II that I was thrust headlong into a household where reflections of the past were gracefully accumulated and displayed as common decor.

My discharge from the Marine Corps came on Christmas Day, 1945, and brought me to a home I had never seen (the family had moved earlier that year) but one in which I would have decades of pleasure and delight.

Upon returning from the Pacific theatre, two and one-half years after leaving Utica, NY, like millions of others who were released from the military at the time, we charged off in all directions. Discharge papers in hand, saying "no thanks" to the last minute invitation by the military to join the reserves, by train and bus we made our way home.

At journey's end, there was an indescribable, exhilarating feeling that gripped me as the train inched up to the station's platform that Christmas night. Union Station, in the heart of Utica, was one of those marvelous edifices that could only be destined to become a landmark in later years. It had huge marble columns, rising to a very high ceiling and marble floors, and sturdy wooden benches. Comfortable looking, it was indeed a beehive center of activities during the war years. Built early in the century, it was a monument to the great age of the American railroads.

Not lingering there to savor its historical and impressive beauty, remembering it only vaguely a couple of years earlier as a blur on my way to unknown military excitement, I scarcely noticed it now.

Catching the city bus from there to the center of the downtown area, known simply but definitively as the "Busy Corner," I got off and stood in the middle of it all. Huge snowflakes were falling and there was already a good accumulation, yet the air was mild, fresh, and sweet-smelling, as a snowfall often is. There were few cars to be seen; those evident moved slowly, being mostly of 1930's vintage. Auto production had ceased after early 1942, discontinued until 1946.

Although I was anxious to get to the home I had never seen, I reveled and lingered there among the throngs of people passing by. It was only 7 P.M. and about me was a sight I had, as a youth, always taken for granted. "Merry Christmas" resounded from all directions.

People were coming and going, mostly from the four large movie houses and the many restaurants that were contained within just a couple of blocks. The snow was softly piling up, being brushed from bodies wrapped in overcoats, scarves, gloves and galoshes. It was not cold enough for earmuffs. The street lights had a nineteenth century glow, dusted with snow, diffusing the light into an amber warmth, which in the heavy atmosphere, resembled lanterns or even gaslights. There was a reverent stillness and hush in the air. Even people merrily and jovially making their way in all directions did not disturb the magic aura of this particular night. With virtually but few cars in the streets, the snow banks now looked whiter each minute.

It was the nearest I could imagine a Dickensian Christmas to be. It wouldn't have surprised me to see Sidney Carton leaning against a lamp-post, mellow and smiling, with a black top hat and a scarf. I could just as likely have seen Scrooge walking briskly by, eager to get away from the crowds.

People made their way into four directions where the "Busy Corner" dissected the city into somewhat distinct entities. Every now and then a bus would appear and fill up, taking people away from downtown and to the poignant, sweet sadness of the final hours of this most festive of days. More than a half-hour had passed as I stood in the shelter of a wooden news stand, my thoughts being pleasantly enveloped in the sentiments of the day. My bus, approaching now, would be going south and slightly uphill through the entire business section, which would give me an added measure of holiday splendor, and a sight that would never be equaled.

The bus made its way slowly up the rise. All of the important stores were located along the way, being especially illuminated with holiday decorations, casting aside the somber war years.

At the crest of the downtown area stood the majestic Stanley Theatre, built around 1926. Above the entrance, outside, were Bernini-like spiral columns. The baroque exterior design was enhanced by a multi-colored mosaic centerpiece, above the marquee. Inside were crystal chandeliers, marble staircases and elaborate mirrors; carved figures, gold boxes, red velvet curtains and thick rugs; leaded stained-glass fixtures of various colors, rococo cherubs and intricately carved configurations surrounding the large stage and an ethereal-looking dome ceiling. It had everything never noticed by kids, as we clutched our dimes for admittance, but what we all look for as adults in our search for quintessential Art-Deco style and architecture.

Passing through the business district, the next several blocks embraced large, turn-of-the-century homes. Many of these elegant, one-family houses had two stories and a large attic. Swinging away from Genesee Street, the main thoroughfare, the bus drove past more fine old homes on both sides of the street, adorned with stately elms, now powdered with snow. From their windows, along with the varied-colored Christmas tree lights, soft-glowing table and floor lamps shone warmly upon the snow-covered window sills. I never dreamed that in the not-too-distant future I would be looking to gain entrance into just such homes, in my pursuit of antique jewelry—and later, antiques of every type.

Now, feeling apprehensive, I wondered what this new "old" house would be like. I was not going back to the old neighborhood where I had spent the first sixteen years of my life. That was a few miles away. Immediately after the war, my brother Vin was astute and fortunate enough to purchase a large, beautiful house, dating from the early 1920's, in one of the best residential sections of the city. This was where I was heading, to be my home for the next thirty years, and here also a few members of the family would enjoy an integral part of their lives. But in the final minutes of the drive, my mind flashed back to the old homestead, scene of my happy youth.

It had been a small house for so large a family. As the second youngest of eleven children, born and raised among eight sisters and two brothers, I was barely aware of the existence of some of them. Always playing outside, it was my oldest sister, Jewell (an appropriate nickname Julianne had chosen for herself), who was always calling me from the streets to come home to supper.

It seems that I was about six or seven when I took notice of my mother. That someone far loftier (than Jewell) was looming from the background, was in charge, in control. She appeared in fuller view as some of us began to vacate the nest. But she was not the one who took off ice-torn snow suits, or wiped thawing noses and unpeeled rubber boots, or washed and fed us. She was busy elsewhere, doing maternal chores while allocating sixteen female hands to the tasks they needed to learn for their future.

My awareness of my father's all-powerful presence came somewhat earlier. As the youngest son, I remember resting my head against him, who smelled wonderfully of strong tobacco and coarse masculinity, leaving me immensely secure.

However, as easily as I could rest my head at his knee in occasional comfort, just as often the five-tailed leather strap—a surefire enforcer of discipline—would appear and more than dust a tender behind when necessary. But it hung nearby, more in dreaded suggestion than actual use, of which we kids were keenly aware.

My fondest memory of my father was of a used bicycle given to me. It had big balloon tires and cost him seven hard-earned dollars. This he did because my best friend across the street was presented with a new one.

My father always seemed to be working. Like millions of immigrants entering America in the early part of the century, my parents set out immediately to begin a meaningful and fruitful life. Good fortune followed him when he secured a job in one of Utica's many knitting mills, that city being noted for its knitted products. He worked practically alone, in charge of operating the power-plant for the entire factory, naming his work "fire-man engineer." This included a lot of coal shoveling into flame-threatening furnaces, which had more than twice scalded him severely. This job he would keep through the Depression, raising a family of eleven children, and finally retiring from there into Social Security at age 65.

Returning daily from a twelve-hour shift, my father would be stern in hearing out my mother's reports on family members' wrongdoing. There and then they would be revealed and settled. In a large family, tattling on one another was common enough because it saved one's own skin. It seems that everyone took turns being bad. However, if there was any reporting, betraying and punishment, it was usually forgotten a short time later.

When disputes, however small, disturbed his peace at home, my father could be quick-tempered. One of my sisters enjoyed telling of the occasion when there was an argument concerning whose turn it was to wash and dry dishes that night. Deadlocked, neither of these two made a move to begin the chore. (Of course boys never touched the dishes, so we enjoyed the fracas.)

My father, usually resting in a chair with a hand-rolled cigarette while surveying the family activities, this time had his patience exhausted. Having enjoyed a cold Utica Club beer from the icebox and a most substantial meal, had heard enough of the argument. Plainly exasperated, he rose towards the table and lifted one end of the tablecloth; swooping it up, he vigorously dumped its contents onto the floor, furiously proclaiming, "Whose turn? That's whose turn!"

Financial assistance came from older family members, some with full-time jobs, others with part-time work. I recall the Depression years as being lean, but we were better off than many of our neighbors. We always managed to have ample food, prepared by plenty of cooks; and, where some families searched for substitutes to spread on their bread, our butter was bought from a large wooden tub at the local A & P store. No food donations needed to be delivered to our door as to those on Relief. The payments on our mortgaged home would always be met on time—although our father worried beforehand.

In later years, all family members would recall our youth with joy and satisfaction; each of us had shared in its trials as in its triumphs. In summation, growing up as a family of thirteen gave us wonderful experiences that smaller families could never realize, nor could we visualize it at the time. Anyone having but one sister or brother to love—or not to love—imagine multiplying that by ten. Apparently that many children did not take a toll on my parents' health. In the large last home they maintained in Utica, my mother lived happily into her 87th year while my father enjoyed full retirement there up to his 83rd year.

From age seven to sixteen I roamed freely, doing what boys in the 1930's were up to, hoping that I could be off on camping trips, away from home. Going "outside to play" meant plenty of rugged physical competition among the many tough kids in our neighborhood.

Some of the most valued memories of youthful days came in grammar school. I walked only two blocks to Kernan, a public school of fine structure with rolling lawns, two gyms, and a sports field for baseball and soccer.

The best recollections have to do with my teachers more than anything else. Their names come to me with affection. While Miss Goodman headed us off in the direction of the printed and written word with pencils and crayons, Miss Scott, a woman of ample size, stern of look, with a rising cone of hair, launched us into Social Studies.

My initial awareness of the beauty of the mature female figure came in the form of Miss Fox, teaching sixth grade. Flaming red hair, a lovely face enhanced by make-up, my excursions into Geography were delightful because she was on the same trip.

While Miss Beach entranced me with her body and her English lessons, Art teacher Miss Drum gave color to the character forming in my soul. I couldn't draw well, but I was fascinated with the blending of the chromatics.

Math teacher, Miss Losey, adorned mostly in low-cut black dresses, gave rise and meaning to the word cleavage. Adding, subtracting and multiplying became great fun.

Most influential in expanding my horizon was Miss Plum, my Music Appreciation teacher. Introducing me to Richard Wagner, particularly "Lohengrin," she instilled pure romance into our tender ears, not to mention the overwhelming orchestral strains that lifted our spirits in crescendo and excitement. It stuck! Many years later the romantic sensuality of "Tristan & Isolde" had convinced me that we were properly guided. Miss Plum, herself, with her impressive stature, might have portrayed "Brunnhilde."

Ancient, wrinkled, skinny, mean-looking as she appeared, purple veins protruding from beneath the thin skin that covered her entire body, she was the oldest teacher in the building. Paradoxically enough, she was the kindest of souls with her soft words and genteel demeanor, evoking compassion from all. Believe it or not, her name was Miss Ripley.

The most adored person of all was the principal of the school, Miss McKernan. Our eighth-grade graduation class coincided with her retirement. Noted for her extreme kindness, fairness and understanding, she blended this with unmatched skillful administration. She was the ultimate boss. Any youth sent to her highly respected office for punishment was handed a heavy ruler and instructed to hit himself as hard as he deemed his infraction deserved.

One may marvel now, thinking back on those times and those teachers, all entitled with a "Miss." While they taught us what they wanted us to absorb, they also endeared themselves in some fashion.

By the time I reached fourteen, four of my sisters had vacated home and city, departing for the New York City area to seek better opportunities than a mill town could offer. Each of them found a new life, two of them soon to be launched into marriages. Another sister left at high school age to become a nun, while my remaining sisters continued their education. My oldest brother still contributed to the support of the family, and my older brother was off to the CCC's—the Civilian Conservation Corps—where many of the youths of the 1930's found employment and adventure.

Three years later, World War II having fully erupted, many of my buddies, youths of seventeen and eighteen, volunteered for the military. Quitting high school or just managing to graduate, they enlisted in all branches of the service. Despite protests from my parents, I managed—not too easily—to enlist in the Marines shortly after I turned seventeen.

Three months of training at Parris Island, ten days of furlough, little did I realize it would be two and a half years before I returned home. Seeing some action in the Pacific theatre, I was among the grateful millions who thanked President Truman for ending the war swiftly.

Returning from reminiscences of my youthful years, now, as the bus driver let me off at the requested address—our new home—I was excitedly impressed with the imposing house, the white porch pillars giving it a classic and aristocratic look. Magnificent in winter splendor, it had a back yard that stretched to the next street, the foliage and grounds giving it the look of a manor within a city.

That would be my home for nearly 30 years, a place to enjoy while launching myself into various adventures. For the present, along with my best friend, Ted Graystone, I hoped to catch up on all the fun and excitement of post-war America. And there was plenty of it. Never again would there be so many bars, dance halls, restaurants and taverns with live entertainment, overflowing with ex-service-men and women. The country was exploding with pleasure and good times, begun from the earliest war years and beyond war's end. Service men and women were rushing home to reunite with their beloved. Once postponed plans were now achieving a reality. Decades later, these same young people would wistfully recall those years as the best years of their lives. In that period, America had fulfilled its destiny as the land of opportunity and greatness.

For those veterans having difficulty adjusting, the government offered a program known as the "52 ... 20 Club." One could collect $20 a week for up to 52 weeks while "looking for work."

Ambition motivating me, I tried several jobs. A knitting mill—No! A copper-rolling mill—No! A construction job—No! A few other part-time endeavors convinced me I needed further schooling.

By concentrated efforts, I turned to finish my last two years of high school through night classes and a correspondence course from the "American High School." It surprised me that I could learn algebra on my own. I then passed a New York State high school equivalency test, happy to end up with two diplomas.

Like millions of returning service men and women, I took advantage of the G.I. Bill of Rights. Having no preference for a lifetime profession yet, I enrolled in Utica College of Syracuse University in Liberal Arts, with an aim at the law profession.

However, while in my second year there, I would listen to the tales at the dinner table of my brother Vin's adventures in exhibiting as an antique jewelry dealer at antique shows that were springing up throughout the country. Even more fascinating were his stories of his old-gold buying days during the Depression, where he got his start. Sparks of excitement stirred deep within me; these certainly were stimulating times.

The Old-Gold Buyers

CHAPTER 4

It was in the midst of the Depression that the government raised the price of gold from $20 to $35 an ounce. When one could no longer use gold coins as a means of exchange.

Thereafter, gold coins were no longer legal tender; the public was told to trade them in at the banks for their new face value, or to puncture them for use as jewelry in pendants or charms. Of course, the latter would destroy their numismatic value, but it was done frequently, nevertheless. (We occasionally come across gold coins that have been pierced or soldered for use as jewelry—a symbol of the 1930's.)

Patriotically inspired to obey the new law, millions of people willingly helped the country get back on its feet financially. Although millions of gold coins were melted down, millions more disappeared into dresser drawers, intact or perforated, for speculation or as souvenirs of a bygone era. Fortunately for the numismatists, an untold wealth of them were tucked away for future trading under mattresses or in banks.

Of much more importance to the soon-to-emerge old-gold buyers was the unimaginable amount of gold jewelry that people possessed, its gold value suddenly enhanced by $15 per ounce. Virtually an unlimited source of gold stored in homes all over the country, the accumulation of preceding generations, heretofore largely neglected.

Coupled with the fact that the Depression—a period that earned a name always to be capitalized—was heading into full swing, with millions out of work and in need of money, it didn't take long for someone to figure out that the public would eagerly sell their jewelry and "old-gold" (as it was to be called universally), for immediate cash. The term became so popular, there was even a cigarette brand named "Old Gold" that appeared on the market.

When bread and butter was needed on the table and the rent or mortgage had to be paid, what good was Grandma's old, heavy Victorian bracelet? Or Grandpa's big gold pocket watch and chain, with that awful, cumbersome-looking fob on the end of it? That pocket watch would now fetch $10 to $20 in scrap value. Another common item found wrapped in tissue paper and never discarded because of sentimental value was Uncle Zeke's old gold teeth and bridgework resting in the bottom drawer. A lot of ears of corn had met their fate with that formidable combination of porcelain and gold. Then there were all those gold stickpins and cufflinks. Imagine how dapper he looked wearing them, before he no longer had any use for them.

All those gold earrings, bracelets, and heavy bar-pins that Aunt Minnie inherited won't mean a thing when she's out hunting for a job. Better to sell them and buy a few clothes; looking neat might help to land some work. Just about everyone owned jewelry of some type—a gold wedding band from someone in the family, and all those old eyeglass frames. Surely they were of gold. They looked it! So went the thoughts of those searching the house for gold.

In the trend of the times, all over the country, scrap yards had been dealing in non-precious metals: copper, iron, steel, tin, plus old clothes, newspapers, etc. (Japan, incidentally, was a big buyer of scrap metals in those days—which would be used against us in World War II.) Unemployed men went knocking upon the back doors of homes throughout the land, looking for scrap metals and "rags." It was a common sight to see men pulling or pushing carts laden with scrap metals, papers, rags and junk of all types—anything to earn themselves a few pennies. Across the country, was there a city in excess of 10,000 population that didn't have a scrap yard or two doing a brisk business?

To be sure, some scrap yard owners soon envisioned a golden opportunity—literally! Out there was a bonanza in precious metal that was overnight enhanced by $15 per ounce. Where hundreds of pounds of junk brought just a few dollars, to have a golden heap of indescribable trinkets measured in mere ounces that glistened in bright yellow allurement sent red blood racing through the veins and left the mind giddy with speculation.

Even more so were jewelry stores across the nation excited by this vast potential. With their own methods, many went about buying old-gold, either by sending representatives out into the streets—going from door-to-door—or by putting signs in the front window of their stores that read: WE BUY OLD GOLD.

These buyers, now getting organized, imagined a descending of a golden aura at a time when a bleak and dismal future gripped the entire country. People needed money in these very hard times! The buyers thought about those millions of pocket watches resting in dresser drawers, being cast aside for a more convenient and cheap wrist watch now coming into full style. The hey-day of the pocket watch had been in the mid-1880's through the 1920's. Every railroad man took exceptional pride in his particular watch, in an era when trains pulled into their respective stations "right on time." The ladies during that period wore lapel watches or those double-chained from the neck, with an ornamental slide for adjustment. Even these wonderful attractions to the fully clothed female bosom were rapidly being replaced by wrist watches. The buyers thought that people would be very willing to sell if someone appeared at their doorstep, with cash in hand.

In an area of my home town, junk yard owners weighed the huge volumes of old clothing, papers and metals on large scales, both outside and in their small office. They had dimly-lit shacks dispersed about the lot, mostly with kerosene lanterns. It was often dark before the push-cart peddlers came in with their day's toil, having stretched the most out of the daylight hours. Men in old, worn caps and earmuffs and weather-beaten faces looked anxiously at the scales as their heap of back-breaking labor was weighed and a piece of paper scribbled upon, giving the amount he would collect from the front office.

In the latter days of the Depression, even kids could get into the act for earnings by picking worms, commonly called night crawlers, for a few cents a large bucket. Grown men and women made themselves a meager living by selling this fishing bait to those who had plenty of time to try their luck at catching fish, in hopes of putting some supper on the kitchen table that night. I have a vivid memory of a man down the street from us who devoted a couple of his rooms in his upstairs flat to his bait business. Pans of dirt, coffee grounds, and water housed his worms and crabs, the latter always fascinating to us youngsters. His sign downstairs on the sidewalk had an arrow pointing through the alley and up the stairs (his only entrance), reading: FISH BAIT FOR SALE—UPSTAIRS.

In time, the junk yards began sprucing up their poorly-lighted, impoverished looks, a sight that was more often located on the outskirts of cities and towns and the last sight upon leaving it. Even though the rusty hunks of iron and tormented chunks of metals still greeted the visitor, other things happened to change their image.

The office, usually at the entrance to the yard, became the focal point. Brighter light fixtures, polished brass spittoons (chewing tobacco was fashionable), and an inside lavatory with soap and towels were added to the building. With a large, freshly-painted sign replacing what was once HENRY & ABE'S JUNKYARD, a formidable fence guarded the entrance to a building now known as WEST SIDE METALS INC.

This central office or headquarters had let it be known that they were now hiring men to train as old-gold buyers. My oldest brother Vin was one of the first to apply for this new adventure, having already tried several schemes at door-to-door selling...with success. He loved selling, even in these extremely difficult times, and he was not timid or afraid to knock on anyone's door. But what in the world were these people—this outfit—doing, he wondered. Buying? Who, other than a junkman or rag-picker could make a living going from house-to-house buying discards?

The central office, he learned, was to provide the men with the training and equipment to go wherever they wanted, soliciting to buy "old-gold." The equipment was not much, but it was teaching them how to use it properly that was important. This included a small set of hand scales for weighing gold on the spot. In Troy weight, these measured from the smallest grain to several ounces. The second most important item was a full-strength small bottle of nitric acid, wrapped very carefully, since it was powerful and burned the flesh instantly. Next was a small, triangular steel file that was used to file a nick into any piece of jewelry, and a sturdy set of pliers.

Since a vast amount of jewelry that these buyers would encounter was not solid gold, it was necessary to test each piece. To the beginner, brass or copper could look like gold, especially if he were more zealous than cautious. There were many other cheap metals from which jewelry was made. They were only after solid gold. This was usually nothing less than eight, nine and ten karat—up to 24 karat—which was pure gold.

The simplest test for solid gold was to file into the metal, be it a bracelet, watch or whatever. The seller was aware that this was necessary and was as hopeful as the buyer that it was gold. Few buyers knew gold by appearance, at first, and unlike today's requirements, much of the older jewelry was not stamped by karat. After filing quite deeply, where some items had two or three layers of solid gold over a base metal, the buyer would let a drop of acid fall onto the exposed section. If it fizzed and turned green immediately, it was not gold. It was wiped clean and cast aside. On to the next piece.

Much old jewelry was heavily gold-filled and quite deceptive. This was especially true for large pocket watches and chains. A beginner's heart could race with high hopes at first sight of these.

In their minds, they "knew" them to be gold. They held their breaths while testing, but their spirits ebbed in a flush of disappointment when the testing bubbled, fizzed and turned green with a drop of nitric acid—the proverbial acid test. They were only gold-filled. An even more degrading term was "gold-plate," a still thinner veneer of gold, of which there was plenty.

The bosses of these operations, after giving a worker as much training as they could without practical application, would send these crews out into the field. If they had their own transportation, fine, but in those days many rode street cars, buses, or got together in one automobile, then dispersed to different sections of town.

They headed for the average looking houses—not too prosperous but not too run-down either. It soon became apparent to the buyers that there were always areas of a territory that looked better than another. But it was stressed by the trainers that they should work each section systematically, not wasting any potential profit by skipping around. Nevertheless, they all soon developed their own systems.

After a few weeks of on-the-job training with large amounts of jewelry, an apprentice could soon eliminate a lot of on-the-spot testing by recognizing what was gold and what was not. Most jewelry, having similar characteristics, fell into one category. Some buyers became exceedingly adept at detecting this in just a few months. Of course, many who tried becoming gold buyers were not capable. Though lured by the word "gold" and driven by lean stomachs, chilly homes, and families to feed, they soon had to drop out of the operations. One needed stamina and spirit to go out "cold turkey" and knock on doors, day after day, with an aggressive but friendly attitude.

Surprisingly, the gold buyer did not need a lot of capital. By spending a few dollars the first day, he could hurry back to the central office and cash in his gold for money. With diligence and effort, he could accumulate everyday working assets.

Of course, many people would not sell anything to a person ring-ing their doorbell. This tended to discourage new trainees and kept the field highly selective. Then, too, there was a lot of inclement weather—certainly true of the winters in upstate New York. Those who endured usually enjoyed their work and realized they were uncommonly talented as specialists in a unique field.

Unlike many other peddlers of that period, these gold-buying crews needed no sales pitch. They were trading "cash for trash." Some even used that slogan in their daily transactions. They didn't have to buck the sales resistance in these demanding times, like other house-to-house solicitors were experiencing. There was noth-ing like—"No mister! Whatever you're selling, we don't want it," which resounded out of more doorways than any other phrase, sometimes without even giving the doorbell ringer a chance. Another remark that frequently came from behind a screen door without hesitation was—"A man was just here selling magazines an hour ago. Nope! We don't want any!"

To avoid being refused entrance without a chance to get any words in at all, my brother invented a little device that worked very well for him. Immediately after knocking on the door or ringing the doorbell, in the instant the door opened, he thrust a small box of gold samples into the face of whoever answered and said, "Good morning, Ma'm (or Sir). I'm in town buying old jewelry and old gold." (Some buyers would mention the name of the company, jew-elry store or refinery they were associated with.) Instantly remov-ing several items from the box into their inquisitive looks, he commanded attention. Then he continued, "I'm buying items like these that you may no longer be using."

With their eyes directed to the samples and their minds working on what it could mean, one would say, "Yes! We do have things like that. What do you want them for?"

In a calculated reply, the buyer might say, "Now that the govern-ment has raised the price of gold, it pays to sell them for scrap, especially if they are of no further use to you."

Opening the door wider, she would say, "Let me look around. Come in and sit down." Off she would go to another part of the house, returning with her husband and a box of jewelry. My brother would then explain to the husband the purpose of it all. No one mentioned "hard times" or "we could use some cash."

Instead, my brother would suggest: "It might be a good idea to sell these items, since they're out of fashion and maybe of little use to you."

Even today, many people in their advanced years can recall these times and proudly reveal that things "were so bad we had to sell our jewelry in order to eat during the Depression."

My brother would then separate the gold from the gold-filled, test when needed, and make an offer. Knowing what the company office would pay him, he had to buy as cheaply as possible, to make some sort of profit for himself as well. He was one of the buyers who soon became exceedingly skilled in recognizing solid gold instantly; testing became less necessary. He became so thorough and disciplined in his system that he felt he had truly stumbled upon something with a future that was quite unlike anything he had done before.

Ingenious as he thought some of his other ventures might be, this one fascinated him the most. An earlier excursion was a partnership in a dry cleaning business. They adopted the slogan: "If Your Clothes Are Not Becoming To You—They Should Be Coming To Us!"

But the business soon dissolved. They "took a bath," as the saying goes, and lost their small investment. After that came house-to-house selling—Watkins Products, magazines, kitchen wares and sundry other items that peddlers were trying to sell, irritating countless housewives in the process.

This new venture of gold buying was his best endeavor and he soon became highly professional, persisting where others dropped out, as the competition increased.

When the gold buying crews returned at night to the office, their day's pickings were separated and they were paid a set fee per ounce, the company figuring in their profit. Some refiners paid more than others. The buyers soon became aware of this and sold to those who paid the most.

Out came pliers and hammers at the central office. The stones— precious and semi-precious—were popped out of their settings. Rose diamonds, pearls, amethysts, garnets, etc., were all forced from their mountings. These could not be weighed and paid for; the scrap gold was all that mattered. Pocket watches, being plentiful and the heaviest, were eagerly attacked with pliers and screwdrivers. The movements were separated from their cases, stems pulled out, metal linings, hands and crystals pulverized into meaningless heaps and discarded. Only then was the gold ready for weighing.

It wasn't long before some of the buyers lamented the fact that so much beauty was being destroyed just to get at the basic intrinsic gold value. My brother was one of the first buyers in our area to do something about this tragic cycle of smashing and melting. While it made sense and was necessary to refine gold teeth, broken rings and countless objects of worn-out solid gold jewelry, he could soon see the pity of putting useful and beautiful objects to the pliers and hammer. Too much of what was being destroyed might be reclaimed and sold as objects of beauty. But how and where to do this? How could he open a jewelry store in the late 1930's? Besides, the gnawing hunger pains of the Depression still necessitated this mass destruction.

The old gold buyers who were hired by or owned jewelry stores were the first to find the solution. They could re-sell right from their stores. Those that could, opened up jewelry stores in villages and cities throughout the country.

In virtually any town where one might still come across a sign such as: B.SMITH ~ SONS—JEWELERS, one could assume that the father or grandfather got his start in the old-gold buying days. Putting signs in their store window as WE BUY OLD GOLD, was the first step towards that end.

It beat knocking on doors. In time, every village and city had their favorite, well-established jeweler downtown who earned the respect of the community. People bought from and sold to these former old-gold canvassers, encouraging the younger generation to carry on in the family business.

As for my brother Vin, who did manage to be resourceful enough to rent a small store in downtown Utica, fate was to direct him in still a different manner. Owning a store gave him a headquarters from which to buy jewelry and old-gold, but this had its limitations. Other jewelry stores were doing the same thing, enticing people to buy and sell with them.

One day, a friend of Vin's who was also one of the original old-gold buyers, stopped by his store and told him about an "Antique Show" that was going on in a village about fifteen miles away.

"You wouldn't believe it, Vin," he said, "but there were people selling antiques from tables. Each one had his own space. There were all kinds of antiques. You should take a ride out there."

Eyes brightened, eagerly getting more details, he replied, "Thanks, Ed, I'll go out there in the morning."

Chicken Dinners And
Cherry Pie

CHAPTER 5

My brother Vin arrived at the "Antique Show" at 10 A.M. Being held in a small building adjacent to the church, the show was just opening.

He paid his 25¢ admission and entered an unknown world. There he found about 20 dealers, each in a booth of his own. They all appeared to specialize in different items, everything having sales price tags attached. Somebody had to be buying.

One dealer had gleaming, highly polished silver; another displayed all colored glass and lamps, next to a beautifully arranged booth with very old-looking furniture, quilts and rugs. Another had exhibits of cut glass, sparkling with the sun rays that filtered through the stained glass window of this old building. Magnificent indeed! As Vin stopped by several booths and overheard conversations, he learned that much of what was being exhibited were objects from the nineteenth century. Polite owners explained this to interested customers.

Vin saw that the exhibitors were selling items he saw every day in homes that he canvassed. If these articles were salable, he thought, someone might have purchased that beautiful pair of heavy gold Victorian bracelets which he so reluctantly scrapped for their gold value only a few days ago.

Even more intriguing was it when he discovered that gold-filled jewelry, much of it equally exquisite, was being sold here. He realized that tons of gold-filled jewelry was being left behind on kitchen tables, when from door-to-door he bought only solid gold jewelry. In another booth he saw a couple of trays of silver jewelry, price-tagged, items he had barely glanced at when buying in homes. He could hardly contain his excitement in these new discoveries—taking in the entire show with heart throbbing and ideas racing through his mind.

Entering several of the booths, he noticed that some dealers would have a tray or two of mixed jewelry up front—an attention enticer. Examining them closely, Vin was utterly amazed to detect that some solid gold jewelry was priced lower than the gold-filled items. It was apparent that the dealers didn't know the difference and it didn't seem to matter. This was confirmed when, after striking up a conversation with a silver dealer, she ventured, "Well, we buy the jewelry in a lot. People sometimes want to get rid of everything and we just include it with the silver we buy. Our customers like to poke around in it. We just price it by how pretty it is."

Obviously, they hadn't paid much for it. But that was, of course, incidental to the business of antiques, Vin thought. Why should they "know" gold? A lot of antique jewelry was not marked, or had tiny, obscured hallmarks on it. One had to have a trained eye and experience to really know jewelry.

What most people didn't know was that solid gold jewelry could oxidize and tarnish just as gold-filled jewelry could, thus, easily be mistaken for something of lesser value. As he picked over other trays of jewelry, he discovered more items vastly under-priced while others were over-valued. For the skilled eye, the show was full of bargains. Just by walking through all the booths that day Vin was able to pluck out more than a good day's pay . . . if he were out canvassing.

He wondered how many more antique shows there might be. This was something new on the scene and the Depression was nearing its end. If he could find out what areas were having antique shows, all he had to do was get there the minute they opened, dash around from booth to booth, and pluck out the bargains.

What would be even better for him, of course, was to get his own booth at these shows. It was more exciting than keeping a small shop downtown. He would be there when all the dealers were setting up, beating everyone else to the punch. Plus, he would have his own exhibit from which to sell jewelry.

Entering a booth, Vin inquired about this immediately. He explained to the man and woman that he was an old-gold buyer and he noticed there wasn't a single dealer exhibiting antique jewelry exclusively. "In your opinion," he asked them, "would there be a market for such a dealer?" They were more than encouraging, thinking it an excellent idea, since it would be a specialty. They handed him a brochure that listed a few antique shows that were to be held in the months ahead.

They didn't know how instrumental they were in launching a young man into a lifetime career, nor did Vin at the time. He was wild-eyed with gratitude and it certainly showed, even to the couple who had so inspired him.

That night, seeking as much seclusion as was possible at a house with thirteen vibrant and varied family members, he managed to find a quiet niche where he could plan nothing less than an entire new life. Pouring over the small but precious list of antique shows that was given to him so kindly that afternoon, he noticed that one was coming up in a couple of months at a nearby village. Sponsored by a church group, it was to be held in one of the parish buildings. He immediately made note of it and planned on driving out there the next morning.

Wearing the best jacket and tie which he usually reserved for church, entirely confident of himself and his background, that morning Vin set out with great optimism. Having no difficulty reaching the committee in charge, his idea for the exhibiting of antique jewelry was greeted enthusiastically.

The show's sponsor was fully pleased to have an exclusive antique jewelry dealer. Since each booth specialized in a different category of antiques, this was a first for them, too. A $5 booth deposit was Vin's ticket to an exciting future.

In anticipation of his first antique show to come, he would try to put aside as many elegant pieces of old jewelry, Victorian period and earlier, as he could buy in house calls. Meantime, he would survive on the scrap gold, which meant having to work harder. His spirits soared even higher, if that were possible, speculating that there could be a vast market for gold-filled and silver jewelry at these shows. These could be bought very cheaply from house calls, since they were largely ignored. When buffed, polished, scrubbed and cleaned, they looked as good as solid gold jewelry—and would sell.

It was a fact that for every solid gold pocket watch and chain, for every pair of beautiful Etruscan-type solid gold bracelets, there was much more the same in gold-filled jewelry. When Queen Victoria appeared adorned in all that massive gold jewelry during the long decades of her rule, new designs and fashions came to be worn prominently. These works of beauty and innovation, of which there were immense quantities, were duplicated and worn by the masses. Much was created in solid gold, but far more of these replicas were necessarily made more affordable in gold-filled content. Although their age and beauty were the same, even jewelers would have to give much of it the "acid test" to see if it were in fact gold.

The next two months were spent with all this in mind, and when the time finally arrived for his own show, Vin was ready to display his jewelry handsomely. He assembled and pinned upon colorful satin strips of cloths his fascinating and resplendent array of antique jewelry. No longer was he dealing in old-gold scrap, just the metal devoid of its sparkling adornments. Rather, they were the genuine, original objects, meant to be worn and appreciated and sold for a good price.

The show was one he would never forget, for in those three days he'd sold over $500 worth of jewelry. Unbelievable! Besides being included into a rather prestigious group of people, each displaying their choicest antiques, he invented for himself the title of "Antique Jeweler." This followed his name, above the entrance to his booth.

In this one fantastic stroke of luck and endeavor, he had carved out a profession that would last him a lifetime.

For the sponsoring church itself, this antique show became a means of earning funds for their various activities. It was to turn into an annual social event that was anticipated more each year. Besides charging each dealer a nominal booth rent, they required a small admission charge from the public. And to make the occasion more festive, various church members concocted delicious lunches and dinners, all of which turned out to be highly successful and profitable.

During the dinner hour, as Vin enjoyed a home-cooked roast chicken dinner, topped off by fresh-baked cherry pie from locally picked trees, he wondered what the crew at the scrap yard would think if they saw him now.

More important, new vistas were opening up for him. Meeting there with dealers from other states gave Vin an opportunity for expansive horizons. They told him about new antique shows being promoted in their areas, from which he could build his own yearly itinerary.

As for procuring stock, there were two immediate sources. (Finding his small store downtown too confining and limited in scope, he closed that.) It became obvious that he would continue buying from door-to-door, not for scrap, specifically, but to buy all the jewelry possible: gold, silver and gold-filled. Having a new sales outlet through the antique shows, he could offer more money to the public for their jewelry, and thereby greatly increase his inventory—as he would his sales.

Secondly, there were probably many bargains, what he now referred to as "sleepers," to be found among those dealers carrying a sideline of assorted jewelry they apparently knew little about. But in 1940, there were not enough antique shows where he might exhibit to warrant full-time attention to just looking for "sleepers." Canvassing, he reflected, would still produce most of his stock, even as plenty of scrap gold could be turned over for instant cash.

Ideas popping one upon another, Vin asked himself: Why just go cold turkey and knock on doors every morning? Why not let people know the night before his seeking to buy their discarded jewelry, and that he would be there the following morning? Advertise yourself, first!

He soon had some handbills printed: BUYING FOR CASH! OLD JEWELRY AND OLD GOLD! Adding on a complete list of the items he desired, then his name and address, and in large letters at the bottom: WILL CALL IN THE MORNING.

Methodically picking out a neighborhood for the following day, he would have someone drop off these leaflets in a number of doorways, where they would be found and read and items searched for that night.

Taking a kid sister, Vin would drive into one of the many local towns and have her insert handbills in the doors. His siblings would often argue over whose turn it was to earn a little change, plus having the pleasure of riding in Vin's new 1939 Pontiac. To more distant places, he had more than enough such helpers who would be happy to distribute these handbills after school.

Door-to-door salesmen being in excess, where everyone else was trying to sell something, it was a novel and receptive idea to have someone insert a notice in your door, offering to "pay cash for unwanted jewelry." How could one fail?

This system worked very well for my brother. Many people awaited him anxiously. He would often be greeted at the door and immediately led to a table that was spread with old jewelry.

As he was leaving one home after purchasing jewelry, what a delight to hear someone yell from the opposite side of the street: "Yoo-hoo, mister! You were here before. We found some more jewelry. Can you come back?"

At times, while in a home, the phone would ring and the owner would reply, "Yes, Ethel, he's here right now. He says he'll be on that side of the street soon."

The old-gold buyers were the envy of the ubiquitous salesmen, who saw how easily these mysterious people gained entrance into so many homes. They literally had a tough time even getting a foot in the door, at times, slammed in their faces.

The mark of a successful old-gold buyer was the brown nitric acid stains on his fingers. So precise was his work—having to file into small items of jewelry, often too much in a hurry to prevent a little spilling—immediately the fingers would turn yellow, then brown and in a few days, finally peel. It was a repeated process. The yellow and brown stained fingers of the old-gold buyers were their trademark, a rare breed indeed.

Although old-gold buyers could be deceptive in their dealings with the unknowing public, all of them were so much in need of a job that they were happy enough to make a fair profit from each home. Besides, when word got around of their success, the competition increased. Where one buyer had been, another was soon to follow. "We just sold our old-gold yesterday to a man that was here," became the dreaded phrase of discouragement to the latter-day buyers.

In the years of World War II, some buyers entered the armed forces or war plants or other essential services. Some disappeared into thin air. When they folded up their portable acid kits and stored away weighing scales, files, pliers, hammers and related paraphernalia, for most it was forever. Some who had caught the "gold bug" during those years and survived the war, came back to it, but in ways they never imagined. Specialists in times of bad economics, the old-gold buyers were a bit of Americana that lasted just a few years, from the early 1930's to the war. World War II finished it. The people who remember these buyers who came knocking on their doors with their equipment and a smile, are disappearing into history with them.

As a teenager, I'd heard these tales first hand from my brother and his acquaintances of the old-gold buying business. And never dreamed that several years later I would pick up where they left off. Even more incredible, that it would become my lifetime's work, watching the antique game grow in all its fantastic maneuverings. Right up through the biggest gold and silver rush ever, thirty-four years later.

Cows and
Encyclopedias

CHAPTER 6

As one of the pioneers in the highly skilled antique jewelry facet of the business, my brother had a distinct advantage by having been one of the original old-gold buyers from Depression days. In time, his eyes became well-trained in spotting gold jewelry in seconds, usually without testing.

There were always sleepers for those possessing this knowledge, since many of the booths at the antique shows also carried a tray or two of jewelry. Another boon was the sprouting up of antique shops all over . . . city and country alike . . . including a tray or show case of jewelry alongside their antiques for their customers' browsing. Vin even built up a regular route of shops that he would check weekly, thus eliminating for himself thereafter the idea of canvassing from door-to-door. Because he bought swiftly, consistently, and for cash, he gained the trust and confidence of many dealers, some who would set aside a box of jewelry for his visits. This got him well on his way to becoming an established dealer.

For many of his earlier years in the trade, he had found only a few dealers who cared about or could fathom the secrets and intricacies of antique jewelry. Several got stung, buying inferior metals for gold—very easy to do—with plenty of gold-filled jewelry around. After a few attempts, they would avoid the risks.

These stimulating and arousing stories from Vin, coming as a regular part of my dinner diet, stirred me in body and soul, which Vin couldn't help but notice. And as I became more interested and sought more knowledge, Vin, never one to vacillate about business, simply said to me one evening, "If you want to try doing an antique show by yourself, I'll give you enough stock and equipment."

Noticing my favorable reaction, he added, "What have you got to lose? Take a fling! I just received a notice of a new show in Dayton, Ohio. My Cleveland shows are good. All the jewelry is tagged; just see what you can sell. Get the feel of it and you'll soon know if you have a flair for the business."

Always one to work fast and efficiently, he had me "off and running" before I knew it. My sales were satisfactory for a beginner, but I was equally impressed with the social opportunities. Meeting the attractive daughter of one dealer, we later became friends and it definitely added more luster to an illuminating experience.

My brother was pleased with my enthusiasm, commenting, "It's easy enough to sell anything that's marked; it's more important to know what you're selling. To do that, you have to learn what antique jewelry is and isn't. It's not that simple to learn, but I can give you a very concentrated crash course. And then, the best way in the world for you to learn how to buy is to go out canvassing, like I used to, from door-to-door."

I was excited about the prospect. My brother had one large room upstairs in our home that was converted into a work shop. There, conveniently, I was going to receive the best of private tutelage, free of charge.

Of course, the first essential was my learning how to test for gold. Everything the gold-buyers of the Depression had to learn initially was poured into my head in a few days. Experience in the field would teach me even more, in less time, Vin assured me. Supplying me with the necessary cash and the few essentials, including the small but important bottle of pure nitric acid, a set of gold-weighing scales and weights, a steel file and a pat on the back, the rest was up to me, whenever I wanted to launch myself.

"Pick your territory," he said. "You don't have to go far. It should be good out there. Chances are there hasn't been anyone buying jewelry and old-gold since before the war."

The crash course was over and I was itching to go. I had dropped out of college, at least temporarily, and there was nowhere to go but forward. I had no doubt that I was shortly going to become an antique jewelry dealer, with expert advice and training at my fingertips. More important, I firmly believed I had the psyche of the push-cart peddler. I'd had part-time experience selling door-to-door while in college, but this was different. I wouldn't be selling a product; instead, I was to offer "cash for old jewelry you no longer have use for."

Behind me were a series of job experiences, one of them was selling the Encyclopedia Americana, from house-to-house. In the few months I was doing that, I'd met plenty of solicitors.

After the war, with the scramble for jobs in the rebuilding of the country with consumer goods, factories were humming and millions of veterans were working at industrial jobs or going to college. With a large labor force, spending money was on the increase. But while a laborer on a construction job was getting about $1 per hour—skilled men more—the classified ads offered $100 per week in commissions for door-to-door salesmen and women.

This opportunity to work out in the fresh air—not factories or offices—and having the chance to become one's own boss, brought out every conceivable peddler. They were selling what was unavailable in previous years or creating new markets, consisting of books, magazines, vacuum cleaners, hair lotions, roofing and siding; Avon products, Fuller brushes, cosmetics, soaps; pots and pans and life insurance. Very prevalent were the assorted religious sects selling Bibles and distributing literature, who gave moral or spiritual lectures at a front or back door, in the interest of saving souls on the spot. Television sets not yet commonplace, people took their pick of other entertainment.

Before the coming of shopping malls and centers, it was common—from the late 1940's and into the 1960's—for a single household to have three or four different types of solicitors in a single day. Getting no response at a door, they even walked out to a person doing some gardening or mowing the lawn. In those days few people feared opening an already unlocked door or to greet a neatly dressed man or woman selling something.

With a smile, a curious housewife might call out several times a day, "Whatcha selling? Someone was just here an hour ago." Rarely was a door slammed in a solicitor's face, except out of slight annoyance or boredom of yet another canvasser—seldom ever with malice. It was a kinder, gentler time!

A solicitor on one side of the street was likely to see another salesperson across the street, or one following in his or her path. They speculated what the other might be selling. Was it a better product? Easier to sell? A more unique gimmick? The religious solicitors usually worked in pairs, were very polite and well-dressed.. The men often wore suits; only on the hottest days would jackets come off, but never the necktie. The "tin men," as roofing and siding salesmen became known, would cruise the area in autos surveying which homes were in most need of their services. Everyone had his trademark, hidden or obvious.

When my friend Ted Graystone and I set out to try selling the Encyclopedia Americana, they were paying $50 commission on each set. It was possible to get three prospects to sign on the dotted line every week and see our "American dream" of making $150 per week fulfilled.

Working for this outfit had us learning the most aggressive salesmanship I'd ever witnessed. Our boss would take a trainee with him to learn from his sales pitch his method of approaching a customer. Because the contract would need to be signed by the "head of the house," our sales talk would have to be given after 4 P.M., when that person was most likely to be there. It was up to each salesman to present his sales pitch, get as many appointments as possible for that evening, and have a contract signed between himself and the customer.

Sporting a new convertible, the boss took along a crew of three or four of us each day. After sizing up a village, we were dropped off at an assigned section. "I'll pick you up about 9 o'clock tonight. Good luck!" he would say, driving off into the summer's shadows.

At my turn to watch him and learn, we drove up to a large farm house, and after calling off a vigorously-barking dog, the housewife told us her husband was in the barn doing the milking. Driving out to the barn, we climbed out of the car and walked in briskly. The farmer stood near the entrance, calming down still another dog before beckoning us into the barn. The boss introduced us as the farmer stooped down to continue his milking process. I stood slightly behind them, but close enough to catch every word. I heard a forceful but very friendly spiel about "your children's education." Then before the farmer could respond unfavorably, the boss spread out an array of colorful literature pertaining to the set of books beneath the cow's udders.

The farmer stopped milking when the boss went into his full sales pitch, while I leaned up against a bale of hay and looked on. Loosening his tie, the boss showed the farmer some impressive pictures from his sample kit, and by now both were on the floor, while the cow resumed swishing flies with her tail and occasionally mooing. Upon the farmer's attempt to interject some words of rejection, the boss heard him out patiently as he loosened his tie. Then, drawing up some words to a friendly crescendo, what I finally heard from the boss, as he put one arm around the farmer's shoulder was, "You wouldn't deprive your children of an education for just a few dollars a month, would you, Mr. Hayes? Here you have at your fingertips a whole world of knowledge in one magnificent set of books. Imagine what they could learn if they read from them a couple of minutes every day."

His informal, congenial, yet persistent sales pitch worked very effectively, sometimes selling two or even three sets in one night's work. Of course, farmers were especially susceptible in those days, many being naturally friendly and even a bit shy, particularly when confronted by a salesman who appeared sincere, intimate and not minding a little bit of manure on his kneecaps or a spray or two of fresh milk.

Now that I was about to launch myself back into the world of the omnipresent solicitor, I recalled those book selling days and thought what a delightful difference buying jewelry would be from selling volumes of words. Or selling anything from door-to-door.

For the canvassers in the cities, villages and towns, however, the increased competition caught the attention of the local governments. Not all solicitors were honest, and to discourage the unscrupulous, who were bound to appear here and there, it became necessary for communities to protect their citizens. Most of them enacted some sort of solicitor's rules and regulations in their laws.

To let the canvassers know about their respective restrictions, these communities erected permanent metal signs, usually black on white, and drove them firmly into the ground at the entrance of the major roads leading into their domains. Many potential solicitors would drive around randomly, looking for a town or village that looked good to them, park their car, jump out and try a few houses. But now they would have to think twice, since the signs were very noticeable and the laws enforced.

The lettering would usually read: NOTICE TO AGENTS, VENDORS, SOLICITORS, PEDDLERS. LICENSE REQUIRED! APPLY VILLAGE (CITY) CLERK. With slight variations, these signs appeared everywhere.

In all my years of canvassing, however, since I was not selling anything but buying instead, I was usually asked to merely register when I applied for a license, and there was seldom any fee. Most city or town hall clerks looked up in astonishment when I applied for a permit to purchase old jewelry from door-to-door. More often than not, they smiled and waved me towards the door, often telling me what they had at home in old jewelry. Some cities or villages brought such good results that I worked them over and over again, as many people were not home the first time I rang their doorbell. A good solicitor works his territory thoroughly!

Thomas Dewey
and I

CHAPTER 7

In need of an automobile, I was delighted and proud to acquire my first one in 1948. This black 1941 Oldsmobile, bought for $900, was in immediate need of a motor job. It left a distinct trail of blue haze, which was not noticed until hours after I bought it. Its previous owner was a single male, once an essential worker in a war plant where he put in far more than forty hours per week. Besides having hauled in by car pools many a Rosie-the-Riveter, he had as many war stories to tell as any combat veteran of World War II. On my part, he and his wartime vehicle equally deserved a Purple Heart, as I later discovered.

My brother-in-law Bob, being a mechanic and a veteran of that war, took pity on me. It took him many laborious hours after his work day to install new valves and rings in the car before he was able to put that heap of metal together to set me in a direction, fifteen miles away, where I was to begin my new career.

It was the day following the Presidential election of 1948 that I parked this mohair-cushioned, resuscitated casualty in the parking lot of an A & P grocery store and walked confidently to the residential area of town, a block away. Not only was this day the first one as my own boss, but one to which the nation awoke to the stunning news that Thomas Dewey was not the newly-elected President—as a Chicago newspaper proclaimed in a famous headline. Instead, Harry Truman had staged a surprising upset and victory.

It was a gorgeous fall morning when I mounted the steps to my first doorbell. Each neat house on the street had a rise with wooden or stone steps leading to the porch. From one window I could see a Tiffany lamp and as I approached the screen door, the mixed aroma of pickles, tomatoes, vinegar and assorted stewing condiments, blending into a wonderfully powerful scent, entered my nostrils.

Every house had a screen door, the inner front door often open, letting out the sounds and smells of harvest time. To this aroma house flies were drawn, clinging to and buzzing about the screen door, as they basked in the last warmth of an Indian summer.

I heard pots and pans banging and caught a pungent fragrance wafting forth strongly and pleasingly. Thus was I introduced to a scene and scent, the likes of which were about to become a large part of my life as a buyer of old jewelry. More of such was certain to come, by the many variations and other circumstances to be found in far-flung places of other environments. But not always as agreeable as this one.

"Who's there?" asked the approaching figure of a smiling, elderly woman, adorned in apron, armed with a large ladle. Reaching the screen door, she greeted me warmly but quizzically as I thrust an open box of old jewelry samples near her inquiring eyes.

"Good morning, M'am, I'm buying old jewelry . . . like these . . . that you may no longer have use for," I said as I poked my fingers through the box, holding up earrings, a pocket watch, a bracelet, and a pair of old-gold specs and a few other items.

"What in the world for?" she asked, as her eyes rose from the box to mine.

Explaining to her that I had customers for such items at antique shows, she seemed even more perplexed, "What's an antique show?"

As she opened the screen door, she said, "Come in here, young man, and let's see what this is all about." Just then her husband came up from the cellar—which was right off the kitchen—with a pan of apples. "Noah, there's a man out here who says he's buying old jewelry. Come here and see what he wants."

Tall and gaunt, country-looking and mild of countenance, he

stuck one thumb through his crisscross overalls and said, "Hmm!" as he reached for his pipe with the other hand.

Explaining to him what I wanted to buy, the woman turned to me to say, "I've got some earrings and rings in my bureau drawer. Let me go look." The man left too, without saying a word. His wife soon returned with a small box of trinkets, but dropped it suddenly to the table exclaiming, "Oh! My pickles are boiling over," and bounded out to the kitchen, pots hissing in the background.

Returning, the man handed me a large, double-cased pocket watch—called a hunting case—at which my eyes popped open and my mind raced excitedly. My first piece of gold! He then spoke his first words, "I forgot all about this. Was my father 's. Doesn't run anymore; anyway, don't need it. Is this what you want? I've got this wrist watch (showing it) which I use now."

Taking the pocket watch from his hand, I found it was heavy. It must have two ounces of gold, I thought. If I offered him $20, it surely had $40 in scrap gold when stripped of its metal movement and other non-gold parts. He accepted my offer casually and said, "That's fine by me, if you want it. Only laying there in the drawer."

When the woman returned, I checked the box of assorted odds and ends of jewelry and offered her $10, since there was nothing that looked heavy. "You may have them," she said, "I'll never use that pair of earrings. Too old-fashioned."

Completing the transaction and thanking them, I headed for the porch, thinking I had never smelled anything as sweet as those sour pickles and whatever else spicy she was concocting. From there, I hustled back to the parking lot, locking those items in the trunk of my car. Talk about beginner's luck!

Picking up at the next house and making my way down the street, I discovered that some people weren't home or didn't answer their doorbells. Others simply said, "No! We don't have anything we want to sell," or, "Off-hand, I can't think of anything." People were friendly and I knew the potential was great just from the response I was receiving. One said, "Oh! There hasn't been anyone around here for years buying old-gold. Is that coming back?"

Another gent said, with a big smile and a puff on a cigarette, "The only gold I've got are these Old Gold cigarettes."

From one woman came, "You mean you're not selling something? I don't understand." I was quite heartened by these words, knowing that in this hunt for gold, I was on to something special. A genuine gold buyer! An antique jewelry dealer—very soon! Might I believe this?

I could hardly wait for my brother to return from his buying trip that night. I would be the one telling of my conquest at the dinner table tonight.

Just before dinner, moments after Vin arrived and went up to his work room, I entered casually and handed him the watch. Without even opening it, he took it into his hands and said, "Nice big clonker! You're going to run into more of these gold-filled watches than solid gold ones. Was that thrown in with some other jewelry?"

When I didn't reply, he looked at me and knew that my heart had dropped to my feet. Not gold? Impossible! I thought.

"Did you buy this for solid gold, Hank? Look, it's very hard, can't be bent. You can bend solid gold—even a large hunting case like this would give a little when you press it—if it was gold."

Then he asked the fatal question: "Didn't you test it before you bought it?" Since I couldn't find words in response, Vin continued, as he opened it, "This is definitely gold-filled. Didn't you file into it like I told you? Here! Read inside the back cover. It says it's a 25-year 14 karat gold-filled case. It's stamped so. You've got to test everything until you get some experience. It's worth about $1.50 in scrap value." By now, he looked as disappointed as I did.

I fumbled for words to tell him that I had been so sure it was solid gold that I didn't test it ... it looked too good. Though I knew those people I bought it from would have easily let me file into it.

"Well," he shrugged, hoping that I was not too discouraged, and said, "You lost $18 on that one. Always use the acid test. This is the prime example of a heavy, gold-filled watch. It looks good; it's not worn at all but there are three layers of gold over a base metal. It fooled you!"

It was small consolation to me that I made about $6 on the other batch of jewelry. Some of that was gold-filled, too, and all should have been tested.

I felt as badly as Thomas Dewey must have felt this very same day. Thinking I had victory in hand—as he—my overconfidence shook me drastically as reality set in.

This error served its purpose. So deeply impressed was I with that bitter lesson that I would rarely again have any difficulty telling the difference between solid gold and gold-filled watches.

Indeed pocket watches were one of the easier items to determine for their intrinsic value. They became very popular at the antique shows in the 1950's and the 1960's. Many that were only gold-filled were as beautiful as those of solid gold, and since there were many more gold-filled—more affordable—we bought all we could.

Fortunately, unlike Dewey, my career was just starting and there would be all kinds of surprises; sleepers and wonderful pieces of antique jewelry to procure in various intriguing and exciting circumstances. But, through the many years that antique jewelry was still available, I never left home without a small bottle of nitric acid wrapped securely somewhere in the trunk of the car. At times, it was absolutely essential to use.

For the next two years, I became a full-time, door-to-door old jewelry buyer. I had an immediate market: selling everything to my brother. Gold! Gold-filled! Silver jewelry! Any condition! It all had some value.

Vin became an expert repairman to meet his own needs, salvaging and refurbishing a lot of broken jewelry—his and mine. At antique shows, customers clamored for his jewelry, even the items Vin had re-styled from other objects. Gold pocket watch lids were

often made into ladies' link bracelets; fancy cufflinks were converted into earrings and bracelets. It was all a woman's world, full
of adornments.

By my own canvassing, I contributed to this effort, buying all the
jewelry I could. And I could see that the old-gold buyers of the
1930's had barely scratched the surface of all the potential jewelry
available out there. Untold wealth in gold and silver, in good condition or disrepair, was laying dormant in drawers—in banks and
homes of the American people.

It was not my interest, however, to exhibit at antique shows, as
Vin did—not yet, anyway! Instant cash and immediate turnover
was my preference. For now, the buying and selling of old jewelry
still remained only a means to pursue the unlimited pleasures of
youth.

Fish Fries—Boiler-Makers
And Opera

CHAPTER 8

In 1950 a totally unrelated development was to interrupt my budding career in antique jewelry. It would encompass a whirlwind of activities I never could have foreseen, sidetracking me for an interval before I was inexorably drawn back into the antique world. But it was a match for the energies I was erupting at this time.

To earn extra cash during the summer months to purchase jewelry in the fall—the best time—I was persuaded to rent a hot dog and refreshment stand near a city park. The pedestrian traffic was heavy during that short season, the center having a large swimming pool. (An equally important factor was my steady relationship with a very attractive blonde.) This venture proved successful and was near termination when another unexpected opportunity literally popped up before my eyes.

Just a few blocks down the street from my stand stood the extending structures and grounds of the New York State hospital for the mentally ill. Passing by it every morning, one day I noticed that they were about to erect a new building there—for the same purpose—on an adjacent lot. A new sign announced the large financial undertaking and named the out-of-state construction company that was awarded the contract.

I was quick to realize that the construction company would require many workers. If I could flip hot dogs for park patrons, so could I provide daily lunches and beverages to construction workers. That very day I drove up to couple surveyors on the job, who pointed out the superintendent to me. Consulting with him about providing the workers with coffee, lunches, etc., he very congenially told me to go ahead and work out the details.

I drove off, elated. But in a little while I became strangely confused. What was I doing? There were going to be hundreds of workers for two years and I was about to exchange an interesting and exciting future in antique jewelry for hustling huge amounts of food for construction workers in upstate New York, where the winters were born in Canada and reached us in their full maturity. Realizing at the same time that my brother Vin would be in warm and sunny Florida for the two coldest winter months, exhibiting at antique shows there. On the other hand, I would have a monopoly on a food concession, allowing me to earn more money to buy jewelry later. So I rationalized. And settled.

All I needed was a small structure to set up my operation. Better yet, I scanned the classified ads for restaurant equipment and noticed an ad for a small, old city bus, having been converted into a lunch wagon, which was for sale at a low price. Moving like lightening to buy it, I discovered why it was a bargain. It had a cracked cylinder block and was useful only as a stationary diner.

Calling on good friend Ted Graystone, a would-be racing driver, he somehow managed to tow me and my vehicle across town. By exuberant and reckless youth and a St. Christopher's medal more for his passengers than himself dangling above the front seat of Ted's car, we managed to limp, jerk, quiver, and lurch—I steering the bus, he pulling the load—onto the job site. Miraculously—it seemed.

Even though we had several hair-raising moments setting it down firmly in place, it served me faithfully for two incredible years—frozen to one spot like a prehistoric creature.

During that time, we had dispensed innumerable gallons of hot coffee into frozen workers through the winter and countless bottles of soda in the summer. We became famous for our Italian hot sausage sandwiches—a hearty lunch in the wintry blasts of upstate

New York. These left a burning afterglow intestinally, and a red ring of tomato sauce around the mouth to confirm the consumer's courage in devouring it.

I made many friends among the workers, several from other states. In the early 1950's, before television became common in the home, people flocked to bars to see sports events, to socialize. Drinking at taverns and restaurants after work became the trend for millions of workers. It was party time for men and women alike.

In this period I was able to buy a new car, and the pursuit of good times pushed any thought of buying old jewelry out of mind.

Fate took an even stranger twist as the construction job neared completion. Knowing my food service was well received by the construction contractor, it still surprised me when I was approached by one of the top bosses out of headquarters. He told me of a huge construction job for which they had just contracted, in Pennsylvania. There were to be many more workers and for a longer period of time. For a percentage of the food concession, would I be interested in setting up lunch and refreshment facilities? The money-making potential was tremendous and besides, I saw it as an exciting challenge. With the nation booming in construction, there was no limit to where I could go from there. Of course I was interested.

Driving down there shortly thereafter, with my current girlfriend, we were both very enthusiastic about this new venture. I had gained a lot of experience in mass food handling and was confident I could do a good job.

I had a definite appointment to see a specific person who would give me all the details. Since I was kept waiting for more than two hours, there came creeping into my mind thoughts that something was wrong. The secretary explained, in a vague manner, that she didn't know why the person I was to see hadn't appeared. After several hours of fuming, fussing and inquiring from a couple of other people, I knew I was purposely being avoided. The only deduction was that since this was such a great financial opportunity for a food concession, there might be a "payoff" from another party-—or something of that nature—and I was out of the picture.

Since no one faced up to the situation by late afternoon, we stormed off to the car, realizing I was completely cut out of involvement.

That event resulted in a deeply seated decision to never again rely upon anyone to help shape my destiny, no matter what; only I would create my future, make my own choices and be my own boss—from now on. My girlfriend went back to school in New York; the construction job in Utica now finished, and the diner business a thing of the past, I was free to do whatever I wanted. Despite this vast disappointment, I had gained an immense grasp of the business world—as of myself.

While analyzing my situation, another compelling and appealing notion was to cross my path, which would sidetrack me from my ultimate destiny for another three years, even as it would in another sense send me towards that end.

A few blocks from the construction job stood a three story building. The entire first floor was a bar and restaurant combined. Above it, were two stories of apartments. One day, the bar and restaurant were for sale. My friend Bill Erickson and his wife Julie—once part of the office staff of the past construction project, and my constant companions for those two years—agreed with me that this establishment would be a very good business opportunity.

This restaurant and bar had been a favorite haunt for many of the construction workers—including we three. It was here that we so energetically had contributed to the reputation of the 1950's as being the "glory years" for the taverns, bars and restaurants all over America, where we so liberally buttressed ourselves with teeth-rattling and mind-boggling Martini and Manhattan cocktails. Two or three of them before dinner would be sufficient preparation for the forthcoming escapades of the entire night.

I was soon convinced that this restaurant would be an exciting and profitable venture for me—my soul stirring again. The newly-opened hospital wing down the street would provide plenty of young nurses as patrons. Nearby, a new General Electric plant had recently begun operations, becoming a major employer in the area. (The once-famous knitting mills of Utica and vicinity were in their death throes or moving South.)

In patronage, I could envision a merging of young male G.E. employees coming into my restaurant for food and fun and the nurses seeking to assist them in that pursuit. Since I was single, free and 28 years old, I further anticipated new avenues of expression for myself.

Even though there was a persistent presence deep within me that kept recalling the greater freedom of the old jewelry buying days, this idea of having a virtual perch for observing people my age having fun, all while operating a potentially profitable business, was overwhelming. Everything before my eyes would be new and stimulating; the excitement and intrigue that this situation could provide was too tempting to resist.

But, I had a problem! I needed $8,000 cash to close the deal. The two years with the lunch wagon had me provided with plenty of spending money and a new car. But, the company I kept was not bent on frugality; rather, that tomorrow would take care of itself. (My pleasure trips to Montreal with Bill Erickson on summer weekends required instant Monday morning replenishment of the till.) Living at home, as I did, with my parents and brother, I had few serious responsibilities and lived quite freely in most respects.

Having no doubt that I would be successful in this endeavor, I took this case to my brother Vin. By now, he had fully established himself in some of the best antique shows in the country. I laid before him the facts and fantasies of my latest venture as he listened quietly. There's an adage which states that a true salesman is an easy mark for another salesman's pitch. This I fervently gave him. But he was always a soft touch anyway—as he was with other family members. Most accommodating.

Looking me straight in the eye, he said, "Hank, are you sure you want to work all those long hours and be tied down to one location?" His question had a tone which assured me that my request would be granted . . . although he had more foresight than I, at the time.

"That place is just waiting for the right person to come along and get it going," I said to him, adding "and I'll pay off the debt in weekly installments." This became true immediately. (In later years when I would again have that confident feeling in making an important decision, I would call it my "Club York feeling," having named the club after the street where it was located: York.)

The deal for Club York was finalized shortly thereafter. I was even more fortunate to have my sister Frances (recently divorced, six years my senior with two children to support) move into one of the apartments above the restaurant. In one stroke, she became manager, head waitress, cook, bartender, and troubleshooter. We became a perfect team. From emergency gravymaker (at one wedding reception we had I accidentally knocked the contents of the large coffee maker into the turkey gravy; she frantically managed to replace it in time for the wedding toasts), to listening to the tales of woe from many of our lovestricken young patrons. She did all of the above for the grand salary of $55 per week, getting a few scattered quarters, nickels and dimes in tips, from 4 P.M. to 2 A.M., Monday through Saturday.

Even with absolutely no previous experience, it didn't take me long to become a bartender, full cook and restaurant manager. Never having drawn a glass of beer from a tap before now, there was plenty of waste before I acquired the knack in not losing too much excess foam. Even worse, my very first night we had an order of four large pizza pies for a softball team that was on its way to the restaurant after a game. Using fresh-mixed dough, the nightmare began when one section of the pie slipped away as I tried to make it hold together in the large aluminum trays. I covered up the holes with tomato sauce and baked them with a prayer—I never saw that team again.

I soon learned to handle most of the cooking, from spaghetti and steaks to turkey, lobster tails and pork chops. We had large and small parties. There were a few hastily-catered-to weddings, a couple of them in blizzard-like conditions, and several others on hot, sultry days. We were always available for emergencies.

One specialty we enjoyed was the Fish Fries on Friday. Among the more lamentable traditions that would be dissolved by Vatican II in the 1960's—in the name of modernization—none surpassed the abolishment of fasting from meat on Friday for Roman Catholics. This was the viewpoint of many restaurateurs across the land that had been catering to millions of Catholics and non-Catholics, alike.

But, for our Friday nights in the 1950's, there were all types of fresh seafood available—in practically every restaurant. Because people were eating meat in much larger quantities during the week, in those pre-cholesterol-conscious days, many looked forward to Friday for a taste change.

Friday also being payday for most workers, to accompany the seafood, there were oceans of beer and other alcoholic beverages to wash down these piscatorial delights. Bars, taverns, and restaurants prospered primarily on Fridays. The aroma of frying fish and French fries (which took me two days thereafter to cleanse from my hair and skin) emanated from the "corner tavern." Thus happily began the nice, long weekend. For many housewives, this was the only day that her husband could take her out to dinner and still feel like he was one of the boys.

From 4 P.M. Fridays we would be busy right up to closing time. For $1.25, at Club York we served a half-a-haddock (freshly delivered from New York City the night before), along with French fries and hand-grated coleslaw, almost spilling over the large platter.

With it, the waitresses lavished smiles and courteous service, coming away with tips of 10¢ and up.

With this great meal, a large glass of beer was 15¢; a shot of Seagrams-7 Crown whiskey was 40¢. A combination of both, known as a "boiler-maker," was 50¢. This was a favorite among workers engaged in heavy manual labor and wanting an immediate high. It was also popular among circulating tavern owners making their rounds, and businessmen slipping away for a few minutes, also undertakers, who partook of bottled spirits to ward off the chill from the cold weather or from his last client.

When there was a lull in food orders and patrons coming in merely for drinking, I would chop up an onion on the grill; within minutes sandwich orders would come flying in.

I had plenty of family and good friends willing to be part-time employees, who enjoyed the chatter at the bar. With their small salary, they always enjoyed the barrel of laughs that came with the drinks—all the fun that makes the 1950's an era of great nostalgia for so many. But, for me, the kitchen was my escape from particularly garrulous customers. I enjoyed the task of cooking more than bartending.

Although we were in a recession about this time, the Eisenhower years were peaceful and bountiful. When I bought my new Oldsmobile convertible in 1954, it was in keeping with the times. Convertibles in this country had reached their apex of popularity and variety in the 1950's.

When I sported a turquoise convertible with red interior, white sidewalls on balloon tires (for $3000 or so), the look of a millionaire's bearing started a trend at the restaurant. Frances, as manager, followed suit, and within a few months six members of our family owned convertibles. Because we worked evenings and nights, by day we were spotted about town driving carefree in the wind. Before long, many of our patrons followed our example. Driving into the parking lot on a Friday night thereafter, the common sight was the assortment of convertibles there. Friends told us that we should have gotten commissions from several auto agencies.

Like others, I bought on time, but with low monthly payments and very little thought, if any, about interest rates. In two years time the car was mine and ready to be traded.

September was traditionally the month when the new cars were presented to the public—unveiled—with each auto company trying to outdo the other. At the time, this viewing of new cars was comparable to our visiting all the Catholic churches in the city on Holy Thursday. A pleasurable obligation.

The entrance used from the parking lot to Club York led people directly to the bar. It was not a large bar and on weekends it was always crowded. There the usual sporting events of the day were discussed among men. The bartender would do well to have not only a smattering of such knowledge, but a receptive ear to family woes or joys as well, plus philosophy, politics, religion, current events, technology, music and such like. Everyone had his own opinion, and I soon learned to shake my head in a manner indicating that I was in agreement. A wise bartender utters one word to every 100 spieled forth from a customer.

The main part of the restaurant had a spacious dining area, allowing a small but adequate space for dancing, offering a couple a degree of intimacy. At that time, there was still a 10% luxury tax on live music in public restaurants and bars. In lieu of this, juke boxes were the omnipresent form of entertainment. Each year the companies came out with still grander models, for the depositing of nickels, dimes and quarters coming from customers' jingling pockets. (Try to buy a jukebox from the 1950's today. It will look good with your Lincoln Town car.)

Dining and dancing, parties and serving drinks at the bar or at the tables, fun for all continued on. We were highly successful and making an abundance of friends; we enjoyed many treasured experiences and laughter—a much needed ingredient in life. Here we

created a habitual gathering place for many people, who like ourselves, were to recall special moments as their happiest. Club York
was the birthplace of many romances that set the stage for more
than a few marriages. People met here and their intimate personal
lives were often revealed to us. Both happy and tragic events had
occurred, the latter much less frequently, fortunately.

What was most bothersome, however, came at closing time.
Outside neon lights were turned off at 2 A.M. Dimming the inside
lights didn't move the hangers-on. Their ploy was to order a round
of drinks a few minutes ahead of closing, knowing we would not
put them out for a time yet. On they danced and romanced—pre-
liminaries to their main bout—while we, the weary management,
tolerated it but not too happily. After a few months, we took action.

Between us, Frances and I devised a plan we thought would
drive them out at the stroke of 2 A.M. Our customers were used to
dancing to the strains of Jackie Gleason's orchestra, hearing the
voices of Della Reese, Paul Anka, Sammy Davis Jr., Jo Stafford,
Elvis Presley and many other popular greats of the 1950's. Some
dropped coins in the jukebox after 2 A.M. just to sit and glow in the
pleasure of these voices, rather than dance.

We'll fix them! She and I were opera fans. We drove to the old
Metropolitan Opera House in New York City with friends or family to catch the opera giants of the day, of which there were many.
Anyone that is a grand opera fan might consider the offers of the
1950's: If we saw Renata Tebaldi as Tosca, we would want to hear
how Maria Callas sounded next time in the same role; or to hear
Richard Tucker next month in LaBoheme, although Giuseppe
deSteffano was very good; we'd seen Rise Stevens as Carmen last
time, and Leonard Warren was to sing next week. So it went.

One day we selected some recordings of opera favorites for our
jukebox. We had some difficulty, however, in persuading a reluctant jukebox owner, who provided us with the latest selections of
the most popular music—which paid off handsomely —to include

these in his machines. "Who's going to play this junk?" he asked smilingly.

"Don't worry, Marty, the money will come in, and your jukebox business will be the better for it," I laughed in return.

Come next Friday night, just a few minutes before 2 A.M., I slipped over to the jukebox and secretly deposited a good hour's worth of coins. It was nearly fifteen minutes before other selections would catch up to ours.

When an opera tune came on, three couples, dancing closely, stopped dead in their tracks, wondering what that selection could be, as Jussi Bjorling—the "Swedish Caruso"—poured forth with a golden-voiced aria from Manon Lescaut. Just as a couple came over to ask me what was going on, they were treated to Zinka Milanov as her soprano voice shook the church walls in Cavalleria Rusticana.

"Sit down," I told them. "Right after this, Mario Del Monaco is going to warm Mimi's tiny frozen hand. Just hold on," I implored them, "and if you think you've got troubles, wait until you hear Madame Butterfly tell you hers."

Two more records still to play, I then gave them the grandest of them all, my own favorite: Birgit Nilsson, rendering her most in the wonderfully sorrowful Liebestod.

"Who died?" one of the young customers shrieked.

Smiling broadly—a rarity for me at 3 A.M. into a Saturday morning—I replied, "Ah! Ha! John. Congratulations! You catch on fast. You'll love her as Brunnhilde."

Our scheme worked! They fled soon after 2 A.M. every weekend thereafter. Accustomed to taking over the dance floor for up to an hour of after-hours dancing, they groaned as they made for the exit—their passions petering out, wondering what had come over the place.

This worked beautifully for a while; then something new developed. Was our scheme backfiring? I noticed that a few customers would still linger after 2 A.M., just to listen to what we played. After a time, they would drop in their own coins, some even playing the operatic arias before closing hours. We also noticed that our clean-ing man had a preference for something lighter in the classical fare, like Fledermaus, while mopping the floor and scrubbing the lava-tories, and keeping the place looking neater. Our customers and friends were hearing their own untapped emotions and passions.

Surely we were the only bar and restaurant where one might cry or rejoice in his beer or other alcoholic beverage while listening to "Pagliacci" tear his heart out in magnificent crescendo. Today I would like to believe that some of my customers' children are now enjoying the likes of Domingo, Carreras and Pavarotti and sopranos as Beherens and Bartoli because their parents relaxed after hours at Club York in the mid-1950's.

All things come to an end, so did our time in this establishment. For all the new friends, exciting times, mirth and merriment our successful business had given us, Frances and I both realized this was certainly not to be a lifetime occupation. After three years, the novelty had seriously begun to wear out.

Had we continued at Club York, I'm sure we could have realized permanent financial security—who knows! I probably would have settled down and even had a family, something I never considered seriously.

Now, just as it was when I was a kid—always "outside playing"—I had the urge to move on. I had a new car, no debts, some cash and plenty of ideas. Selling the restaurant business and clearing my debt to my brother meant I was free again.

Home at the dinner table, Vin's adventurous travels in the antique show circuit once again commanded the conversation and my attention. I would watch him on a gorgeous, Indian summer day (as other times) pack up for an antique show several hundred miles away. Convertible top down, antique jewelry and equipment in the trunk, in an utterly relaxed and jovial mood, off he'd go.

When he returned from one of his trips, I related my intentions of going back to buying jewelry from door-to-door. He accepted this calmly and, no doubt, expectedly. There was no preaching, like: "I told you that the work would be endless and very confining."

Instead, he said, "If you're going back out there buying jewelry, you know I'll always buy anything you get. Or, if you decide to exhibit at your own antique shows—there are more and more new ones springing up all over the country, I'll let you know which I believe are most promising." Once again, I was fortunate enough in walking out the front door one day and starting another career the next day—on my own.

Frances, luckily, who had been so capable and important to me in the restaurant business, was also quite ready for a change. She'd had a previous background of secretarial work and had no problem getting a pleasant desk job locally. She could be depended on. The Club York experience she, too, would treasure.

I Could Have Made "The Guinness Book Of Records"

CHAPTER 9

Nearly everything I would have to do with antique jewelry and antique shows in the next twenty years might be called the springtime of my maturing years. And the advancement of America, as well. The economy ever rising with the growth of new inventions and the development of housing and new industries; in the antique world, alone, equally significant was the proliferation of antique shops.

This time span, up to the fall of 1979, was the formative years of the antique business—one might say—a foundation to what this business would become.

Throughout the cities, villages and countryside of America, people were opening up antique shops as a legitimate business venture. They were converting their homes (parlors, attics, cellars) garages, barns and front and back lawns into display areas for antiques: family accumulations and passed-down antiques of earlier eras. To which the public was welcome to come and browse, to buy and sell.

One reason for this was the movement of city dwellers to the suburbs and the availability of the more desirable modern furnishings for their homes and the unloading of "old stuff." They were newcomers to the field—housewives and their spouses—who knew little about the antique business. But they drew those who scoured the countryside seeking a sign in a window, on a tree or pole reading: ANTIQUES.

Outdoor antique flea markets first appeared in the mid-1950's. In time some of them were to become as good, as famous as some of the indoor antique shows. (More on this in a succeeding chapter.)

Among other newcomers attaching themselves to the field of antiques came the "bedroom dealers," the "antique pickers," and the specialists. And in the forefront of the antique show business were the promoters. Trying to cash in on America's latest game, they portrayed pioneering ability and pompous pride in their ambition for personal achievement and cultural enhancement— and come they did.

America grew to love antiques and for the next 20 years the field expanded in a fairly predictable fashion. It was only at the end of 1979, when the financial world inflated frighteningly, that the antique profession would follow suit and give birth to a new era that would alter the trade drastically.

It affected me directly. I had been around to witness the old-gold buyers evolve into antique jewelry dealers—from the late 1930's up to 1979. Those who chose to hang on and could master the skill of being exclusive antique jewelry dealers during that time had entered a privileged category.

* *

Upon my return to canvassing (through the 1960's and the 1970's) I found some notable changes. In soliciting, a steep decline had taken place; there were fewer solicitors, those selling everything from pots and pans to religion. Pesky as some had been, back in my earlier gold buying days, I missed their hardy and persistence presence. Inevitably, the shifting of families from the cities for the finer homes in the suburbs and the appearance of shopping malls had much to do with it, leaving poor pickings for many a door-to-door salesman.

But this was a boon to me, having the path cleared of: "Someone's at my door, Muriel; I'll have to call you back." Even the NOTICE TO PEDDLERS AND SOLICITORS signs, once so visible, were being removed of further use. My applying for a license to buy old jewelry had the town clerk perplexed at my request, but permission was rarely refused.

What had changed even more was people's response. When they came to their doors, they, too, were puzzled when I inquired about old jewelry. For the changing times, I would need a new method of approach. What's more, I wanted to cover as much territory as possible to make up for lost years, to travel farther and constantly. I knew the jewelry was out there!

The system I invented, simple and to the point, sure to gain their attention, would serve me well. I could still use flyers but the approach would be different.

On the newly printed flyers I would list near forty specific items of jewelry I was seeking, plus those customary eye-catching objects: DENTAL GOLD . . . BROKEN JEWELRY . . . SCRAP GOLD. Of bridgework and other dental gold, there was always plenty, attesting to the days when gold was lower priced and widely used in that profession. The bottom line of the flyer reading: FREE ESTIMATES . . . NO OBLIGATION . . . LICENSED. These pamphlets could be used in another fashion, rather than left outside the door the evening before, as in former times.

Reaching a desired neighborhood, I parked my car promptly at 9 A.M., not to return until 12 noon—for a lunch break. I worked one side of the street then the other side.

To each door opened to my ring I bid the person a "Good morning! I'm buying old jewelry and scrap gold that you may no longer have use for. And paying good prices!" Opening up the small box of samples I carried with me (Vin's technique of earlier days), I held forth a ring, a bracelet, to their attention, hastily adding, "I'll be back on this street after 1 P.M.; I have other calls in the neighborhood. Meanwhile, you might look around to see what you have." I handed the person one of the flyers for instant scanning.

I found it best to make an appointment for later that day than to expect them to initially allow a total stranger into their home. This procedure gave them time to think it over without pressure.

This simple and courteous system enabled me to get several appointments for that afternoon, doing away with what was once "cold turkey" house calls.

Rare were the times when my appointments produced nothing. I jotted down the house number as I backed away from the door. Just as important, they now had in hand my name and address; if they had questions about my legality, I could be checked out.

Appearance—as well as manner—a freshly-laundered shirt with tie (jacket when cool), plus a splash of cologne were effective aids in beguiling a potential seller when making house calls. I still like hearing "What's that you're wearing? It smells so nice."

Another rule was to never "waste" any territory—no skipping around haphazardly—never missing a single house on any street I was working.

Nor did I bypass funeral homes that appeared on my route. It afforded me a challenge to inquire of them for objects like gold teeth and old wedding bands as I drew forth samples into their icy glares. A brief encounter here would break up my routine and provide a few chuckles for me along the way.

Continuing my daily route, where a response was, "No, we have nothing to sell," to get a smile from them, I had a lure and a line for that, retorting, "As a last resort, do you have any discarded bridge-work or gold teeth?" At the same time I drew out a huge, gold-encrusted molar or a partial bridge with a couple of gleaming yellow gold caps that struck the eye. With a smile or laughter came a response: that the dentist had simply thrown out their old gold bridgework into a waste basket or handed it to them wrapped in tissue. Many would ask for them, implying they would keep them for souvenirs. Thus there arose the prevalence of gold bridgework tucked away somewhere in dresser drawers.

Going through this gold teeth routine via a screen door one fine day, the woman behind it replied, "Well, as a matter of fact, young man, I have an appointment with the dentist later this morning, to have some gold bridgework removed." Hesitating a moment, I relished what I was about to ask, "I happen to have appointments on this street after 3 P.M. Why don't I just stop back then?" To this, she shrugged her shoulders and said, "Why not, I guess." This was my first time to buy gold bridgework that was still nearly warm and not too far removed from its last meal.

Returning for an afternoon appointment, a prospect's jewelry was ready for me, spread upon a table. If satisfied with my cash offer, I asked them if they had other items put away elsewhere. A search might produce the best pieces. For those objects first agreed upon, it was best to pay cash immediately, further instilling confidence. It got to be fun for many, a treasure hunt, this second search for other pieces and getting a second cash payment.

It was more the rule than the exception for people to invite me (they still do) into their bedrooms. Spilling everything out on bedspreads or nearby tables, we searched together. "Look into those drawers, too, and see if there's anything you can use," was the frequent invitation. (Whenever other dealers inquired how I got some of my best antique pieces of jewelry, I simply replied, "The secret of it is, you have to get into their drawers!")

Just as often, when something was plucked from nowhere, the seller might say, "Oh! I forgot about that." Or, "No! That's not for sale." Quite frequently they ended up keeping much of what was "discovered," but this was to be expected and I was able to purchase more by telling them, "I only want to buy what you might want to sell." A powerful word—might—no pressure.

Although I made no obvious attempt to conceal my method of canvassing to procure my stock in trade, most dealers knew nothing about it. I kept it to myself. Why should I share my fun! My workable buying pitch.

There was, however, one secret that all antique jewelry dealers shared in common before 1980—before the gold and silver rush. For those 20 years preceding, with the emergence of antique shops and shows all across the country, there was an unlimited and surprising storehouse of "sleepers" to be found.

* *

Talking to an ex-door-to-door salesman in our shop recently, after he finished bragging about the success he'd had selling "in the old days," I said, "Well, it wouldn't surprise me if I'd made the Guinness Book of Records for the number of doors that I've knocked on or doorbells I've rung."

"How do you figure that?" he asked, not too happily.

"Well," I replied, amused, "I rang my first doorbell in 1948. Subtracting six years for other ventures, I once figured, over a period of 25 years or so, I've knocked on about 500,000 doors."

Looking at me in disbelief, he said, "You're not telling me that you got into a half-million homes trying to buy stuff?"

I laughed, "No! Not everyone was home, but I still had to try. Let's say that I banged on that many doors."

Antique
Show & Sale

CHAPTER 10

Success in my system of canvassing had me ready to set up a permanent itinerary of antique shows. Beginning in the fall of 1958, believing I could get a jump on the Florida winter season of shows, I packed my baggage and equipment into my new, sleek, yellow and white Pontiac Star-Chief convertible and headed to Florida.

Arriving in Ft. Lauderdale on Labor Day, the sun broiling the earth, I immediately drove to the beach and jumped into the ocean. The water was as hot as the air and the next few days brought torrents of rain. I wondered what on earth I was doing here this time of year. Under these circumstances, I couldn't get out to canvass. Sitting in my car, windshield wipers furiously working, I decided to drive to California—leaving immediately.

I thought the climate would be more suitable at this time of year for canvassing. Another compelling reason for driving out there was that a former girlfriend lived in the Los Angeles area. Being out of contact with her for at least a year, it did not surprise me when I learned that she was married.

California's weather was wonderful, ideal for soliciting. I found people receptive, concluding that I could work anywhere I chose. It was easy enough to find a refinery in downtown Los Angeles where I could turn my scrap gold into cash. By soliciting diligently, I soon accumulated enough antique jewelry to exhibit at an antique show—but where?

Seeking out a small community antique show, I became acquainted with one of the dealers. Since she had antique stock other than jewelry, she allowed me to share the expenses and exhibit jewelry from her booth at a bigger show in Los Angeles.

Fortunately, I was able to exhibit in two other antique shows within a 50 mile range that fall, convincing me that I could work in California permanently. Antique shows in 1958 were "catching on" everywhere, new shows starting up in the West as well as back East. But, there was not a solitary soul in the entire state that I could talk to, except as a stranger.

With winter coming on, thoughts of Florida and friends I knew living there became increasingly enticing. Plus the memory of the good times and the pleasures the area afforded, convinced me to return. Florida, here I come!

Catching a little sleep at truck stops along the way, by Thanksgiving Day I was gobbling down a dinner in a diner in Abilene, Texas. In three days I was on the west coast of Florida, where I chose to dally for a while.

Knowing that St. Petersburg was famous for its retirees, I thought it might be interesting to see for myself. Looking over the downtown area, my heart leaped with excitement. Row after row of benches along the downtown streets were overflowing with elderly people claiming this retirement paradise. Not only were the streets, stores and restaurants occupied with aged citizens, but when I came across a large jewelry store in the heart of downtown, my eyes danced from window to window in glorious amazement.

Surely this city had to be the Mecca in America for antique jewelry. The windows displayed trays of Bohemian garnets; pairs of bold, ornate, solid gold Victorian bracelets—in their original boxes; heavy, intricate gold necklaces in various shades of gold and elaborate designs; innumerable jeweled brooches; row after row of antique rings and splendid antique diamond pieces; plus an array of solid gold pocket watches and chains. Prominently displayed signs were placed in windows: WE BUY OLD JEWELRY.

Cruising the residential area close to downtown, street after-street I found neat, single-family homes, with an air of heavenly solitude and not a child or toy to be seen. What conditions could be more ideal for a firm, bell-pushing index finger? There obviously had to be boxes of old, stored jewelry just waiting to be plucked from these homes.

Exploring the local beaches, I found a small fishing settlement with the appealing name of Pass-a-Grille. Its idyllic setting and golden sunsets over the Gulf of Mexico lifted my exuberance ever higher.

Checking into a very reasonably-priced room at the only hotel, from their I would conduct my canvassing every day with renewed energy. All through December I went into St. Petersburg by day— the results of my endeavors being as good as anticipated—and returned at night, with very little to do. This situation persuaded me to consider canvassing here but four days a week, and make Ft. Lauderdale my headquarters for long weekends. Although I was fortunate enough to meet someone with whom to celebrate New Year's Eve—the only waitress at a small diner—there was not enough action otherwise to compel me to stay the full week.

I knew that my brother Vin would by now be in the Miami area for his three winter antique shows, which gave me a good reason to leave on the following weekend.

In Ft. Lauderdale, I was lucky enough to find an efficiency for $80 a month, from there I could return to St. Petersburg weekly.

I drove around Ft. Lauderdale, amazed to see how it had grown since I was there several years earlier. Cruising the residential sections, I was further pleasantly surprised to find how many single-family dwellings were inhabited by a large influx of senior citizens; even as outside the city, entire new retirement communities were being developed. I wasted little time in getting a solicitor's license. There proved to be plenty of antique jewelry available (and other antiques as I was to discover much later). No need to return to St. Petersburg.

Meeting my brother in Miami, where he stayed for the season, he invited me to display my own antique jewelry along with his at the only three antique shows being held in the area. But now that I had a vast field from which to buy and sell, I opted to free-lance and procure my own yearly itinerary of shows, as Vin was doing.

Antique shows became the culmination of my achievements in successful canvassing, the dealers rushed to my booth ahead of opening time, to buy from me (what they might sell for yet a higher price), knowing I purchased my jewelry directly from private sources. A great combination, house calls and shows, were to be mine for many years.

Not only were antique shows an exciting way to make a living, but the travel and social life surrounding them were added inducements. It is truly show business!

The shows were often held in the best downtown hotels. Dealers were given a special rate, allowing them an opportunity to live it up a little. And they did! Those dealers who exhibited in the winter and summer resort antique shows followed the sun and the wealthy. Living at least on the fringes of high society.

In the late 1940's, Kate Smith had been a fixture at the New York City shows. In the 1950's and 1960's, Liberace could be seen taking in shows at a fast clip, a very keen eye out for the rare, unusual or spectacular. And Barbra Streisand, lovely in black, was seen examining antique silver in the booth next to us. Then there was David Brinckley strolling through the 26th Street and Sixth Avenue Sunday Flea Market in Manhattan; and surely that was William Buckley Jr. looking over nautical items at the Stamford, Connecticut Marina Antique Show in September. The dealers had an exciting moment when Elizabeth Taylor came by the back entrance before the show opened at the Hyannis, Cape Cod Antique Show & Sale in July, looking over some antique books.

There was always a chance of a famous person, a Hollywood star, appearing at many of these shows. A buzz could be heard here and there as people, touring the aisles of the show, tried to catch a glimpse of them. Some dealers reveled in luminaries as customers, and saw themselves as "show people" hobnobbing with the elite and prominent. (Alas, my idol, W.C. Fields, was never spotted at any shows in which we exhibited.)

Aside from the glamour and the financial prospects to be made from a show, each city or village—whether held at a hotel, a church, a synagogue or civic building—had its special attractions, which was equally important to the antique dealers. They sought out the best restaurants, the dancing and the night life after the show. There was plenty of these, according to one's budget, and the word FUN was associated with ANTIQUE SHOW.

By the late 1960's, the "ANTIQUE SHOW & SALE" had reached its zenith in popularity. Shows were being promoted at the most desirable places possible. But the antique show promoters' ambitious endeavors to produce ever more of them in every hamlet and city—churches, synagogues, State Guard Armories, hotels, motels, ballrooms, and auditoriums—became redundant. Wherever one show became successful, another was soon to follow. America had become hooked on antique shows. And the idea that money, excitement and prestige could be had by promoting more shows would lead to vigorous competition later.

Regardless of the changes that began to appear, I would continue my regular circuit of soliciting and exhibiting at antique shows up to my mother's death in 1975. After my wife and I sold the big house in Utica, N.Y.—Vin and my father were deceased by then—it became our opportunity to move to Florida.

There was no warning yet of the forthcoming boom in the precious metals market, although gold then—mid-1970's—was a free commodity in the markets, hovering at near $100 per ounce.

In 1978 we bought a condominium on Pompano Beach overlooking the ocean, making that our permanent residence. Soon thereafter, we leased a shop from which to operate our business.

This new setup would eliminate our northern shows and it had already been proven that this region would be excellent for buying jewelry. Indeed it did so, but it also became a part of the scene for the destruction of the antique jewelry business, itself.

Gold And Silver
Rush

CHAPTER 11

While on an Alaskan cruise a few years ago, the tourist stops included Gold Rush towns, references to the Yukon, and other points of interest relating to those famous days in the late 1800's.

Lounging in our deck chairs, I asked Jane which she thought had been the biggest gold rush of all. Thinking momentarily, she replied, "I don't know! Up here in Alaska, I suppose. Or maybe California?"

"No," I informed her, "It happened in 1980. In America and all over the world."

One of the most amazing facts about this epoch is how easily the "1980's gold and silver rush" had faded into history, with very few if any accounts depicting its brief yet astounding impact on the world markets at that time. Yet, not surprisingly, the people who were embroiled most actively in this period would probably be the ones least likely to recall it publicly. Those having made the largest fortunes of all in such a short period of time would have no need to broadcast their exploits. However, they will always recall privately and fondly the crazy shenanigans of this era, relishing their profit and the fun the precious metals frenzy had provided, yet shaking their heads in disbelief.

Those were the days! It all happened so fast that the federal, state and local authorities could barely digest what was going on before making an attempt to regulate the vast buying and selling of all precious metals. Spontaneous, hectic, giddy and unpredictable as that time was, those who had participated in it may look back at its incredibility and realize they were a part of history.

Near the end of 1979 and for the next year or so, all those who were in the metals, jewelry or antique market and in any relating occupations were implicated in the spiraling adventure. Those of us who were directly involved feel it will never happen again—not in the direction it went.

Since gold was allowed to be traded on the free market, from a low of $35 per ounce in 1934 to about $100 per ounce in the 1970's, it began to skyrocket in 1979 and by January of 1980 it was priced in excess of $800 per ounce. Silver was about $2 per ounce in the 1970's. By early 1980 it began to soar, reaching a plateau of $50 per ounce.

The rise was phenomenal, also being linked to the low value of the dollar. It was frightening to turn on the TV daily and hear the networks start their news programs citing the day's decline in the value of the dollar. Those dealing in gold, silver, coins, bullion and stock became delirious with excitement and the mad scramble was on.

As the price of gold soared, a pair of brothers in Texas, named Hunt, began buying up vast amounts of silver daily and driving the price steadily upwards.

One could pick up major newspapers and read of predictions that gold would rise to $1,000 and even $2,000 per ounce. For a time, even people of vision believed this. If so, imagine the chaos within the jewelry business. A simple, plain wedding band of gold could cost $500.

One had to be in the business to fully appreciate the exuberance of it all. High inflation sent investors rushing into intangibles and antiques. Diamonds and other precious gems gained tremendously in value and demand; brokers would draw up portfolios for anyone wanting to get in on the action. People knowing nothing about these markets wanted to be included, and so the fever became highly contagious.

A flawless, top grade one-carat diamond, loose, unmounted, folded within a piece of tissue paper, was being offered for an astounding

$60,000 to anyone foolhardy or rich enough to "invest" in it. The same stone today would be priced in the neighborhood of $14,000.

* *

By sheer coincidence, we had leased a shop in Pompano Beach just before all this began in September, 1979. Our original plans were to open an antique jewelry store for the purpose of buying and selling. We were in a prime area for purchasing privately, surrounded by condos inhabited by older, wealthier people. Using local newspapers to advertise our venture, we forged ahead confidently.

We visualized operating a shop dealing exclusively in antique jewelry. Having traveled over 40,000 miles a year exhibiting at antique shows, I felt it was time to settle to something permanent and more promising.

Having returned in early October, from an antique show in Stamford, Connecticut, we energetically began furnishing the new shop. First, we had an artist do a fine job of painting a large sign of bronze coloring, show-window size, and placing it above the shop front. In huge darker lettering was PURNIE'S ANTIQUE JEW-ELRY, with a large pocket watch and chain drawn below. The shop faced four lanes of traffic and pedestrian sidewalks.

Earlier that year, while in Myrtle Beach at an antique show, the dealer across from us had a large, old Persian rug which I thought would look well in the living room of our newly acquired condo, a few blocks from the shop. The show was not the best for many dealers, mainly because of inclement weather. So, on the last day, between the re-packing of our merchandise for the haul to our vehicle amidst a drenching rain, I made a couple of trips across the aisle to ask the owner of the rug, "What's your best price?" Still not low enough, not until the rain increased and spirits ebbed did the dealer finally make me an offer I couldn't refuse.

That rug ended up not in our apartment but in our new shop. And if ever an Oriental rug was to live up to its name for durability and resistance to wear, this one more than proved itself over the next five years. Furthermore, with its vivid beautiful colors and, on the walls, several paintings borrowed from my artist-sister Edith, the shop had an aura of elegance. We needed that! But before we had a chance to put any display cases of jewelry into the store, the sudden rise in silver and gold prices altered our plans. We needed the shop, but only for the public to come in to sell their items. After hastily adding an antique sofa, a few chairs, a couple of desks and operating equipment, there would be nothing to suggest we were a jewelry store. That was not to happen!

Besides myself, there was Bruce, my nephew, and his brother-in-law, Ron, as my staff. Both had recently moved to Florida. Friendly and courteous, Bruce knew absolutely nothing about the gold and silver business, but he was to get the most intensive on-the-job training one could hope for, and in the shortest time possible.

Ron, having been a police officer in a New York state village, became our coin buyer and security guard. He made a good appearance at the front desk of the shop. Burly, amiable, with a full head of curly reddish hair, his looks concealed the challenge that sparked from his eyes, for he wore a gun around his midriff and was ready for action, were it required. That appearance also belied his true nature, for he courteously made all customers feel at ease and comfortable.

My wife Jackie was only called upon to help sell at the area antique shows, which were coming up soon. Interestingly, we were the only buyers around to have a "maitre d'" in Dave, a friend who daily frequented our shop. A gentleman in his late seventies, his background was as a retired New Yorker and a former bar owner in Manhattan, a concert violin player, an excellent shoe salesman, and an inveterate card player. Always a lady charmer, he fit in especially well with all the retired New Yorkers in the area, his accent making them feel at home. With a full head of wavy silver-gray hair, Dave had a quick smile which partially revealed a small fortune in gold teeth becoming more valuable each day.

With our staff and "maitre d'" firmly in place, we launched ourselves into the sudden activity in the silver and gold market. As the first salvo, a man walked into our shop, excited about the rise in the price of metals, and sold us an entire tray of heavy, solid gold high school rings. He had been a salesman of those items. These were samples he still had on hand. Now retired, seeing our ad, he was happy to be rid of them. We speedily popped out all the stones, which were synthetic anyway, and took the rings to a refinery in Miami. Making a fast, appreciable profit, it immediately became evident that had we kept them a week longer, we would have made considerably more.

As 1979 neared its end, things were beginning to explode; more silver and gold was coming into the shop from the general public. The stir among the dealers in gold and silver went from a buzz to a roar. All the jewelry stores and antique dealers dabbling in these metals in all forms threw their doors wide open to the public.

Newspapers across the country blared out daily headlines: GOLD REACHES $200 (. . . $300 . . . $400 . . . $500.) SILVER SOARS TO $30 PER OUNCE (. . . $40 . . . $50.) DOLLAR TUMBLES. INFLATION RISES. Over and over again, day after day, the metals market captured the headlines and the dealers rejoiced in delightful delirium.

For a ready cash flow, there soon was no need to run to a refinery in Miami. Dealers new to the game would stop at the store daily, asking to buy our scrap gold and silver on the spot, at that day's market price. Sheer volume enabled an instant profit.

Aside from the scrap surge, we also purchased re-salable items of jewelry and silver. More antique jewelry came in during that period of time than we could have imagined. Having antique shows in the area, one every month at Coconut Grove, we had an instant market at all times. Any attempt to put price tags on jewelry or silver objects was futile; the value became obsolete overnight. Ever upwards! It was confusing, but none of the dealers were complaining. A well-worn phrase heard was: "The merchandise is coming out of the woodwork!"

Good fortune was theirs—the antique dealers in Florida—where the major winter antique shows were being held. Not only were gold and silver objects in demand, but people were investing in antiques of every kind, also sending the art market into its long, spectacular climb.

Besides our own customary American dealers racing around buying from each other, the first large influx of European dealers began flowing into the South Florida antique shows. The English! The Italians! The Germans! Who next? Initially they were not too important to the American dealers. Everyone was plunking down cash on the counters and hauling the merchandise away, turning it over as fast as possible and in whatever language prevailed.

When handling a piece of gold jewelry, the first question a buyer would ask the seller was, "How much does it weigh?" But, as antique jewelry dealers, our prime concern was always the beauty, rarity, provenance and age of the piece, with weight being of far lesser concern. However, with escalating gold and silver prices, weight became an important factor in any kind of gold jewelry—unfortunately.

Numerous dealers, never before interested in jewelry or silver, suddenly became entranced and bewitched by them because of their high demand. One needed only to learn how to test for silver or gold and how to weigh them. It was very easy to learn the fundamentals, and with cold, hard cash, anyone could open up a store, a shop, an antique booth, rent a motel room or any facade where the public could be invited to enter and sell their precious metals. The doors of opportunity were thrown wide open for anyone wishing to invade the field and make himself plenty of fast money.

**

What a bonanza the newspapers were reaping in advertising revenue! Teams of buyers set out to travel around the country, renting hotel and motel rooms, or opening new stores, all advertising: WE BUY GOLD ... SILVER ... PLATINUM ... JEWELRY ... COINS ... DIAMONDS ... etc.

Practically every jewelry store had some kind of window sign asking for the same items, also using the newspapers to advertise the fact.

Many stores required a crash course of their employees, teaching them how to buy precious metals. Men and women, young and old, they were taught the difference between "sterling" and "silver-plate." They had to learn that there were 20 pennyweights to an ounce of gold, that pure gold was 24-karat. They had to master the art of reading 10K ... 14K ... 18K. They were trained to gently file into an object and touch some acid to it to determine if it was solid gold. They acquired the skill of taking a hammer to a pair of candlesticks and wrestling the sterling silver from the resin-weighted material inside. They had to become adept at using a pair of pliers to knock out the semi-precious stones from a bracelet, or to separate the gold from a dental bridge. In far too many instances, they had to learn to become blind to an object of antique or modern beauty, to see only its weight and "scrap" value.

The back rooms of countless jewelry stores and other buying locations were alive and vibrant with relentless crushing, smashing, banging, pulling and ripping apart the most diversified objects ever made of gold and silver!

New buyers would set up in a vacant store, not far from another buyer, to catch some of the overflow. Lined up in the streets with bags of silver and gold objects, people waited their turn to sell. One day a sign appeared overnight in a vacant store across the street from our shop with an arrow pointing upstairs. Two buyers had magically appeared with large WE BUY signs. Anyone, it seemed, could procure an occupational license and become happily involved.

Among the most innovating buyers, soon to become a commonplace sight, were the itinerant GOLD ... SILVER ... COINS solicitors who went from town to town, city to city, or wherever else a cluster of homes might be. They would rent a hotel or motel room, or suite—to appear more impressive—and run huge ads in the local papers and on TV proclaiming something like: FIVE DAYS ONLY! ... IMMEDIATE CASH! ... GOLD ... SILVER ... DIAMONDS .... COINS ... etc. They listed everything they were buying, from dental gold to precious gems. Most important, they would post the current price offered for gold and silver by weight.

One city might have several buyers scattered about simultaneously, each running ads in the same paper: Full-page ads, half-page ads, and smaller ads. A "motel" buyer could move out of one motel after 5 DAYS ONLY, drive a few miles down the street and do just as well in another neighborhood for 5 DAYS ONLY.

The public learned much about pennyweights, grams and ounces by reading the papers, and could check out what each buyer was offering that day. It was quite common for steady customers, who walked by our shop regularly to just poke a head in the door and ask, "What's silver doing today?" or "What's gold today?" One dealer, bored in the frequency of answering the last question, gave this reply in jest, "Gold is a yellow metal, heavy, malleable, soft and valuable, like it was yesterday."

Much was changing among precious metals buyers and antique dealers. So engrossed were they in market prices, even nature was being slighted. Dealers no longer saw sunrises and sunsets. Seasons became irrelevant. Simple salutations were discontinued; it was no longer customary to say "Good morning, Al, how are you today?" Instead, one dealer would greet the other with a sprightly demeanor, asking "Al, did you get the spot gold price from London yet?" (Whose price was five hours in advance of ours.)

The competition became so furious between the buyers that they began to include something novel in their advertising: WE WILL PAY FOR YOUR GAS, or WE WILL PICK YOU UP AT

YOUR HOME, or FIVE BUYERS ON PREMISES . . . NO WAITING IN LINE, or FREE COFFEE.

One dealer had his secretary send out a business letter to the area dentists, quoting the prices he would pay for their discarded dental gold. There was talk of another dealer mailing similar solicitations to funeral directors: OUR REPRESENTATIVE WILL CALL AT YOUR PARLOR TO PURCHASE GOLD.

There had to be names for all these maverick buyers. Locally, even the Sears store opened up a GOLD AND SILVER BUYING DEPARTMENT, near a heavily-trafficked escalator. One of the more exciting objects one buyer purchased there was a large, sterling silver ship: sails, masts, and all. Uncommon items became commonplace.

Above hastily-rented vacant stores, signs could be quite innovative and flashy, like: 1980's GOLD RUSH or GOLD BUYERS OF BABYLON, or GOLDIE'S NUGGET NOOK, or THE GOLD SHAFT, and more than one THE GOLD MINE. Wherever someone posted a sign, the public would soon be trudging there with bags of gold and silver.

Not along snow-swept mountains in California did they pan for gold. Or the Yukon! Those had been nightmares. For these yellow-metal grubbers of the 1980's there would be no bracing against the elements; no Arctic blasts and sleeping in tents along a frozen creek or river; no pick and shovel or panning for gold in frigid waters; no fear of baying wolves on a lonely mountain, nor the night prowlings of a grizzly bear; and no rugged, snow-covered mountain to face in the morning in hopes of finally claiming the mother lode.

Not at a distant place were they, but at home. They sat amidst the comforts of a modern office, a store or motel room, in the dignified atmosphere of a reputable jewelry store or the homey surroundings of an antique shop. Here the riches from private collections were dumped on formica or wooden tables near the blinking of the most up-to-date electronic weighing devices and the fast-figuring calculators working out transactions into penny-weights, grams and ounces, which were ultimately traded for cash.

Here there were only the moving of chairs by men and women, well-dressed or casually attired, serving an endless line of customers to whom they addressed the initial bland question of "Who's next?" They were the assayers. Whatever location they purchased from was their "stake."

All buyers advertised "WE PAY CASH." The plainly visible mounds of cash stacked in crisp new bills laid out in denominations were what enticed people in. Of course, there stood at least one armed guard close by the operation, as duly advertised.

The cash flow daily was in the thousands for even the smaller buyers; for the big operators, some with several employees, it came to hundreds of thousands, and more. Few buyers had time to ponder how long this bonanza would keep up. All predictions were upward, optimism being the prevailing attitude.

The public, in the millions, unable to resist selling something, was having the time of their life. They sold useful items, along with those of no further use since there was never a better time to sell scrap silver and gold.

Many knew that for a single silver spoon, even twisted or bent from the dishwasher, one could get at least $10 immediately. One silver dollar, of which there were untold millions, could bring at least $15. One gold dental cap could buy a good lunch for yourself and friend.

Neighbors telling neighbors, selling became contagious. "Matilda, I just sold my sterling tea set for $1500. Why don't you get rid of yours? I'll go with you—it's sort of fun."

It didn't matter if the sellers knew whether their items were solid gold or sterling silver. "BRING EVERYTHING FOR A FREE APPRAISAL," the ads urged. People dumped their jewelry boxes on bedspreads, looking for high school and college rings, or any ring at all. A simple gold wedding band found in a box after Aunt

Sarah's death could be worth $50 in scrap. Class rings were the first things to be tossed into the "melting pot"—there were so many of them. If there was any tearful nostalgia over an old antique brooch once belonging to Aunt Abigail, tossed on some scales, it was surprising how easily sentiment flew out a shop or motel door when a voice said, "We will pay you $250 for this brooch."

**

We knew a few antique dealers who originally started out as dealers in coins exclusively. They were the first to get on the gold and silver bandwagon, since everyone had some silver coins to sell, dimes to dollars. In a time when the weight of the coins was suddenly worth far more than their face value, regardless of their condition, people stampeded to sell them. The buyers advertised constantly in the local newspapers, clearly stating what they would pay for every denomination of silver and gold coins, also encouraging the public to bring in anything else in jewelry and precious metals as well. This gave them on-the-job training for their future as antique dealers.

Overnight, in a world full of silver coins, small coin collectors became experts in gold, silver and gems, with them well on their way to changing professions. The motel coin buyers had an immediate advantage as they moved from one location to another, into "virgin" territory. Everything was done in the open. From armed guard to the line-up of chairs in the motel hallway near a room entrance, customers waited their turn, clutching their bags of silver and gold.

Entering the room, the beds would be holding a quantity of large white plastic buckets boldly marked, indicating: DIMES and QUARTERS and HALF-DOLLARS and DOLLARS; also 10K and 14K and 18K; DENTAL, etc. As items were purchased from eager sellers, the buyer would whip out fresh, green bills, then turn away to fling the objects into the appropriate bucket. "Next!" was bellowed out to a seated customer, awaiting a turn to spread out his/her treasures. Of silver: candlesticks, compotes, silver spoons by the pounds, goblets, kettles, tureens, mirrors, cups, hairdressing sets, flatware, serving pieces, etc.

Gold items were of equal diversity, the likes of which many buyers had never seen. Advertisers enticed people to search their bank vaults for the inherited and the forgotten objects of jewelry passed on through the years.

Articles such as: Snuff boxes and enameled cigarette cases; gold mesh purses with precious stones, often bearing a Tiffany or Cartier mark, or that of a famous European maker, as Faberge. Out came the millions of gold pocket watches few used anymore, and the long-chained Victorian womens' gold watches with jeweled or enameled slides. More were intricately designed necklaces and very heavy gold lockets, often with pictures or braided hair locked within. So the list continued: Bar-pins and brooches of every description, millions of rings, bracelets and earrings of yesteryear. All were thrust into eager hands, causing eyes to sparkle in the pleasure of seeing, of handling, and finally owning these coveted treasures coming from people unknown.

What person back at the turn of the century would have ever dreamed that the gold stickpin in the shape of a horseshoe set with diamonds, so cherished and proudly worn, would end up 75 years later in a "bedroom" sale to a total stranger for "INSTANT CASH?" And what woman who so elegantly had adorned her wrists with a pair of antique Etruscan-type bracelets, given to her by her mother, and so prized, could have imagined that they would end up in a busy antique shop and sold for a thousand dollar's value in gold weight?

The newly trained buyer would be required to test most of these frequently unmarked antique pieces of jewelry, to determine their gold content, and toss them into the bucket. Many who inherited these pieces, cared little else who might wear the bracelets, or whether they were melted for their scrap value. It was the same with the buyers, unfortunately. They were there to buy. Examine! File! Drop acid! Weigh! Make an offer! Pay in cash! Not necessary to smile! Throw in designated bucket! Next! Over and over again.

Because there was so much more in silver, by sheer weight and quantity, who could ever calculate the enormity of this market? There were pictures in newspapers and magazines of dealers from London to New York, from St. Cloud, Minnesota, to Opa-Locka, Florida, smashing sterling candelabras and other objects. Often by people who, only a few months earlier, were book dealers, assorted salesmen or cattle barons.

We knew a few dealers who had a couple of rooms in their home stacked high with antique silver items—their way to become "rich." We also knew smarter dealers who had huge inventories of silver, purchased years before at $1 and $2 per ounce, now in their senior citizens years, who were spending most of their time unloading it all when silver reached $35 an ounce and more.

*

Back in a motel room, two itinerant gold and silver buyers, Sam and Tony, are exhausted after two days purchasing from a constant flow of crowds, and are thankful that it is nearly time to lock up for the night. Both double beds were covered with containers of loot, while the room was stacked with bags, boxes and buckets of gold and silver. Having dismissed an armed guard for the night, Sam wipes his brow and asks Tony, "Where the heck are we going to sleep tonight? We've got two more days here."

"Don't worry," a fatigued but very happy Tony replies, "as long as we have pillows, we can sleep on the floor."

"Well, since our van is right outside our window and we have cots there, why don't we take turns staying with the goods?"

"Fine! Get me the guns!"

At 3 A.M., Tony comes in and says, "I can't sleep thinking about all that stuff that's going to be coming through here tomorrow. And the next town we go to, we'd better get a bigger room, something more classy. What's on TV?"

**

Things were happening so fast that running out of money was quite common, making expeditious trips to the bank a constant necessity. The cash flow was enormous; dealers needed stacks of $100 bills to operate every day.

Friends of ours, on their first attempt at buying from a motel room, soon learned the thrills and hazards of doing business there. They were among the first antique dealers to run a full-page ad for buying gold and silver—THREE DAYS ONLY—in a small but prosperous city in upstate New York.

Having what they assumed was ample cash, many thousands, they were overwhelmed by the response of the public on their first day of buying. They were exhilarated but nervous as they looked at the bags of silver and gold stacking up to one corner of the room, and they with just a few thousand dollars left for the two remaining days.

Their was plenty of cash in the basement of their antique shop back home, but that was 125 miles away. Checking his watch, eyes wild with worry, the husband grabbed his car keys, and before bolting out the door, he said to his wife, "I've got to go home! I'll be back in time for opening tomorrow. Don't open that door for anyone, Lucy—and you know there are a couple of guns in the suitcase."

"Don't worry about me, Ernie," his wife replied. Being antique gun collectors, they had all types of operable weapons at home, and they were accustomed to living somewhat dangerously. Dashing off on an important business mission was just routine.

But this was mid-winter and upstate New York was the playground for capricious weather. Ernie was halfway home when he hit a stretch of wide open highway where winds from a nearby lake were noted for blowing snow drifts at any time. Where pavement was bare he found patches of ice and snow, but he calmly lit a cigarette and turned on some lively music.

Going around a curve, he suddenly froze in his seat at the sight of a tractor-trailer ahead that had apparently jackknifed and was blocking half the road. Could he stop in time? Not daring to brake fast, he pumped his brakes and hit a dry patch, but not enough to avoid another streak of solid, icy pavement, which spun his car completely around. As the trailer loomed straight ahead, several feet away, in those few seconds he saw his entire life fleeting by. The bags of gold and silver left in the motel with his wife . . . gone; his exciting life as an antique dealer . . . gone; a big casket loaded down with flowers . . . lots of flowers and people in church.

Dazed, unhurt and unbelieving, he soon saw his headlights reflecting upon the hood of the trailer, only inches away. Muttering, Hail Mary, full of grace . . . he realized he was alive, and had come to a stop.

Vastly shaken, he got out of the car and saw a tow truck and police nearby. With flares now burning, he was waved on, moving around the end of the truck. There was barely enough room but he held his breath and squeezed by.

Resuming a slow speed, he knew he would soon be out of the exposed area and into a more protected wooded section of the highway. Having thanked God, his thoughts soon drifted back to his mission. He took no time out then to marvel at how his thoughts could change so rapidly from the ethereal to the earthy; his only concern was getting home safely. Soon he was picking up speed.

When he arrived, the house and the shop never looked better. Reaching for a bottle of Jack Daniels, he poured a very generous drink and sank into a sofa, the warm glow of the liquid soon spread through him, soothing his nerves.

The next morning, he arrived at the motel early enough, loaded down with thoughts of all the treasures that would be forthcoming in the next two days. By going on a path from city to city, he had a hunch he was on the right track for buying gold and silver. Maybe last night's experience was meant to be. Was that a warning? He should take more time out to meditate. Did he go to church often enough? Surely not! It could have been curtains for him had he hit the truck broadside. And even though they already had a successful antique business, this gold and silver thing could make them really rich.

Noting how people poured into the motel room that first day, their arms loaded with bags and boxes of stuff, he knew he and Lucy could do one of these a week, even bring some help along. Cash? Bring it by the carload! They were in the big times! He hesitated a couple of seconds before going into the motel room. He knew there was something he was trying to remember about last night before he finally fell asleep in a pleasant stupor. It was his trying to remember what came after Hail Mary, full of grace . . .

The general public was never more weight conscious. Not about the pounds on their bodies but the price of gold and silver by the ounce. We had many repeat customers come into the shop who were as well-versed in the technical weights of gold and silver as some of the dealers.

A charming housewife who ordinarily spent her time pouring over the exact measurement of sugar, salt, butter and flour by the tablespoon and cup for baking cookies was now conversing in a new language.

"Hello, Gertrude! I just saw in this morning's paper that silver is up to $37 an ounce. Yesterday it was $32, and I noticed that YOUR GOLD MINE is paying $1 more per pennyweight on 14-karat than THE GOLDEN CALF paid us on Monday. Let's get a few things together and scout around today." (Our phone would ring constantly from people seeking information such as, "What are you paying a pennyweight today for 14-karat?")

Mildred would take a shower that morning, then weigh herself. On the same scales, she carefully placed the silver tea set she and

George had bought on their honeymoon at $4 an ounce in 1950 in Mexico. With coffee in hand, she would read the daily silver and gold quotations, then get dressed. Picking up Gertrude, they arrive at one buyer's store with heavy, tightly-held bags. Mildred asks, "What's silver today?"

After weighing the reply, Mildred, backing out, looked across the street to THE SILVER VEIN, saying, "Let's not go there! When I took my silver flatware set there the man threw it on and off the scales so fast I couldn't read what he weighed. They're in such a hurry that you've got to watch them."

Chicken Deals And
College Grads

CHAPTER 12

As the gold and silver rush grew more hectic in early 1980, and the ever-forming lines of people set out for places to sell their valuables—across the country—Dave, our self-appointed "maitre d'" served us well at our shop. He would appear each morning and socialize, at the same time sizing up the situation. As a customer entered, he would say, "Please have a seat, Madam, someone will be right with you," or "You're next, sir, just step into the back room."

Always the gentleman, the ladies enjoyed the courtesy and attention he offered them, guiding them gently by the elbow to the buying room. To someone's impatience at waiting, Dave would say, "They'll pay you more than anyone else . . . it won't be long." Hearing this from the back room, I winced, reminding him later, "Don't talk it up too much, Dave!"

One day I overheard him tell a couple who were waiting with two large bags of silver beside them, "It will pay to wait. They treat you fairly here. Other places might give you the chicken deal."

Hearing this for the first time, I later spoke to him privately, smiling, "That doesn't sound kosher to me, Dave. What do you mean by that?"

His reply: "When I worked part-time in a poultry market in New York, way back in the 1930's, when the customer wasn't looking, the owner would put his thumb on the scales with the chicken. Times were tough then and every finger and feather counted; a few pennies more here and there would add up."

"What's that got to do with silver and gold?", I asked.

"Well," he laughed, "I go around to see some of these other buyers we know, and watch them when they weigh silver. It comes in so fast. They throw it on the scales, some pieces slip off the table, or get mixed up with the silver plate. With all the stuff around, nobody seems to notice. Everybody is in a rush; there are lines of people and it's easy to do all kinds of chicken deals, but this time, you subtract instead of add weight."

"If that's the case, Dave," I laughed, "there probably isn't a single buyer today that doesn't have some kind of chicken deal going. Look at the competition! Everything's done in such volume and haste that all kinds of 'mistakes' can and do occur, intentionally or not. These are unusual times. Open up the Wall Street Journal, or the New York Times, or any of the local papers. You'll find all sorts of new investment companies involved in precious metals."

With the value of precious metals rising daily, people were eager to invest in silver and gold stock and bullion. Many were afraid they would be left out if they didn't invest in something immediately.

When the gold and silver rush made a disastrous downward turn later, there were innumerable sad stories to surface, and more tales embarrassingly concealed. The biggest chicken deal perhaps was one that occurred locally. People who thought they were investing in bars of pure gold were mortified to learn later that the new investment company vaults contained not gold, but only wooden bricks painted a tantalizing yellow.

By and large, however, these were happy and profitable times for the sellers and the dealers. Silver and gold items purchased at much lower prices years before, were now sold at the highest prices ever. One of the most frequents laments still heard is, "We should have sold our gold and silver back in 1980."

**

We were kept advised constantly of what was going on by the regular dealers who came into our shop daily to purchase from us.

It no longer was surprising to hear that GOLD GALORE down the street had bought a complete set of Russian enameled spoons as "some type of cloisonne" that turned out to be Faberge. Tales were told of rookies or experienced buyers who didn't notice until later that the heavy sterling silver tea service bought for scrap at $1800 had early English hallmarks and was worth far more as an antique. Much of what was bought was purchased as scrap, but not everything purchased as scrap was resold as such.

As gold peaked, new buyers would come into the shop every day. Well-dressed, valise in hand, they would present us with a card: PARAMOUNT PRECIOUS METALS, INC./HIGHEST PRICES PAID FOR GOLD, SILVER, PLATINUM, etc. Each buyer would claim "WILL PAY YOU MORE FOR YOUR SCRAP!"

Among the greatest casualties of the times were high school and college rings. Anyone over the age of eighteen could see a buyer, have a ring weighed and sold for instant cash. Did anyone bother to ask: "Hey, Mom! Do you want that old class ring?"

One baby-faced nineteen year old asks, "How much can I get for my college graduation ring?" Weighing it, the buyer hands it back, saying, "$120 . . . after you graduate."

Another conspicuous victim of the gold rush was the "grand-mother bracelet." After the young men and women came marching home from World War II, got married and had children, as proud parents they presented the doting grandmother a birthday gift of a small disk of gold with a head silhouette of a grandchild (another year, the bracelet, plus another gold disk as each grandchild was born.) Here were all the little darlings, dangling on a bracelet, with their names on one side and the other side proclaiming "Love to Grandma." This assured the parents of a place in Grandma's heart or a chance to vie in the family hierarchy for Grandma's favors. Grandma could recognize instantly the little tykes: "There's Billy with the cute chin," and "Look how sweet Polly looks with her pigtails."

Some bracelets became quite heavy with the propagation of the family name, Grandma proudly wearing the treasured ornament with eyes twinkling and heart leaping with joy and pride. Something to cherish forever.

That is, until 1980! Grandma and Grandpa were by then out to pasture in Florida; the "kids" and the grandchildren phoned dutifully from Cleveland every week. Everything had been taken care of in Florida: the condo, the bank and stock accounts, properties, burial arrangements, leaving nothing more to be done.

Then Grandpa died in his sleep and the "kids," in soft tones, invited Grandma to "come live with us if you like." The "kids" on the other end of the telephone line smiled at each other when they heard Grandma reply, "Oh! I would never be a burden to anyone. Besides, I love it here and I have a lot of friends. We're always busy."

Same subject, another dialogue: "Hello, Mildred! Did you see in the paper where gold is today? I'll pick you up at 10:30; we can go over to that gold place on Atlantic Blvd.," says Sarah. They arrive at our shop and, after a brief wait, Dave escorted them into the back room.

After Mildred finished selling her items, Sarah emptied her purse of several pieces of jewelry on the table. We quoted prices on each item, but when it came to her "grandmother's bracelet," she held it back and said to Mildred, "I don't know if I want to sell this bracelet. What do you think, Mildred? It has all these silhouettes of my grandchildren. Isn't it sweet?" as she held it up for us to see.

"It's darling," Mildred agreed.

"Whatever you think," I volunteered.

Holding it a little longer, Sarah said, "I guess I'm just being sentimental, but I believe I'll keep it." About ready to put it back into her purse, but noting its heavy weight, she asked, "Just out of curiosity, if I were to sell it, what would it bring?"

Placing it on the electronic gold scales, I offered her $925, whereupon she ceased putting it away. Turning to Mildred and placing it on the table, she said "I really don't wear it anymore and the grand-children have about grown up. What do you think, Mildred?"

"Well, I'd get rid of it, if you're not wearing it anymore," replies her friend.

"You might as well have it," she tells me, with no noticeable tears or visible pangs of regret, nor with one last glance at the profiled heads of the beloved little angels. "Where shall we go for lunch" is heard as they leave.

Another treasured keepsake that became a major calamity of the times, that speedily went into the melting pot, were the innumer-able "charm bracelets." These charms were usually individually purchased and added on to a heavy, gold-linked bracelet having an opening between links to allow the adding on of more charms.

Women and men—some widows and widowers—would come in and plunk down a heavily loaded bracelet with many assorted charms. Collected as souvenirs of world travels with the spouse over a lifetime, the charms might be the Eiffel Tower, the London Bridge, the Leaning Tower of Pisa, shamrocks, gem-studded miniature birthday calendars, llamas from South America, boats, dancing bal-lerinas, hearts and similar items. All of which held fond memories in gold replicas, purchased with love, joy, happiness and passion.

The bracelets represented forty, fifty or more years of marriage and cherished meanings in two lives—the blessings, strife, travels and money-making—all that could be embodied in as many gold charms as a single bracelet could contain.

Bracelet in hand, the seller pondered it further, and relived some memories as she fondled each charm: a gold and pearl wishbone; a garnet birthday charm; a heavy gold cupid with its arrow, along with a "Love Always, Sol." Such mementos could have her reaching for a hanky.

"Can you just take this one off, please, the enameled cat?" she would ask. "We always had cats." Out came the pliers and the cat was tenderly but hastily detached from its lair of forty years. Onto the table and carefully wrapped in tissue, I handed it back to its mistress. Then, "Oh! One more! The one with the diamond stickpin soldered on it. Sol loved it!" she said, holding it forth. Out came the pliers again, the woman reclaiming a second charm. As the remaining charms and bracelet were dropped into the electronic weighing bucket, they gave forth a loud clink and clank. Barely concealing a surprising "Oh" as we offered her $1600, she topped the deal with "It was getting too heavy for me anyway. Just as well I sell it."

Another couple that entered our shop, both in their middle seventies, were pleased to tell us that they are newly married and have decided to sell some jewelry they no longer wanted. Among other objects, they each had a well-loaded charm bracelet from a previous marriage. Smiling and nodding affectionately towards each other, they separately replied when I quoted them a price, "that'll be fine." Walking out happily, the sentiments appeared to be less relevant.

Who knows how many millions of charms had lost their enchantment and ended up in a crucible? Certainly most gold buyers would agree that charms had been among the foremost martyrs in jewelry that vanished forever. Today, there is a demand for old, intact charm bracelets from the 1940's and 1950's. They have regained a prestige and nostalgia that makes them quite salable again—if they can be found.

Bags and boxes of such items had entered our doors. For some original owners, their disposal put an end to an important part of their lives. Yet, less often was the occasion sad, since people knew there had to be a separation from material things sooner or later. And what the heck! The price had never been higher.

At this point in time, since our shop never had an opportunity to become a retail store as originally planned, we likened ourselves to a no-frills funeral parlor. With chairs lined up on both sides of the wall, a Victorian couch set to one side, drapes drawn to keep out the hot western sun, and people solemnly awaiting service, the portraiture was not too far fetched. The thick, rich-looking Oriental rug further contributed to such an atmosphere. Although humans were not the subjects here, to be viewed for the last time, there was surely a lot of gold and silver objects headed for an end to a meaningful form and a resurrection into another.

**

One day during the height of the gold rush, a customer came in with just one object to sell. As usual, we had been busy at a steady clip; upon his turn to deal, he said that he was disposing of some Russian objects of art for an elderly neighbor who was confined to her house.

From her elegant collection, he handed me an elaborately enameled silver-gilt Easter egg. These had been highly symbolic in the Russian Orthodox Church and very popular in the days of the Czars. Intricately designed, the colors were of vivid red, blue and white. It opened into two halves.

Never having seen one like this before, I checked it for identifying marks. The man offered no information; his task was to sell it only. I soon found the Russian mark for silver, and, scrutinizing it closely, made out further Cyrillic imprints. I remembered enough about Russian lettering from my brief study of it in college and could decipher the name K. Faberge in Russian. There were a couple of other letters, somewhat worn, which intrigued me further.

The man had a swarthy look and a Slavic accent. Perhaps the south of Russia, I thought, which made the encounter more interesting. In heavily broken English, he conveyed the message that the woman had other valuable objects but wanted to sell this first. Her asking price was $2500. But I immediately thought it could be worth considerably more, being a Faberge piece.

I knew I had to make an instant decision since he could take it to any number of places in the area. "Look," I cautiously remarked, "I like it but I don't know what I can sell it for. (which was true) Would you take $2,000 for it?"

He was not eager to accept my offer, which heightened my interest. "She has other things if you buy this," he said, and waited, completely relaxed. I hesitated and further inspected it, if only to stall for time, and because a couple had just walked in with a heavy bag of silver. He suddenly said, "Okay! Make it $2200. You take it!"

Perhaps by buying this he would bring me other Russian treasures, now that we had initiated a business deal. Besides, there was a constant cash flow and it was a fun risk. Paying him off quickly, I was happy with the thought that I now had a valuable Russian Easter egg, by no one less than Karl Faberge, himself, with the maker's mark nicely incised within it and worn enough to make it all the more authentic. A nice addition to my collection of antiques at home and a great conversational piece, I thought. I would hang on to it for the time being. Twice the size of a hen's egg, vividly colored and obviously painstakingly designed and beautifully crafted, it was greatly admired when I showed it to a few people that day.

Setting it aside for a few weeks, with no definite plans for its future, I considered sending it off on one of Bruce's (my nephew) trips to New York City. The object was to take it to Sotheby's and get an estimate on its value. We had a parcel of antique jewelry to be sold there to some of our regular customers, and this would be a good time to check it out.

At Sotheby's, the expert on Russian objects took one look at it and asked Bruce, "Are you up from Florida?"

"Yes! Why?" he replied, wondering what difference that would make. The appraiser disappeared momentarily into another room and emerged with an identical egg in hand.

"This also came from from Florida and it is an excellent reproduction of a Faberge egg, with nearly the exact silver content, measurements and an amazing amount of beauty and even marks that appear worn, but nonetheless, not the real article. A great looking counterfeit, in other words," he concluded.

Continuing, he answered the forthcoming question, "If your egg were authentic, it would be worth about $10,000; as it is, it's worth whatever you can get for it. This reproduction I have might be worth up to $1000, if I can find a buyer."

It was about Easter time when I got this information, and the only dialogue I would have on this piece thereafter had me referring to the object as the "egg I laid." Since it would no longer be any fun to own, I told my nephew, "Let's just get rid of it at the next antique show, if we can."

It went to a couple of shows before we finally sold it to a dealer for $800, as a reproduction. He walked away mumbling something like, "It's stamped Faberge, and that's all . . ."

**

Back when gold was only $35 an ounce, there were few antique dealers who specialized in antique jewelry exclusively, while dealers in other antiques handled but little if any jewelry. Most antique shows and shops carried a general line of antiques.

But in 1980, there came a turning point in the careers of many antique dealers. Those who carried silver with their antiques, often now saw it as suddenly worth more for scrap than what was asked for it as a useful or ornamental object.

Looking upon their wedding bands of gold, it occurred to them that they, too, might be worth more for scrap than what they had paid for them. With the result that cut-glass dealers, for instance, who sold their wedding bands for its higher scrap value, could be on their way to becoming gold dealers. Could anyone blame them?

Those who noticed what was happening at jewelry stores in any city and town across the land—the lines of people out to sell their gold and silver—seeing the jewelry dealers at shows briskly and happily buying gold and silver, they too wanted in on the action. Why not?

When the gold bug first descended upon the antique dealers of America, it gave them a new appearance and outlook thereafter. Suddenly the field was exploding with jewelry experts.

Enterprising jewelry equipment sales people were soon going from dealer to dealer selling them acid, scales, portable and permanent weighing devices—the latest in electronic technology. Overnight they learned to test for gold, sporting brown-stained fingers and burns, but smiling joyfully.

At the antique shows, dealers who once encouraged customers to enter their booths to admire their crystal, porcelain and other fine antiques, now relegated them to second place as they set out showcases full of jewelry up front, where people could easily hover over them.

Consequently, we no longer recognized many of our old antique dealers by the new names above their booths. What was once CALICO CAT was now JUDY'S GEMS; and PAUL & PAMELA'S POTPOURRI became EAST END ESTATE BUYERS. A couple dealing in antique miniature figurines, under the name of DELICATE AND DELIGHTFUL, were hardly recognizable at the next show, stacked to the ears with showcases of jewelry, under the banner: ADVENTURES IN GOLD & SILVER. Long known for their selection of country antiques, ELLIE'S COUNTRY STORE became ELLIE'S ELDORADO. Gone were the old wooden butter churns; Ellie herself was now decked out in many ounces of gold, and her husband, handling his end of the booth, was surrounded with objects of silver.

To the new style jewelry dealers, it mattered not if the jewelry was antique or modern, as long as its value could be determined by weight and easily sold. Their identifying feature was a jeweler's magnifying loupe worn around the neck—many were of 14K gold, with a corresponding 14K gold chain. If a customer asked to see a piece of jewelry, it was handed directly to them in a sober demeanor and a single comment that "it is 18K gold weighing 34 pennyweights." The beauty of the object was secondary, nor did it matter whether the item was a bracelet or necklace.

With their newly acquired skills, these dealers could walk into pawn shops, antique shops and shows, or to other buying locations and purchase gold and silver. Selling it from their own booths, they had become jewelry dealers.

Two of my favorite dealers had adjusted to the gold and silver rush in a most representative fashion. Not having been to their shop in months, I noticed the change instantly. They once ran a shop full of bric-a-brac and furniture beneath a sign reading GWEN'S GARRETT (painted in green on a large wooden frame). But not anymore.

There was now a huge, blazing neon light covering half the store front. Multi-colored tubes of glass ran around in circles and squares, announcing to the world that this was THE BOULE-VARD JEWELRY EXCHANGE. Directly under it, in flashing lights were alternate colors of neon: WE BUY DIAMONDS-GOLD SILVER/IMMEDIATE CASH.

Walking in, I was greeted by the son, who had been in college the last time I was there. Lou and Gwen worked very hard in the antique business to send him to law school. Moments later his mother entered and greeted me enthusiastically, saying, "Henry, you remember my son, the lawyer, don't you?" Giving him due recognition and eyeing the cases of jewelry and silver throughout the store, I congratulated her on their new enterprise.

Her son, smiling broadly, winked at me and gripped his mother firmly by the shoulders as he said, "Henry, this is my wonderful mother, the 'EXCHANGE.'"

She became the first of many "EXCHANGES" that were to spring up all over. Ten dealers would rent a store or buy out a building and overnight become an "EXCHANGE."

Dating back to the early part of the century, "EXCHANGE" was an eye-catching and practical name for the jewelry dealers in the Bowery section of New York City. But now we had "EXCHANGES" making their appearance among the palm trees and ocean-caressed condos of Florida, as elsewhere in the country.

**

With gold at its peak value in the winter of 1980, the antique shows of South Florida experienced their most hectic and prosperous season ever. For the first time in memory, there was absolutely no time for dealers to idly stand around and talk about business. Customers were on the floor in droves all day long and every day of the show. Everyone was eager to invest in something as inflation soared. Gold, silver, art and practically anything in antiques was snapped up. No salesmanship required!

Every antique dealer seemed to produce his own essence; what he or she was doing at the moment was vital. There was no time to waste; they were part of a world-wide financial shakeup that had even the smallest flea market dealer, set up in the most obscure meadow or parking lot, feel an integral part of something that was overwhelming.

At the same time, European dealers in antiques, silver and jewelry were beginning to be seen in large numbers. In the previous thirty years, the major dealers we had done business with were from New York, Chicago and California. Those were mutually profitable and satisfying relationships, and when one American dealer was suddenly gone, another would appear to take his place.

Amidst high currency rates, we unexpectedly found ourselves facing European dealers, mainly the English, German and Italian. In accented German, they asked: "How much is the garnet necklace?" Or ... that gold cameo pin and earring set? Or ... that pair of bracelets?" A pause for the use of calculators, then, "Okay, we'll take it." Just like that! If those four words, "What's your best price?" were to vanish from the face of the earth, if but briefly, this was the time.

So suddenly had foreign dealers appeared on the American scene, the American dealers, who paid in good, solid business checks or cash, found themselves in brisk competition with international dealers, who were laying down inordinate thousands in hundred dollar bills. Consequently, some dealers, taken by surprise, asked themselves, "Hey! What's this? Where did these Germans come from? Thirty-five years ago we were exchanging bullets, now they're dealing out dollars and whisking away all the antique jewelry."

The English dealers, in vigorous and polite tones, would inquire, "What are you asking for that sterling silver tea set?" After a response and a bit of calculating, "Fine! We'll have it!" It was a surprising reversal of the 1950's, when opportunistic Americans stormed the war-ravaged shores of Europe to relieve many of them of their antiques.

As fast as the exhibitors at a show sold their antique wares to this influx of international dealers (as to others), so they hustled about the floor of the show seeking to replenish their stock and promptly sell it at a quick profit. Later, a prominent antique jewelry dealer would tell us that the winter show of 1980 at Miami Beach was profitable "beyond my wildest dreams."

Certainly, there were many others who had similar experiences, which spoiled them for future shows. These particular circumstances would surely vanish into history, probably never to return.

Following the success of these antique shows, the exhibitors searched for more sources, wherever more gold and silver might be found and purchased from an eager public.

Even businesses totally unrelated to this market, with a grain of knowledge and some extra cash, could set up a section of their premises for the purchase of such desired items. They might be a vacuum cleaner store, a hardware establishment or a dry cleaning outlet, advertising with a sign in the window.

Especially busy were the flea markets. The gold buyers would set up a tent or a stall, a couple of chairs or tables, the necessary equipment, and they were in business. A large sign stretched across their allotted space would read: WE BUY GOLD AND SILVER! From the thousands of people pouring through the area every weekend, they had gained access to a new source of supply.

From flea markets to distinguished auction houses, from jewelry stores and motel rooms to antique shops and shows, there was gold, silver and antique fever to electrify the air. Who took time then to worry how it would all end? Everything was going up!

**

Behold the cliche: What goes up, must come down! It was no tremor that shook the metals market in March of 1980; it was a vibration of high seismic proportions. Without any warning, the bubble burst on a weekend, dropping silver from about $50 an ounce to $16. The newspapers blared out in headlines, exploding the full story, which revealed the Hunt brothers' attempt to "corner the silver market" by buying up vast amounts of silver.

With the tumble of silver, gold dropped $200 an ounce in a few days, causing an onset of gigantic hangovers. Many dealers, caught with large amounts of silver, were suddenly stunned with immense losses.

We were a small operation, with a constant daily turnover like many another business, so there was no drastic suffering for us, just amazement and eagerness to learn all the details.

Questions arose: What would be the expressions upon the faces of the procession of dealers who would come through our doors on Monday morning? Or those of private investors who came into our shop regularly—clerks, small business owners, druggists, grocers, laundry operators, mailmen and the like—who had been investors in the market? What toll would this weekend exact?

For some, it was incredible that the market could collapse overnight, without any warning. One of our steadiest buyers of silver, stopping virtually every day to purchase our scrap, kept insisting that "the market will come back, turn around and go up again—this is merely an adjustment." His verbal attitude remained so for months, although his eyes were beginning to show a vacuous stare.

"The only thing that's going to turn around, Mike," I repeatedly told him, "is good old Mother Earth." The lightening-like days of running from place to place with metals in one hand and a briefcase full of cash in the other, had come to a screeching halt, for him and everyone else.

What remained was to sit back and analyze, like it or not. As rapidly as the gold and silver buyers "came out of the woodwork" to set up shop wherever they desired, so they quickly fizzled and disappeared. The ubiquitous ads in the newspapers like: FIVE DAYS ONLY ... BUYING FOR IMMEDIATE CASH ... GOLD ... SILVER ... JEWELRY ... COINS ... ETC., had vanished from all parts of the country. Gone were the lines of people clutching bags and boxes of silver and gold, and hustling around to compare prices.

We knew many private investors who had hung onto their silver items waiting for the price to go even higher. Their sense of speculation was severely shattered when the market crashed, leaving them literally holding the bag. But there were many too embarrassed to discuss it publicly, while those who had made fortunes quietly fled with their riches.

Paradoxically, even though the silver market had tumbled so violently, gold was still very high, at $500 to $600 for another year or so, and people were still interested in selling at that price. It was silver that would never recover, plunging ever lower, to finally settle at about $10 an ounce—for awhile, anyway, until it went even lower in the following months.

The growing fear was that the price of gold would go even lower, which kept the jewelry market fairly active. The demise of the temporary establishments was good for those of us who had permanent business locations. Of course, no longer maintaining anywhere near the feverish pace as before, our buying settled into a moderate pattern.

By 1982 gold would slip to $500 and fluctuate thereafter for the remainder of the 1980's. A crisis with Russia or other sporadic events would cause the metals market to rise or fall somewhat, but after 1990, gold slipped well below $400 an ounce and silver would hover around $4 per ounce. The hullabaloo was definitely over.

The biggest impact that brief period had on me personally, happened on a recent trip to upstate New York. One of my best friends had been an itinerant motel gold buyer, from start to finish. As we reminisced about those hectic gold and silver days, smiling broadly, he said, "There must have been something wrong with any dealer who bought gold and silver in those days and didn't get rich!" Lighting a cigar, he waited for my account.

"Well, Charlie, you're looking at a guy who didn't. My helpers were trained from scratch and we were getting many people into the shop, of course, and saw plenty of action. We had plans for expanding the business—advertising like the others—but then the market collapsed and caught us and everyone else by surprise. Who knew it would happen so fast? So what the heck?" That was the only answer I could come up with, feeble as it was.

Walking towards the shop one day in the summer of 1982—with gold fluctuating near $500—I glanced up at the large sign over the front door—PURNIE'S ANTIQUE JEWELRY—with our large logo beneath it: an antique pocket watch and chain. We thought the sign was unique when first placed there. But was it still appropriate for our business or was I kidding myself? Where would I get enough antique jewelry to fill up a store now, or half fill it?

It became evident, from experience and conversations with many other dealers, that untold amounts of antique jewelry from the Georgian and Victorian periods had been sold, and a large share melted. Much of antique jewelry, being massive and heavy, had a high gold content and in many cases was as valuable in scrap metal as it was as a piece of jewelry. So why should the buyer bother to preserve it as jewelry and something useful? Far too many didn't and that sealed the fate of the antique jewelry dealers as a separate and elite breed, so to speak. From now on, the remaining dealers would have to search far and wide for their merchandise. So much of it had also gone to Europe during the rush, thinning out the American supply and ultimately making the price of antique jewelry even more expensive in the future.

The real effect, however, of the gold rush in the antique trade was to catapult more dealers into the jewelry business. Gold at $350 an ounce, new or old, was easier to handle than furniture or glass and bric-a-brac. Not to mention more glamorous. At the antique shows, many dealers, along with their special line, have at least a small case of jewelry at his booth entrance, where one may easily see it.

There is little doubt that antique silver had ultimately suffered at least an equal fate. However, since there is far more silver by quantity than gold and much of it serviceable, more of it had been preserved.

Even though an intolerable amount of antique silver pieces, some quite rare, ended up in the melting pot—in the name of innocence, ignorance or greed—much more had escaped such a destiny. Millions of people, of course, never sold any gold or silver during the rush—for many reasons—thus carefully preserving their treasures for future generations.

Antique silver today, however, brings higher prices than ever; attesting to its importance, fabulous pieces still filter into the trade constantly.

With many a glittering name-sign dismantled from a dealer's storefront, and jewelers taking signs out of their windows, and housewives going back to weighing peaches, plums and tomatoes instead of gold and silver, that era finally ended like a Western movie: Some people slipped away without any notice; others rode exultantly and much richer into the sunset. The majority of the participants will have a longing look of nostalgia or regret, their eyes misting or smiles appearing as they recall that happy, hectic and hallucinatory spasm of time.

"Make My Day!"

CHAPTER 13

Any ideas of developing our shop into an antique jewelry store was abandoned, gone with the fading of the gold and silver rush. Instead of only jewelry, why not broaden our scope and buy and sell a general line of antiques, but keep jewelry, modern and old, as our main interest?

Turnover would be no problem, since we had a few good local antique shows where we still exhibited. But, just when we were about to stock up the empty store with antiques, we learned that the building had been sold and no leases would be renewed. That ended that!

My two co-workers were no longer with me. Having families to support, Bruce and Ron returned to the North.

I now found myself in need of a business address, an office and a shop from which to display, sell and advertise to buy. It wouldn't do that I, like so many others, flee into the night, completely erased from the face of the earth.

Many of my major decisions in life came on impulse, but they usually resulted in appropriate and favorable results. By driving about in my car, relaxed and looking around, I could usually find solutions. This happened soon enough!

Just three miles south from our former shop, in a busy tourist area close to the beach, I saw a store set back from but in view of the main highway. I remembered being in there once before with a friend. Knowing the owner, she had recently spoken to him about me. Perhaps we two could strike up a deal.

Following a couple of visits with Shelby, the owner of this shop, we easily entered into an informal, verbal partnership which bound neither of us to anything permanent. I would contribute towards the store rent; we would split the advertising expense to buy merchandise jointly, but still allow each other to operate separately in whatever manner we chose. It was a good, loose arrangement that turned out to be mutually advantageous for nearly two years. And a lot of fun!

Oddly enough, my partner was one of the ex-gold buyers who had gotten his start by setting up in various motels during the rush. Having previously owned a cattle ranch in Mississippi, he had moved to Florida just as the boom in metals started. Proving that all types got into the gold rush, he mastered the art of buying "precious metals" and opened the present shop for that purpose. Advertising to buy jewelry and other antiques, I spent a large share of my time away from the store, making house calls, while he spent long hours in the shop. We loved the arrangement!

The first thing that commanded my attention when I initially negotiated a partnership with him was a large, hand-printed notice on the front door of the shop that read: I KNOW WHO BROKE INTO MY CAR. I WILL BE READY NEXT TIME! There was no lack of character here and it was apparent that a dull association was not to be ours.

The first problem to overcome was that of a language barrier. That is, we both spoke English, but I came from upstate New York and he from Mississippi. He had less difficulty interpreting my words than I did his. His Southern accent had me often asking, "What's that again, Shelby?" Not because of the words, but the sing-along accompaniment: from a lilting high to low at a good pace, with an accent. It set him apart from the many Southerners I'd known. His manner was always witty, his mind exceptionally keen and mathematical, which worked as fast as a calculator when conducting business. No one could fool him on figures. Curiously, he had the face of a winged celestial being, a 60 year-old cherub—

if you will—but a tongue capable of spewing forth a fountain of the King's English that reached into the bowels of our great language.

Because of his witticisms and old plantation charm, our shop became a hangout for a cast of characters that could be extracted from either pleasant dreams or nightmares. He was a soft touch for a sad story, and gave generously of his time and self. He had a huge, swivel-type leather chair, one that would make Archie Bunker's look new in comparison, sitting in the rear of the shop, where he had a commanding view of all activities. This throne had sagging armrests, scratches, a few holes that revealed the interior parts and other wounds that seemed to gasp and groan at each shifting of his weight. Few others ever sat in this chair, it tacitly being guarded by a large, old wooden desk with locked drawers. Nothing on it, however, could ever be easily found, with its everyday accumulation of potato chips, Krugerrands, receipts, silver dollars, tools, soda, a loose diamond or two, the remains of yesterday's pizza and a loaded gun buried somewhere beneath it all. The walls surrounding this area were completely covered with photos of family and friends, showing his roots were an affectionate part of his past.

He would be found sitting between two telephones, one of which was usually in use, held firmly in place between ear and shoulder with his head. A visitor would often be seated in the prime chair directly in front of his desk. Thus set up, he conducted his daily affairs with a profusion of words and actions that seldom ceased. Here was a place from which to dispense or hear woeful tales, seek advice, laughter, gossip, rumors, truths, falsehoods, or business events. But he could just as suddenly spring from his chair, shuffle to the jewelry case, and give his full attention to whoever came in to buy or sell something.

He was seldom without his cowboy boots, his corduroy pants and a flannel shirt, making a striking contrast to the casual apparel or skimpy bathing suits most people wore as they walked past the shop.

Upon his throne he sat with his analytical and sharp mind—perhaps with a hint of his stint at Harvard—and traded stories, opinions, suggestions or any other service people might require of him. When he walked about the shop, it was not with a Gary Cooper stride, although he was tall enough and of ample build, but rather a Fred Sanford shuffle, which contributed to the "ol' country boy" image he liked to project.

Soon after I moved in, he told me about the robbery he'd had. Someone had broken into the back of his car and stolen some jewelry; although he couldn't prove it, he felt sure it was someone in the neighborhood. Thus the sign in the window, which remained there for a couple of weeks.

In fear, each night he took most of his more expensive jewelry home with him. Since his robbery, he was fully prepared, packing a gun with him as he loaded his car each night. Let them come; he was ready. But for the present, he was looking for the gun—last seen on his desk near a large box of animal crackers he kept for his grandchildren.

A gun would never be far out of sight. One was at hand when he stood at a large glass showcase, near his chair, where he dealt with a customer. What looked like a wooden outgoing letter box concealed the weapon that could be grasped in a moment from where it was casually covered by the Lifestyle section of the daily newspaper.

Our business relationship worked out better than we had thought possible. I was out much of the time buying merchandise (responses to our ads), then displaying it from my showcases at the shop. This showed the cowboy-recently-become-gold-dealer how to become an antique dealer. He caught on rapidly, as he warned me he would; even as I, in this new setup, was gaining experience and knowledge about antiques in general. What we didn't know about them, which was considerable, we could ask the many "experts" who trudged in daily to socialize or buy and sell antiques. Their diverse knowledge was always accessible to us, whether we wanted it or not.

At one time, there was a movie showing in which Clint Eastwood had his gun aimed at an adversary, beckoning to him: "Go ahead! Make my day!" The implication being: one false move and he would blast away. It became a popular expression, like "Where's the beef?" Even the President said, "Go ahead! Make my day," concerning some legislation, a warning that a pending action wasn't to his liking.

Because of the incidence of increased robberies during and after the gold rush, many jewelry stores and shops had installed buzzers near their outside entrances. Anyone seeking admittance would press the buzzer and wait for someone inside to release the door lock and let them in. It being a common security measure, we ourselves had one recently installed.

Returning to the shop from a house call one afternoon, I noticed something new there. Near the inner side of the buzzer was a new sign. Apparently Shelby had it mounted that morning. It was a large, colorful picture of a gun pointing directly into a person's face, saying: GO AHEAD! MAKE MY DAY!

Customers seeing it upon entering the shop would smile and react appropriately—often with laughter. This pleased Shelby, as he still hadn't settled his score with the one who stole his jewelry—and probably never would. In any case, the sign was a strong warning.

Our finest jewelry was placed in the front window where people constantly stopped to look. Shelby took great pride in presenting his best items there and he would open the door to anyone wanting to inspect them firsthand—just push the buzzer. Women were especially attracted to the display, of course; it had Shelby opening the door and, with a wide and friendly smile, call out, "Y' all come on in, ladies. You can't see anything out there. I just know two nice girls like you can make my day."

This and other such light banter, always complimentary, was very effective; and I knew, after many observations, that there were many repeat customers who came by for some much needed flattery.

During the winter season he would often spend much time near this window, elbows on the case, ready to lure in customers.

One afternoon close to Christmas, Shelby beguiled two well-dressed ladies into the shop as they were admiring his finest assortment of gold jewelry from the window. "Y' all too pretty to be standing out there in the warm weather. C'mon in and let's see how beautiful some of this jewelry looks on you," he said, as he opened the door, allowing the two elderly sisters to accept his invitation.

I was, at the time, polishing some jewelry in the back room, but would walk in and out for the half hour they were trying on several items of jewelry. And heard Shelby pour forth compliments effortlessly, in rhythm—honed hush puppie and catfish utterances that entranced the ladies, from whom there came giggles of delight. In truth, he admired the ladies in a natural way, evoking a beauty in manners which hadn't been visible in decades.

"Y' all make that bracelet look so pretty, M'am," were words that no one else could get away with.

Graciously opening the door for them after they had purchased a couple of items, directly next to the words GO AHEAD! MAKE MY DAY!, Shelby smiled as they looked at the sign. Then, "Thank you ladies. Y'all certainly made my day."

Charmed by him, as they each tried to speak first. One hastily saying, "Well, that's very nice of you, but you've made our day, too. Hasn't he Agatha?"

**

During the period in which I shared the shop with Shelby, we employed a saleslady named Arlene, on a part-time basis. Shelby had at one time suffered a mild stroke but it was not debilitating and he hardly missed a day's business. What effects it still had, aside from a minor limp, he covered up stoically. In the first few weeks of his difficulties, Arlene had assisted him, but in no way did this impair his sweet, Southern manner or his raging, profane exasperation—whichever the situation called for.

I was not there on one particular afternoon when Clint Eastwood should have been. Arlene and Shelby were merely getting through another day's work when two young men entered the shop. The buzzer system at the time was out of order, but that wouldn't have mattered anyway, since we always let in anyone who pressed it.

Engaging Shelby in a normal conversation—Arlene nearby—the two men asked what he might have in diamonds. Shelby went to the safe to open it up. At that precise moment, a third man burst through the door with a drawn gun.

This man then ordered Shelby and Arlene to drop to the floor. Shelby immediately complied, but managed to pull a gun to the floor with him, wrapped in an old flannel shirt. No one was aware of this. Arlene stood frozen against the wall, too terrified to move. As she later told me, she called upon her strong Christian faith to get her through this horrible ordeal. The men momentarily neglected her as two of them ran around to the jewelry cases and the other to the safe. This all happened in the front of the shop. Two smaller rooms in back, one leading to a rear exit, were not noticed.

In such an electrifying atmosphere, anxious to get some jewelry into their sacks, none of the men noticed that Arlene had disappeared. Prayerfully and miraculously, she had silently inched her way to the back door.

This door was always bolted with a sliding, heavy iron rod that had to be unlatched from the inside. It held sturdily enough to get more than a grunt from Shelby and myself whenever we had to open it.

Arlene, being petite and more attuned to plucking a cherry from a Manhattan than engaging in such menial chores as dusting the shelves in the shop, pulled out the iron rod from its base with superhuman and unfathomable strength and ran out the door and into the alley, screaming "WE'RE BEING ROBBED!"

Meanwhile, Shelby, forced down onto the floor, was trying to get his gun into some kind of position to fire, all the time being threatened: "Don't move!"

Suddenly, one of the men noticed that Arlene was not up against the wall where she had stood petrified. "Where's the girl?" one of the men yelled at Shelby.

Propped up on one elbow, Shelby bellowed back, "She's gone to get the cops!"

That was enough for the men to flee out the front door, dropping some of the jewelry. By now, Shelby tortuously managed to raise himself and fire a couple of shots.

Fleeing in different directions, the three men soon disappeared. Arlene then appeared at the front of the shop. Police cars were now pulling up from everywhere. Shelby, also unharmed, went to the front, fully expecting to see some results from his off-the-floor, rapid-fire blasts at the bandits. No bodies! Gone! What happened?

As reported in a small local paper later: "After an hourlong chase, a Deputy, with the assistance of seven police, found one of the suspects hiding under a dock. With seven police officers standing on the bank of the canal with guns drawn, the bad guy proceeded to swim the canal, emerging on the opposite bank and ducking through back yards. A new perimeter was formed and he finally walked out, right into an officer. Later that night, the armed suspect was tracked down to a motel room, a pass key was inserted into the door, the door burst open and the baffled suspect found himself sitting on his bed staring at eight drawn guns. The third suspect was identified a few days later."

Phoning me at home shortly after this happened, Arlene emotionally exclaimed, "Get down here, Henry, we've been held up!"

"Where the hell have you been?" Shelby calmly and smilingly asked me when I made my appearance.

Seeing that they were not harmed, no matter what happened, I merely replied, "Well, I haven't been too happy with the tone and action of my piano lately, so I had the tuner over this afternoon. It looks like I missed out on a lot of action here, though."

There was a lot of glass all over, no blood, but two of my large jewelry cases had been shot-up. "Did you get any of them?" I asked, knowing full well how lucky he and Arlene were to have come through uninjured or worse, yet thinking the situation could stand a bit of levity now, to lessen the tension.

"Naw! They got away," Shelby replied with a deep scowl.

"So you mean, Shelby, that all you did was to shoot up two of my cases? That's it?" I asked in mock-heroic disbelief.

Not catching my wink at Shelby, Arlene looked over at me and exclaimed, "I don't believe this! We could have been killed and you're worrying about your showcases! Really."

Carrying it a bit further, I said to Shelby, "How are you going to explain this to your friends back on the ranch? Here you were, ten feet away from your target and you missed. What are you going to tell your old college buddy in New York? What kind of cowboy are you?"

Of course, I realized that had Shelby been his old self, before the stroke, he probably never would have hit the floor; instead, he would have blazed away—point blank. That would have really "made his day."

To compound his frustration at the robbery, when Arlene and Shelby were called down to headquarters to identify one suspect in particular, they were unable to do so.

In the immediate days following, this tale had to be told and re-told to all our customers. We got the buzzer fixed, if only to make our regular patrons feel safer.

Before this event drifted into memory, Arlene expressed one peeve to me. Just because she worked for us part-time didn't mean her part in the hold-up not be shown some consideration. Saying, "Henry, with that full case of jewelry Shelby has up front, you'd think he would give me a gold bracelet or a pair of earrings or something like that. After all, I probably saved his life."

"I agree with you, Arlene." I said, trying to appear as earnest as possible, "but you know Shelby. He's still upset about the whole thing and it hasn't dawned on him to think of anything like that. Why don't you go over to his jewelry case when he's there and pick out something. Tell him you'd like that particular piece the next time you're held up. You know he's very generous."

Afraid of a repeat assault, we armed ourselves further, placing a sawed-off shotgun in a back room, next to some Lay's Potato Chips. Who knew what would be required should there be a next time.

For a while, of course, there was much more caution. If anyone came through the front door carrying a briefcase—even in the highly unlikely event that he was selling the Encyclopedia Americana—there would come a voice from the big leather chair saying, "Pardon me, suh, but I wouldn't open that case too fast if I were y'all." Gently said in a friendly, easy manner, who could take offense from a cherubic visage, augmented by a polite Southern drawl?

It was the younger males coming into the shop that received the most scrutiny, especially if their shirt-tails were hanging out. "Well, now," he might say with a friendly grin, "you look like a mighty nice boy. Ah just know Ah don't have to frisk y'all, do Ah?" At the same time he would rise to stand near the outgoing mail box.

Things finally calmed down after that incident and, as usual, Shelby got ready for the Christmas business. The front showcase was filled with his best jewelry from which, in the months of November and December, he would sell to the maximum. This kept him out of the big chair most of the time and alert to those pausing to look at the jewelry showcase as prospects to be enticed inside.

One particular morning, having no house calls, I sat back and watched unobtrusively as Shelby beckoned to two ladies to enter the shop. His manner of indulgence being irresistible, within seconds he had them trying on jewelry, and without fail the usual words spilled forth, "Y'all sure look pretty in those earrings; I just know your husband is going to be mighty pleased when he sees you wearing them tonight."

"Oh! I don't have a husband anymore," the woman answered. Standing back to get a better look, Shelby replied, "None o' mah business, M'am, but Ah can't imagine why men wouldn't be chasing you all the time, unless y'all are keeping it a big secret." To which the ladies responded in pleasure.

Although the ol' country boy conversed leisurely with the ladies, adding up the figures, the sales tax, and gift-wrapping the jewelry was the speediest part of his business transaction.

As they were leaving, the woman named Maude said to her friend, "Isn't it nice to hear something other than 'Have a nice day,' Matilda? Did you notice he said 'You made my day.' Charming fellow!"

Moments later, a young man approached the shop door; seeing the sign GO AHEAD! MAKE MY DAY!, he disappeared in a flash.

**

Shelby was to meet his match in a person named Jeanette—his nemesis. There would be no bewitching or flattering her into buying any jewelry. An affluent lady in her early eighties, living in the area, she enjoyed the art of haggling over the price of a piece of jewelry as much as any dealer, if not more. Often with better results.

They would do their bargaining over each item she bought out of the front window, there atop the jewelry showcase. Such transactions could consume up to an hour. She would examine the piece from every angle, then wrangle over the price. Before leaving, they would have coffee and pastry, she always allowing the "gentleman" to pay the bill.

Once or twice a month, however, she would return a piece of jewelry, simply because she wasn't pleased with it. At first, Shelby became immensely irritated, but eventually he found a system of trading with her that was mutually beneficial. Both were now playing the game.

One Christmas season she bought two or three items of jewelry at a time, not returning them later to trade for something else.

Then, one day Shelby noticed an antique ring on a young girl who came into the shop. Recognizing it as one he had sold Jeanette recently, Shelby said, "That's a mighty pretty ring, young lady, is it a family heirloom?"

Pleased that he had noticed her ring, the girl replied, "Oh! No! Not at all. There's this rich old lady that comes into the store where I work. When she wore it one day, I admired it, so she was nice enough to sell it to me. She must have a lot of jewelry in the bank because she also sells to other people in the store."

We soon discovered that although "she" was known to be "eccentric and rich," when properly approached she was friendly enough to sell her "family treasures."

Next time she came into the shop, Jeanette said to Shelby, "You've got to give me better prices. I'm your best customer. You know I buy a lot."

Without giving her the slightest hint that he knew she was a "walking estate sale," Shelby replied, "Jeanette, y'all got me down as low as I can get. Don't you want me to make any money?"

"Never mind!", she answered in turn, "If you want to keep me as a customer, you have to do better."

"What are you doing with all this jewelry, Jeanette? You haven't brought any back lately," Shelby replied, smiling slightly.

Not blinking an eyelash, she went on, "Well, I'm getting older. I'm going to be eighty-three and I'm putting it in the bank for my grandchildren, so that's why you have to charge me less." Quickly adding, "I think I'll have an English muffin today, instead of Danish. Tell them not to burn it!"

**

Jeanette often did small errands for Shelby. Patronizing the same bank—directly across the street—as he, she sometimes did his banking. During the Christmas rush, he had a fairly large amount of cash and checks from the previous day's sales.

When last I saw her, she claimed not to be feeling too well; presumably a "bug" of some type, was her complaint. Not seeing her around for a few days, I asked Shelby if she was ill.

"No, she's not sick, Henry, she was in earlier and I gave her some deposits to make. Why? What makes you think she's sick?" he asked me, stopping in his tracks.

At the time, one of regular daily visitors named Bob was there and caught the drift of our conversation. He knew Jeanette very well and said he saw her the other day and "she looked terrible."

Shelby hastily said, "Don't tell me that, you guys. I sent her out to the bank across the street more than a half hour ago with a lot of cash and checks. She should have been back by now, even though she likes to stop for coffee."

With that, he went out the front door, looked across the street to the bank, and walked up and down the shop front, scanning all directions.

By now Bob and I decided to make this episode into a prank. When Shelby came back in, we both feigned deep concern, one of us saying, "Gee, Shelby, I hope nothing happened to her. Even though she's only eighty-three, you never know! I think she said she had pains in her chest, or something like that, when I saw her the other day."

"Don't worry about it, Shelby," the other said. "She's probably in that big new shopping mall."

Suddenly sirens were ringing and getting closer and in a few seconds an ambulance, in full blast, pulled up into the driveway across the street and went towards the rear of the bank building. There was a lot of commotion and people gathering around in groups.

"What's going on over there? One of you guys run over and see what it's all about," Shelby demanded excitedly as he picked up the phone that was ringing.

Bob and I dashed out and joined the people there. An elderly lady had apparently taken ill and was being placed in the ambulance. She was conscious and we could see that it wasn't Jeanette.

We walked back slowly and detected Shelby from the shop, straining his body over his jewelry showcase, trying to see what was happening. Crossing the street, we shook our heads side to side as we entered the shop. I said, "We're not sure what happened, Shelby. I hope it wasn't Jeanette, but they did have an old lady in the ambulance."

"Jeanette! Oh my God! Don't die on me!" Shelby moaned as he thrust open the door and ran out to the bank's driveway. By now the crowd had dispersed and the ambulance was speeding away, siren blasting. Apparently trying to get some information, Shelby disappeared.

Moments later, Jeanette sauntered into the shop, coffee and sweet rolls in hand. "Where's Shelby?" she inquired. "He owes me $4.78 for this."

"Why don't you go out into the back room and set up the table and napkins. He'll be right back," I told her.

We ushered Jeanette out of sight and a short time later Shelby came in, face ashen, muttering, "No one knows who the lady was. She collapsed before she entered the bank. I'll phone the cops and see if they know."

"Did you see any money or checks scattered around, Shelby?" I asked. "I thought there were people picking up papers or something like that when we were over there."

Just as he was about to pick up the phone, Jeanette innocently came out of the back room and said, "Shelby, it's all set up in the back room. You owe me $4.78. What was all that noise and commotion about over there? Was somebody sick or hurt? You don't look too well yourself, Shelby. You'd better take care of yourself."

**

The antique game is a juggling of opportunity, luck, timing and knowledge. Soon I grew restless with my sharing of the shop with Shelby. After two years or so, I was ready to move on. I needed to give myself a speculative fling, get a place of my own. I had been developing a larger appetite for delving further into antiques, all of which called for a change.

The sources for antiques were all about us—that had been proven. Having specialized in antique jewelry, I had also become a victim of its depletion, caused by the 1980's gold and silver rush. As trends go, objects from the 1940's, '50's, and the '60's were now suddenly "hot." Items we once wouldn't have given a second glance were now called "collectibles" and were widely sought after.

Jewelry—modern, vintage, costume, and antique—would be my first preference and become the nucleus for my venture in a new shop. In the two years at Shelby's shop, I had learned about the potential for buying antiques in general, as proved by the response coming from our newspaper advertising. I was ready to diversify, and to start a shop of my own.

Just three blocks from my home in Pompano Beach is where I decided on a location for this new enterprise. I put up a large sign advertising ANTIQUES above the storefront. I aimed to specialize in "house calls" to buy antiques for the remaining years of my career and I was not shy in referring to myself as a "general practitioner"—a dealer of all types of antiques. Soon I would be allowed entrance into innumerable homes and exposed to more fine antiques than I could have hoped to see otherwise. This greatly enhanced my education in antiques rapidly.

Upon signing my lease for the new shop, response to advertising to buy antiques was everything we expected, and more. The area dealers became aware of my new status as a general practitioner, drawing every type of dealer into the shop. It became as much fun as it was profitable, thus finding a silver lining in the decline of the antique jewelry market.

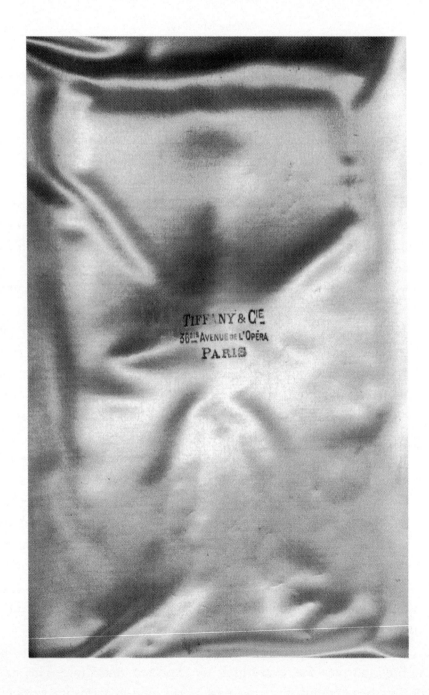

The Tiffany Necklace

CHAPTER 14

In their pursuit of antiques, the lives of antique dealers are sometimes seasoned with experiences of exceptional exhilaration. In
my long career of canvassing from door-to-door, I can recall several
adventures that left an indelible impact on me. But none is remembered more vividly than my two-day episode in the acquisition of a
necklace. So beautiful and rare is it—an Art Nouveau necklace sold
by Tiffany's in Paris at the turn of the century—that I could never
bring myself to sell it, even to this day.

From the moment of my possession over 35 years ago, it has
seen the light of day only about ten times. The previous owner had
also sequestered it, relegating it to the coldness and confines of a
bank vault.

I realized it could have sold at auction at any time and brought
me a handsome price; instead I let it rest in a bank, satisfied to
know it was mine.

I recently placed a photograph of it in a glass case in the shop,
behind some crystal. Those who recognized it as something extraordinary were amazed to learn I still had it.

I acquired it in the early 1960's. Those were probably the best
years of my canvassing; there was still plenty of antique jewelry
available in private homes. At the time I was living in New York
State and enjoyed soliciting in the North in the summer and
Florida in the winter. I had a very successful system of canvassing
that worked out wherever I decided to go.

New York State had many wonderful cities, towns and villages
that I worked over and over again for several years. I was as familiar

with their names, streets and districts as I was with their distinct odors and fragrances, their commercial or industrial prominence, or any other feature that set them apart.

Even now, decades later, it is easy to recall them: Surely it was in Canajoharie, the moment one entered the town, where the nostrils filled so easily with the essence of Beech-Nut chewing gum. And wasn't it the city of Fulton, with its aroma of chocolate products, that tugged at the sweet tooth. Who would not remember the colorful sight of Newark, N.Y. in June, the "Rose Capital," the perfume of roses permeating the air? Who needed air conditioning on the hottest day in August when one could sit on the north end of Seneca Lake with the city of Geneva as a backdrop, and cool off from the breezes that skimmed the lake's entire length? The name slips my mind, but in this mixture of nature's scents and mankind's industry there was a village where one needed to clothespin the nose while riding through it in a convertible, top down. Other cities and towns, as well, added their particular contributions to the senses of sight, sound, smell and feeling. Ask any professional solicitor!

Wherever my quest for antique jewelry carried me—California to the Northeast to Florida—my senses would be filled with these portraits. And for 200 years and more, antiques were brought to these places from all over the world, and ended up in both great cities and hamlets alike.

**

It was a sunny morning in June in upstate New York when I climbed the porch stairs to a typical residential home in a well-cared for neighborhood. There, a gentleman in his early eighties, was reading a newspaper on a porch swing. Although he was a bit hard of hearing, I showed him some of my samples of gold items, to get the drift of why I was there. He went inside and came back with his wife, who asked me to come into the house.

As they went in search of what they might sell, I was struck by the interior furnishings—never to be forgotten. Unfortunately, at that time, I was only interested in and knowledgeable about antique jewelry.

However, what I saw there impressed me immensely. There were antique Oriental rugs throughout the house. Hanging in gold antique wooden frames were many oil paintings. Three or four Tiffany lamps stood on or near tables that held various bronze creatures—a tiger on an elephant's back was particularly awesome. There was nothing new in this house. Although I had been in countless homes with various antiques, all that was seen here was exceptional.

This was verified when the man appeared first, with a box of stickpins and cufflinks, all in gold and small gems. In the other hand, he held a large hunting case pocket watch, which turned out to be an 18-karat gold Patek-Philippe, considered to be one of the finest watches in the world.

When the man's wife came down from upstairs with a box of assorted antique jewelry, there was no need for me to make an appointment for that afternoon. After purchasing the watch from the gentleman and reaching an agreement on price with the woman for "things I will never use anyway," she added, "I have a very beautiful necklace in the bank downtown. I could show it to you after lunch if you're going to be around." Agreeing to this instantly, I went to an early lunch, then drove to a park to read a magazine until the appointed time.

As is so typical of upstate New York in summer, the morning could be clear and sunny, then, within a short time, change drastically. When I returned to the lady's home, the weather turned from cloudy to gloomy, then to a heavy rain. Low-flying clouds darkened, then thinned out, only to roll over again in a black mass.

The lady was ready, with an umbrella; we had just a few short blocks to drive to the bank. On the way, she explained to me that she and her husband had reached the age where they had decided to dispose of their antiques.

Upon entering the small bank, all the employees noticed us, some calling out greetings to her, as we entered the tiny booth with her safe deposit box. After going through a few papers, she produced an antique jewelry box, explaining that she had "inherited this from a relative who traveled widely." As she opened the box, the most impressive example of Art Nouveau jewelry I had ever seen greeted my eyes.

The necklace, intricately designed in gold, was interspersed with six miniature enameled starfish, embedded with small diamonds. From it hung a heavy, diamond-studded starfish pendant and in the center was a lovely enameled lady's head, her flowing golden hair suggesting the head of a mermaid. A large pearl dangled beneath the pendant. It was in the original box. The cover's interior contained the lettering: TIFFANY & Cie, 36 B15 Avenue de L' Opera, Paris.

Someone had the good fortune to procure this extraordinarily elegant necklace from Tiffany's in Paris near the turn of the century. Unbelievably, here in my hands I held a treasure in this small compartment at a bank in a little but beautiful village in upstate New York—close by the Barge Canal, on a very dismal and rainy afternoon.

I was aching to gain more information about it. Who bought it? When? Where? Why? And so forth. However, I knew from past experiences it was imperative that I remain calm and even detached when any interesting or desirable piece of jewelry was being offered for sale.

When I once raved about a pair of antique gold Victorian bracelets I was shown in a home, the owner suddenly turned and said, "Do you know, you're right. These are really beautiful. I guess I won't sell them after all; my granddaughter might appreciate them someday."

With the necklace, I did not betray my inner desire, my excitement to own this prize. Luck was with me because this turned out to be one of those unusual circumstances when I did not have to make an initial offer. As I hinted about what price she expected for it, she totally surprised me. With a calm dignity that befitted her demeanor, she emphatically stated, "My neighbor likes it very much and offered me $450 for it, but I will not take a penny less than $500. You may have it for that right now."

I couldn't believe my ears. Although back then, 35 years ago, $450 was a lot of money to spend for one piece of jewelry. In one of the European auction houses, about 1947, a Russian Faberge Easter egg had sold for about $10,000. In the early 1980's, that same object of art was purchased for over one million.

Suddenly my mind froze in horror, as my hand reached into my pocket and I felt the frightening thinness of the cash I had with me. I had purchased jewelry exceptionally well these last three days, rapidly calculating that I undoubtedly didn't have what was needed. Turning away, I managed to check my cash and saw that I only had about $200. I couldn't expect her to take a personal check from a total stranger. I told her the truth, that I had been away from home buying for three days, including what I'd bought from her that very morning, and was somewhat short. "May I leave you a large deposit and return tomorrow morning, Friday, with the cash?" I asked hopefully, trying not to reveal my anxiety.

"That won't be necessary, young man," she replied, completely composed. "I'm in no hurry. It's been in the bank so many years it doesn't make much difference now. Whenever you come back."

Thinking of her neighbor, I saw a risk, should she hear about my having been there. Certainly she would come up with the extra $50 in a hurry. Fibbing, I said to her, "I'm staying overnight in Geneva (50 miles away) with a friend. He'll cash a check for me and I'll return the first thing in the morning with $500." With a nervous laugh, but trying to appear nonchalant, I added, "Unless your neighbor comes over tonight and wants to buy it at your price."

Luckily her reply was what I might have expected, "I'll just leave it right here in the bank and we can come back tomorrow," dismissing me with a smile. I sighed deeply as I turned away. The tellers acknowledged our departure, and she assured them of our returning in the morning. (I wondered if bank tellers could tell what was going on when they saw prominent customers come and go with strangers. One can bet they did a lot of speculating among themselves.)

Back at the house, I escorted her to the door, saying, "With all this rain, it's just as well that I am only going to Geneva. See you in the morning, Mrs. Meriweather."

"Have a pleasant evening," she nodded.

Putting the car sharply in reverse, I raced back to the main highway and headed for Utica, about 200 miles away. The darkness deepened as the rain pounded incessantly on the roof, but the windshield wipers revealed a mirage of clouds "lined with silver."

Arriving home a few hours later, I related the day's events to my brother, whose smile showed me that he knew I was now permanently gripped by the fever of the antique jewelry business. I tried getting to sleep as early as possible, wanting that night over with, for a slight tug of fear gnawed at my stomach.

Leaving home very early the next morning, I was back at her door promptly at 9 A.M. My heart dropped when she answered the door saying "Oh! I'm sorry," then vanished for a few seconds. Reappearing, she said, "I forgot my hat. Come on in for a couple of minutes." Whew! My stomach recovered!

At the bank we went through the same procedure as the night before. Was it my imagination that all eyes were upon us as we entered the cubicle? As I handed her the money and she gave me the necklace, we turned from business and chatted about the rain that was now into its second day. Bidding her adieu, I drove to the park and stopped for a long, good look at MY necklace.

It was Friday. I'd had an exceptional week. It was still raining. Heading for Utica, I contemplated how much I enjoyed being a professional door-to-door solicitor. One never knew what treasure would appear.

When I showed my prize to my brother that night, he admired it effusively, of course, and was happy that I acquired something so rare and beautiful. Nodding his head in praise, he added very seriously, "Hank! Don't sell this necklace! Hang onto it!" I too felt the same way, young as I was; it could mean a lot more in time. What would it be worth in the future?

But I would enjoy using it before committing it to a secure place. We were to exhibit at an antique show in Morriston, New Jersey, in a couple of weeks. Why not have my future wife, Jackie, wear it on opening day? Anticipating the appearance there of a married couple who specialized in Tiffany and other art glass, we stopped at their booth the first day of the show. The woman always wore elegant antique jewelry.

Within seconds they both noticed the necklace on Jackie. They did as all dealers do and asked the question: "How much is it?" coming as near as possible and admiring its beauty.

"Not for sale!" was my happy reply.

Jackie, smiling, certainly felt just as delighted as I did about it. Cornering me alone minutes later, the husband couldn't believe that I would refuse his offer of $3500. "Let me know, first, when you decide to sell, Henry," he said.

The necklace was then put away for another decade or more, along with other lesser select pieces of jewelry I had gathered. Upon moving to Florida in 1975, after selling our family home in Utica, the necklace was merely shifted to another vault. With all the intensified business activity that followed, the necklace was thereafter all but forgotten and did not see sunlight again until 1983.

**

On that occasion, I took a friend with me to New York City, not having been there in several years. Driving there in my 1976 Cadillac convertible, with its top down on a brilliant summer day brought back memories of many previous trips. It was fun, crossing midtown Manhattan during the mid-week bustle, seeing someone attempting to climb over the hood of a car to cross the street, and finally inching our way to a parking lot.

Although it was a vacation trip getting out of Florida for a few days, there was no reason for not doing some business, I'd decided, as I packed a couple of large canvas bags with jewelry and silver to take with us. The necklace rested safely on the bottom of one of the bags, well-protected and secure. I still knew a few dealers in the city and brought several items that could be sold easily. It was always a matter of "what's your best price?" anyway, and I acted accordingly.

My friend, an inveterate smoker, took this inopportune time to be in the midst of one of his many "quitting" periods. As all smokers know, this is an indescribable limbo, and they themselves can only hope for the best in this challenge.

Being an especially heavy smoker, he did very well. Being the passenger, it had to be especially difficult (hands free), but I dared not to congratulate him, for fear of stirring up his fonder memories and have the whole "quitting" scheme go up in smoke. After parking the car, we made the rounds to a few dealers and had a successful first day, especially in selling the antique silver items.

Although I still had no intentions of selling the necklace, I wanted to show it to a few of the more prominent dealers. Being professionals, they expressed admiration, but like myself with the woman I bought it from, they dared not to "rave" about it. By keeping cool, they probably hoped I might consider selling it. There was no harm in making offers, however, and one dealer said he would pay $17,000 for it. We politely thanked him and left.

Stopping at another jeweler's, the owner being an old acquaintance from the antique shows of bygone years, we had a different experience. He'd bought a lot of antique jewelry from us in the 1950's and the 1960's, and it was obvious that he had come a long way: the store was in a great location, fashionable and expensive to operate, no doubt, and the merchandise reflected that.

Although he was glad to see me, items of jewelry we showed him were: well, ahem!—not in his league anymore.

Okay! Fine! So long, Dave. Nice seeing you! Great store you have here!

Getting our near-empty sacks together, I hesitated as we started to leave, and said, "Oh! I nearly forgot, Dave! If you have another minute, you might be interested in seeing this antique necklace I have here."

The three of us then stood closely together as I casually opened the box with the "starfish lady." At the sight of it, he didn't even attempt to conceal his pleasure and surprise; he'd handled too much antique jewelry not to recognize something rare. And without the slightest hesitation, he happily inquired, "How much?"

Not waiting for an answer, he called out to his secretary, "Jean, come in here and look at this. Sit down, Henry," and he drew up chairs for Dan and myself. When I handed him the necklace, he and Jean admired it lavishly, facial expressions reflecting appreciation for it as a work of art.

"How much, Henry?" he asked again. Although his store contained a wealth of choice jewelry, his instinct for an extraordinary antique piece surfaced and it was as if we were back at the antique shows in New York a couple of decades ago.

In those days, he was one of our better clients, paying higher prices than the average dealer. Consequently, he had every reason to believe that it was merely a matter of price haggling before the necklace would be his.

"Just showing you, Dave, I knew you would appreciate it. It's not for sale! I sort of enjoy having it. I merely thought I would bring it along and show it to a couple of people in New York," I said impassively. Not giving him a chance to reply, since his face expressed involuntary disbelief, I hastily packed the box, grabbed his hand and said, "Thanks for your time, Dave, absolutely wonderful store you have here." Throwing the bag over my shoulder, I turned, smiled, and said, "I sure miss the good old days." Then we disappeared into the throngs of people, leaving him gaping after us.

**

The people we wanted to show the necklace to were two major auction houses. At the first one, a young, pretty girl came out and politely seated us. After looking at the necklace and stating how beautiful it was, she simply said, "We can put a reserve of $5,000 on it if you decide to leave it for auction."

My friend Dan, inwardly very nervous that day—nicotine withdrawal apparently in full control—bolted from his chair, face flushed. He couldn't get the words out fast enough, "$5,000? We were just offered $17,000 from a dealer down on 47th Street. I can't believe . . ." he trailed off as the young lady and I tried to calm him down. She quickly said, "Just a minute, sir, I'll bring my supervisor in," departing hastily.

Returning in a little while with her superior—also a young and charming lady, but obviously the boss—she left the room and Dan immediately asked the "head of the antique jewelry department" (as she turned out to be), "Is there a cigarette machine in this building?"

When I explained his plight to her, she came up with an instant remedy for his staying "on the wagon." Excusing herself, she returned with some plain white paper, rolled it up into the shape of a cigarette, handed it to him smiling irresistibly and said, "You don't want to start smoking again, sir. Just put this in your mouth and pretend it's a cigarette." It was a genuine effort to help him, I thought, and a smart way to conduct business.

Upon examining the necklace, she spoke of its elegance and implied that the young lady who quoted the $5,000 was not that experienced in this type of jewelry and was not aware of the potential value of the necklace at auction. "I understand," I replied.

"We can certainly start our reserve at $17,000, or more, if you like," she said, appearing to be very interested in having it. Leaving amiably, I told her I would consider her auction house when we finally decided to sell.

Outside, Dan let out his disbelief in a volume of words as we went to the next auction house. "Wow! You'd better know what you have when you go into these places! Suppose we had left it there for $5,000 with the first lady?" Shaking his head, he went into a tirade of speculation. Finding a cigarette vendor on the street, he puffed himself back into stability and happiness. Even though I knew it would be merely a matter of time before he started smoking again, I was sorry the necklace had been the catalyst.

At the second auction house, the necklace was received with praise and enthusiasm, at a suggested minimum of $20,000.

Since I was merely seeking reactions and had no intention of leaving it anywhere at this time, we stopped at Tiffany's next, believing they would be interested in viewing an exquisite Art Nouveau necklace sold from their Paris establishment back at the turn of the century. Unfortunately, the person in charge of the antique jewelry department was on vacation, so we didn't take it out of the canvass bag.

On our drive back to Florida, Dan, who was new to the antique world, kept repeating how shocked he was at how dealers conducted business.

"Well, Dan," I tried to conclude, "I'm sure if you know what you have, or a good idea of it anyway, the auction houses will try to get the highest price possible. That's what the antique game is all about, more or less, to buy as cheaply as possible and sell it for the most you can get. We all try."

He kept shaking his head in skepticism the entire length of the Jersey Turnpike, while puffing gloriously on his cigarettes.

A few weeks later we had calls from both auction houses follow-ing up on our encounter. From another source, a woman said she had recently opened up her own gallery and knew some people who would be interested in the necklace.

That winter, I took it to the Miami Beach Antique Show & Sale for the first time, to display it only. There in our booth, merely to attract attention and get the public's reaction, we had an offer of $50,000. Certainly the rarity of the item was being recognized.

I enjoyed this bit of fun, but being very busy, the necklace was again relegated to cryptic confinement, where it rests today.

Part II

Bric-A-Brac

The Bench

CHAPTER 15

Having a shop of my own, at last, met the needs of a changing antique world and the changes I needed. I was to deal in a general line of antiques—a "general practitioner"—a challenge I was ready to meet. My continuation of house calls would open my eyes to other antique treasures, such as crystal, porcelain, paintings, rugs, etc., as well as jewelry and silver.

Besides having a large concentration of the elderly, Florida also harbors the famous and the noteworthy, all of whom are enjoying their last days in a favorable climate.

Our shop stands in the middle of a shopping center of thirty stores. Through windows across its entire front and halfway along the other side, we have a broad view of the business area and much of the parking lot. Next to us is a sandwich and yogurt shop and a few steps away, a supermarket. If location counts, we have it. Except for the doldrums in the summer months, we can look outside and see much activity, which leads to some interesting experiences.

Outside our front window, protected from the elements by an extended awning, is a sturdy concrete bench—one of several about the shopping center. Streams of people walk by it every day, making it a focal point of action. The bench may be vacant, or suddenly occupied by three or four people, or by a solitary soul.

From the bustle of the worldly stage comes a variety of people who chat, rest, pause for a bite to eat, sip at soda or from a paper-sacked can of beer, or merely pause to reorganize their thoughts and get their bearings. From the bench they are launched in all directions, which may be thousands of miles away, or as close as two blocks.

During the winter months we are able to leave our front door open, which allows us to hear on-going dialogue, or shut it off if desired. The activity there is like a TV show, without commercials.

On they come, the day long: the rich and the poor, the bearded or the baby-faced; an occasional vagrant, or the socially elite; someone elegantly dressed, or one shoddily clad; a man passing by with a cane, or a woman sporting a wig as she is pulled by dogs; American tourists and foreign visitors; the overly-dressed and the vastly under-dressed as they head to or from the ocean; the lottery ticket scratchers and the ice cream cone lickers; some appear intently in thought, others may look vacuous. To this small oasis they come, a shelter from the chilly weather, the blazing sun or the appearance of a sudden tropical disturbance.

During the hours of a normal work day, our shop can be quite busy. But at intervals, the people-performances outdoors run continuously from the bench a few steps away from our windows. They sit and read, philosophize or argue, laugh or appear downcast. Some may be a healthy group of college students or well-coiffured ladies awaiting cabs to whisk them away to their luxurious, high-towered condos. Men and women push carts of groceries to be loaded into curb-side Cadillacs or Toyotas. To the bench come French-speaking Canadians chatting cheerfully while waiting for the Montreal papers to be delivered to a nearby drug store. Police will sometimes have a suspect seated on the bench for interrogation. A couple will stop to finish out a noisy argument, then hastily move on, allowing another pair to sit, hold hands and kiss unabashedly. Honeymooners also come to sit quietly, whisper and be completely oblivious to any onlookers—as many who sit on the bench appear to be.

Old timers having escaped similar benches in the North for a few months here, take their place daily on the sun-warmed bench. They chat about winter snowstorms and all else their winters bring, then count the days up to Easter when they may return, like robins, to their summer habitats. People come with racing forms; while area working boys and girls, neatly dressed, make use of the bench to munch on health salads, or sneak a cigarette while awaiting impatiently Friday's work day to end.

From whatever walk of life they come, the bench is a readily available respite from the day's activities. Un-observed from inside our shop, we are involuntary intruders to moments of secrecy by these impromptu actors. A few of them, in the ninth decade of their lives, stop by at least once a week to let us know they are still alive. One old man with an unshaven, grizzled face, ambles through the supermarket, revealing nothing of his past. He carefully checks the price of Quaker Oats versus the cost of Farina, then stops to squeeze the fruits and vegetables. Now looking gaunt, tottering and nearly ghost-like, he could very well have once issued orders from the bridge of a battleship during World War II. Where once his eyes had scanned the beaches of Normandy or the Pacific horizon at Midway, he can now barely lift his head to avoid a collision with another grocery cart. Where once he had pondered over momentous decisions, involving the lives of many, he is presently occupied with a few plastic bags of groceries which will provide him sustenance for a few more days.

Resting on the bench, bags beside him, looking at nothing in particular, no one comes by to greet or recognize him. Everything is in the past. Perhaps just as well, too. How can one reckon much beyond the 1990's when one's life had reached its worthy achievements in importance some fifty years earlier?

Soon an elegantly dressed lady walks by the shop, wearing a wide-brimmed hat and gloves, off to luncheon at one of the fancier restaurants. As she passes a youthful bathing beauty, her mind may wander back to the days when she was a stunning Ziegfeld girl, or an opera star.

Like clockwork, a well-known author strolls by slowly each morning. Unassuming, yet steady and exuding a bulwark of confidence and character, he pleasantly returns the greetings of the many who recognize him. Newspapers and groceries under arm, he is returning to some writing in progress. He is another of the many people in the area who utilize their time creatively, contributing to life's pleasures and meaning.

Among others come a number of business executives, former sportsmen—football and baseball players, boxers; also restaurant owners, lawyers, judges, artists, politicians and other celebrities. They come with legacies that span the country and the globe, giving us an immense aggregation of diverse talent. For they enter our shop—some of them—in response to the small sign in our front window inviting them to browse.

A bench sitter may be a Holocaust survivor with a tattoo attesting to the ultimate traumatic experience. Still another was one of the first German infantrymen during World War II to reach the outskirts of Leningrad. Lucky enough to survive, he reached America and became prosperous, albeit minus an arm.

Sad tales and glad tales, we in the shop have lent an ear and eye to the telling of our country's history since the turn of the century. How appropriate that a shop dealing in antiques also deals with the aged. How lucky we are to be so well located.

Some use the bench regularly, seeming to have a claim on it. If not daily, they certainly will appear sometime during the week. If someone joins them, it adds something to the day's routine.

By age brackets, those in their seventies are the "rookies." They don't brag about their age yet, hoping to stay as young as possible. "Old" in Florida means being in your eighties. But not until they are in their upper eighties and beyond do they publicly boast about having lived for so long. When they are taken for a younger age by ten years or so, they beam happily as they proudly reveal their true age. They repeat the same routine the next day. The older they are, the more frequently it occurs.

Bench sitters in the upper bracket automatically receive the most respect. Since many have some difficulty hearing, their conversations are loud and are easily overheard. It seems that one gent has been telling people his age is 88 for several years. He needs a calendar for Christmas.

Although they mention their longevity with pride and satisfaction, happy at being in good enough health to sit out there and joke around, most are reluctant to reveal their backgrounds and financial status, especially the latter.

The man with the well-worn baseball cap, who comes by faithfully at least a few times a week, is far older than his un-wrinkled face reveals. Well into his eighties, he was the inventor of a collapsible table, an idea that made him financially successful and had afforded him early retirement. He would never disclose any of this casually.

As we came to know him, he revealed his wild and exciting youth, a background of boats, wine, women and frolicking, mostly on Long Island. Even today he would be the envy of any young man. A natural mechanic, Jim solves our technical problems around here, answers our phone when necessary, and is currently discussing the pros and cons of getting married again. At 87, and a widower, he is fair game for matrimony in Florida's society. In our discussions of marriage, I advise him, "Well, Jim, if you're not that enthusiastic, don't rush into it. Now, if you were Charlie's age (96) then maybe you shouldn't wait too much longer." Things happen fast here! Jim is keeping steady company with a lovely lady he met recently and they seem to be enjoying a happy relationship.

Charlie is our oldest steady visitor. Not wanting to spend any time on the bench or encourage conversations with strangers, he comes directly into the shop several times a week and claims the most comfortable chair. He is past the stage where longevity is the most important topic for discussion. There seems to be something about reaching 90, those in that age bracket seldom bring up the fact, unless asked. Perhaps they surreptitiously wait their centennial year before again flaunting their age about in public.

Another gentleman, Al, a jewelry designer from New York City, soon to be 95, eagerly anticipates his yearly cruise with the Elks Club, accompanied by a lady friend. His complexion could be the envy of many men in their sixties, and when he approaches the shop arm in arm with his younger partner, he steadfastly supports and directs her.

Sarah, a refined, little lady, age 93, comes to our shop frequently. She looks like a vintage doll, usually wearing a protective sun bonnet. Keeping trim, she swims daily in her condo pool. When I approached her recently about the four or five men in her age bracket who were single, she sweetly replied, "I'm not the least bit interested, Henry. I had one wonderful man and that was good enough for me!" Any guy would be lucky if he won her affections.

The wealth of characters and personalities that come to rest on the bench daily makes us appreciate the wonderful legacies these eldest of citizens contribute to our life. These people don't just sit and stare into the shop reading the sign that says: WE BUY ANTIQUES—JEWELRY—GOLD—SILVER, etc. Our business and personal relationships with many of them have developed into mutual deeper meanings, creating friendships and happy associations. Every antique shop should be as fortunate and have a large, concrete bench facing it. As the world passes by, one can then grasp it!

"Don't Tell Me You're
Still Alive!"

CHAPTER 16

For forty years the name, PURNIE—ANTIQUE JEWELRY, has hung in plaques above booths in antique shows all over the country. After several years in this location—the same name above the door—we are often surprised at who notices it and pays us a visit from the past.

On more than one occasion someone has stumbled in and said, "Purnie! You must be the same one we knew back when ..." Then add, "I thought you'd be dead by now."

This was deeply impressed upon me at a recent Miami Beach Convention Center Antique Show & Sale. The co-owner of the show remarked that only three of the original exhibitors are left, including he and his wife—more than thirty years later.

No! We have not all departed to that "great antique show in the sky." Many are still scattered around the country, mostly retired.

We are down to exhibiting at only one large show each winter, mainly to keep in touch with show business. Thus showing those who remember us that we are indeed still alive and kicking, and happily keeping abreast of things.

Although I am no longer astonished when someone from the past walks through the door, it was still a jolt when two older gentlemen came into the shop one day and I heard one of them shout, "Where are you, Purnie? Is it you?" I came from behind a counter; he squinted at me for several seconds, took his cap off and turned to his companion and said, "This guy is the shrewdest antique jewelry dealer around." Then bringing himself closer to my face, he asked, "Don't you remember me?"

Studying him closely, noticing the full head of reddish gray hair, a ruggedly handsome face and an imposing overall stature, I still didn't recognize him.

"You're Vin, aren't you?" he continued, "don't you remember me? You used to come into my jewelry store in Utica to buy antique jewelry." Nothing registered in my mind until he finally said, "Andre! Andre's Jeweler's!"

Incredibly, my mind wandered back to the days after World War II, when my brother was taking me around, hoping to get me interested in the antique jewelry business.

"I think it's coming back to me now," I said. "Didn't you have a jewelry store somewhere downtown?" Pausing a few moments, I continued, "But you've got me confused with my brother. You guys used to haggle over jewelry prices." Thinking even harder, I continued, "Boy! Do I remember you now! Talk about shrewd. Between the two of you, no dealers had a chance in the Mohawk Valley or anywhere else. No one knew much of anything in those days and there was little competition."

"Oh!" he replied, "then you must be the kid brother, but I don't remember you at all. I'm 84 years old."

"You couldn't have been in the Utica area very long, Andre," I said. "I vaguely remember your place."

"That's right," he replied, "we tried to open up a classy shop there, but it was hopeless. We stayed a few years. We handled all kinds of jewelry, silver, fine arts and antiques and we were doing very well. Then they opened up an ice cream store next to us. People would come in, licking on those cones, dripping chocolate all over my fine porcelain and paintings. We moved to Florida— Miami Beach—and had a gallery right on Lincoln Road. That was the best place to be in the winter."

After his initial burst into our shop, and since he was living in the area, he soon became a frequent visitor. Now retired, it became obvious that he had done very well in the antique business.

With his years of contacts down here, he soon began buying a few items of jewelry from me and would in turn sell them at a fast profit and return to us for more. Thus proving that dealers hate to give up the business, regardless of their age. Now he was haggling with me, as vigorously as he had done with my brother, 45 years earlier. All the characteristics of the typical antique dealer became evident in our transactions. Age had only made him more astute and retirement did not mean he had lost any of the tricks of the trade.

With each visit, he unfurled more tales of woe. His antique shop had specialized in jewelry, silver and fine art. He was one of the first in the area to sell paintings to affluent people moving to Florida.

"Know what one dealer said to me?" Andre asked me one morning. Answering his own question, "Oh! You're the dealer who made everyone rich!" His expression downcast, he continued, "I was buying important paintings and selling them to rich people moving down here. I had to beg people to buy paintings; they didn't know anything about them. Later, many were valued at hundreds of thousands of dollars. I can show you pictures of our antique shop, with a lot of the originals. All I've got left are some photographs. A few of my paintings became worth more than a million dollars each. Sure, I made some people rich."

When Andre sold paintings from his gallery in the Sixties and Seventies, he had no idea, like most people, that the Eighties would bring an explosion in the art world. Art prices soared unbelievably and unrealistically.

When he retired just before the boom, paintings by artists he once owned had leaped sky-high in value. He left the profession when art was catching on, in a grand, though grotesque manner.

"I sold beauty," he said, "then after 1980, people were only interested in names. Who's the artist? That was their concern, not the painting's visual appeal or artistic value. They bought for speculation and investment. How much would it be worth in the future?"

At each week's visit, he would unveil more bitter tales. I would remind him that "these things have always happened. That's business! All dealers make mistakes."

Studying Andre closely on his numerous visits to our shop, and negotiating with many other dealers during the course of a week, he summarized the life of many antique dealers I have known.

Listening to his laments about selling antiques too cheaply, too soon, too impulsively, and often to a public that had to be educated and persuaded, I became aware that most dealers suffered these moments at one time or another.

One day, as he was examining an antique diamond ring from the case, I observed his facial expression at length. Like all experienced dealers, his scrutiny of the object was an art in itself. As he turned the ring completely around in one hand, the other holding his magnifying loupe to one eye, his expressions changed ever so slightly. A light frown, a raised eyebrow, a bland look of approval, or a sudden rejection upon finding a flaw, were all done without a trace of emotion, and never a smile, especially if he were inwardly pleased with the item. His hands were steadier than those of many a younger man. Who could count the number of objects of art that had passed before his eyes in similar fashion over the years?

Unfortunately, he could not escape the memories of the paintings he'd sold which turned out to be extremely valuable years later. He would inevitably return to this subject wherever he could capture someone's attention. To make matters worse, one of those paintings worth well over a million dollars in today's market was hanging in a home just blocks away from his own.

I could easily put myself in his place. While I've made no million dollar mis-judgments, to this day I find myself making at least one major mistake and several minor ones every month: Too much; too little; too soon; too late. Trading in antiques often calls for snap decisions; regrets or applause come later.

Tiring of his complaints, I finally said to him one day, "Andre, quit griping about all the blunders you made in business! You're not the only one. How about the great scores you've made? We both are living comfortably. Why don't we tell each other about the wonderful antiques we bought for practically nothing that turned out to be valuable. We've purchased things at very low prices, even without knowing their true value, and them resold them at fantastically higher prices. How about that? All dealers have their exhilarating tales of conquest, but we don't often mention them, do we?"

He didn't reply, but I knew by his faint smile and distant look that he was recalling visions of many pleasurable and exciting acquisitions that came his way. Surely many objects coming into his possession had made his heart palpitate, his head giddy with stimulation, even cause his ordinarily steady hands to tremble slightly with delight. It's happened to us all!

"Look at yourself, how great you look," I exclaimed. "Here you are," I continued, "84 years old and you still come into antique shops like this, scrutinizing dealers' merchandise, haggling over prices. You're still trying to make us pay for your mistakes," I said with a smile.

Noting a change in his eyes and his face at this disclosure—although he tried to conceal it—I added, "I know plenty of men who had to retire in their sixties and so do you. They ended up chasing golf balls all day, getting into their wives' hair and spending their nights playing poker for nickels and dimes. They look older than you. When you leave here, you know you're going to make a fast profit on this ring you're looking at. And, after you sell it, you're not going to rush off to some early-bird dinner, stand in line at a cafeteria, like a lot of sunset citizens have to do. You'll pick up your wife Agnes and head for your favorite steak house. You can bet on that!"

Finding it difficult not to smile, however slightly, he didn't reply. Retaining the ring in his hand throughout this conversation, he finally found his tongue, saying, "You know this diamond is off-color. Now give me a realistic price!"

"I've already given you my 'off-color' price. How much lower do you think I can go?" I asked. I already knew the answer to that and how this charade would end. At least this small success should take his mind off his past blunders momentarily.

Putting the ring in his pocket, thus consummating the deal, he sat down and asked, "How do I look? I don't think I'm going to live much longer." Not much, I thought. The older they get, the better they look.

"Eye-Gotts"

CHAPTER 17

A friend of mine from the North, now spending his winters here, came into the shop one day for the first time. Having retired from the accounting business, he knew virtually nothing about the antique business. Staying for a couple of hours, he was just as intrigued with some of the customers that came in as with any of the merchandise. We have a few comfortable chairs about the shop for visitors and patrons, and Roger was soon relaxing thoroughly in one of them, enjoying the ambiance.

One day as he and I were chatting, two ladies entered. One of them asked, "May I just browse?"

"Of course," was the instant reply from Roger—by now looking as if he worked here. He arose to greet them from his favorite antique chair.

One of the women, whose name was Irene, said to her friend, "Oh! Look Rosie, in that jewelry case. I've got a brooch just like that from my grandmother." Pointing into the case, she asks me, "How much is that cameo with the lady's head, the one that has a little diamond in it?"

"$375," I reply.

Thrilled, she looks further; spotting an antique lapel watch, she excitedly inquires, "How much is that watch? I've got one that my Aunt Alvira gave me."

"It's $450," I answer.

"Oh! Rosie," she almost shrieks, "I got the same thing in the bank. I better get it out and wear it if it's worth that much."

Now fully inspired, Irene stands back and gives an all pervasive look about the shop, rejoicing at everything in sight. Eyes gleaming with rapture and wonder, she comes upon a full set of sterling silver flatware and calls out, "Rosie, look at that! It's Kirk silver! I've got that! I'm originally from Baltimore and that's where it comes from. I got it from my Uncle Ephram and Aunt Hortense. How much is that set?" When I tell her, she is completely ecstatic, saying, "I'm so glad we came in."

Now fully launched, she guides Rosie around the shop, pointing to several items, getting more excited each time, saying, "I can't believe it! I got the same thing, only a little different. I've got an Oriental rug like that one, only blue, and a pair of candlesticks like that from Grandmother Ursula, only taller; and see those plates, I've got a set just like them, only with gold trim."

Glancing up at Roger, I smile inwardly as he gives me a perplexed look. He's not met this type of customer before. His eyes follow them around the shop in disbelief.

Tugging at Rosie as they went about the entire shop, only now in a slightly lower voice, Irene says to her friend, "I got so much that looks like everything in here. Isn't it wonderful? I got to get some of these things out and start using them. I didn't know they were so valuable. Can you believe it?" she repeats as Rosie patiently and wordlessly circles all the shelves and counters throughout the shop with her friend.

Starting to leave, then spotting something else again, her eyes sparkling, she makes several more attempts to leave, but each time stops to say another "I got."

Inching slowly towards the door, Irene's face is flushed with glorious inner revelations. Suddenly glancing at her watch, she grabs the muted and hapless Rosie by the arm and exclaims, "Look at the time! I hate to go but I've got to roast a duck for tonight."

Steering Rosie towards the door, Irene turns around to us and, beaming radiantly, says, "You don't know how much we enjoyed looking. It was exciting, wasn't it, Rosie?"

No doubt feeling much richer in many ways than when she first entered, Irene looks at Rosie intently and asks, "What's wrong, Rosie? You look awfully tired."

Discovering she still has a voice, Rosie manages to utter, "I got a headache!"

Roger shook off his stunned silence when he saw me, with an unexpected smile, bolt towards the door and confront the two women. "Glad you came in, ladies," I said, blocking the exit. "We overheard you mentioning all the wonderful antiques you've got and it sounds great. Now, if you have anything you might want to sell, let us know." Thrusting a handbill into their palms with a list of items we purchase, I continued, "Call me anytime for a free estimate. We make house calls every day." They exited, reading the list as they stumbled out, and Irene's last words as she was reading the list were "I got . . ."

"What the heck kind of customers do you call those two?" Roger asked, hands on hips and shaking his head. "The way you pounced on them as they were leaving, I didn't know what you were going to do."

"Well, Roger," I replied, "in the antique business, we call these people "eye-gotts." They flit around pointing to nearly everything, and their eyes get bigger each second. They spot items similar to what they have and keep repeating, 'I've got this and I've got that,' until they say it so much that it comes out: I got. The way their eyes pop open, we spell it eye-gotts. You'll get use to it. Every antique shop has them."

"But if people walk around and price things, how can you buy from them and make money if you tell them the prices?" Roger asked. "Isn't it like giving them a free appraisal?"

Smiling, I replied, "Sure! So what? Giving a free appraisal is part of the game. The main thing is to get into their homes to see their antiques. People are usually reasonable when they're serious about selling. That's why we don't mind too much when the eye-gotts come into the shop, even though it gets tough on the ears after awhile."

I told Roger about one of the best examples of this I had ever seen. It happened at an antique show. A woman entered the booth across from us with a pad and pencil in her hand. The dealers owning the booth, a married couple, had the habit of sitting directly across from each other at the entrance to their exhibit. Each would have a section of The New York Times firmly in hand. They were known for their high quality antiques and knew the public would recognize that fact the minute they entered the booth.

At antique shows, some dealers seem to defy anyone to enter their booth unless they're serious buyers. They give the appearance to the public that their mere presence is something to be appreciated.

As they sat reading, the woman entered and wandered slowly about the booth, scrutinizing their shelves of antiques, then at intervals jotting down something on the pad. Since I was not busy in my booth at the time, I watched, amazed that they had not detected her presence yet. This should be interesting! Resting my elbows on the counter, it was several moments before one of the dealers noticed the woman as she picked up a red Oriental vase, turning it over to check the price.

With a horrified look, the wife, dropping the paper to the floor, sprang from her chair and accosted the woman. Just inches from her face, she looked down at the woman's list of items and it became very clear to her what was happening. The man arose, suddenly sensing that there was something questionable, terribly wrong, and hurried over to them. Focusing on the pad in the woman's hand, her face flushed, the wife sternly proclaimed "Madam! We charge a ten percent appraisal fee. May I have your list so we can do so? We're not paying rent here to pass out free information!"

Mortified, the woman did not know how to answer. Flustered, red-in-face, she left the pad and pencil on one of the tables and managed to stumble back out of the booth, without breaking anything, returning to the safety of the crowds. She had learned something frightening and yet interesting about antique shows and dealers.

"Bee-Backs"

CHAPTER 18

Roger was in luck. He was about to meet one of the most noted characters in the antique world. Two days later he was in the shop, helping me unload some merchandise I'd just bought. Noticing that someone had entered the shop, I called out to him, "See if that lady wants anything in particular, would you Roger? I'll be right there."

Roger had a knack at initiating pleasantries with people coming into the shop—he was not as jaded as I had probably become. He was chatting amiably with a well-dressed and highly perfumed woman in her early sixties, when I entered the room. His eyes shining brightly, he nudged me aside and whispered, "She looks like she might buy a lot. Having just come in, she already seems very interested in a few things. She's not said a word, so I know she's not an "eye-gott".

Strolling further into the shop and noticing a marble-top table, the lady exclaimed, "Oh! Just the size I've been searching for. We had one in the family. But someone else got it and I've been trying to replace it ever since. How much is it?" Upon my reply, she pondered seriously, "That's not bad at all for that. Let me think about it for a moment." Moving along slowly, she seized a tall, sterling silver flower vase, saying, "Isn't this lovely? Just what I needed for my foyer. How much is it?" She nodded approvingly as I gave her a price, seeming pleased. As I glanced at Roger, he gave me a wink and a smile.

Stopping at an ornate mirror, she put a finger to her lips, studied it for a few moments and said emphatically, "Yes! That should fit right in the corner of my bedroom. You have no idea how long I've been looking for just that shape. I think it's the exact size, too. Do you have a tape measure that I can use?" Roger dashed to the desk drawer and had the tape in her hands before I could even ask him. Jotting down the measurements, she saw the price tag and said, "That seems very reasonable. I'll never find another one at that price." Roger was beaming. He hit my elbow knowingly and whispered, "Didn't I tell you?"

Looking at me intently, he seemed disappointed that I didn't share his enthusiasm about this person who seemed like such a good customer. Then he instantly became cheerful again when the woman came upon the jewelry cases and excitedly said, "Oh! I didn't know you had antique jewelry here, too. I just love it."

Studying the jewelry intently, she pointed into the case and stated, "I can't believe it! Aren't those long, pierced earrings Bohemian garnets? They must be. I have my grandmother's antique necklace and the red stones are the same. I've been looking for earrings to match for ages. I've simply got to have those. May I try them on?"

"Certainly," I replied, handing them over and trying desperately to be a little more attentive.

Up and down, back and forth, she bobbed her head in the mirror, now turning around, then looking from the rear, smiling and nodding her head in approval as she adjusted her hair-do in the process.

She was a portrait of satisfaction as she admired the way the earrings dangled. I was mildly surprised that she didn't bother to apply make up, as well.

Suddenly looking at her watch, she frowned and said, "Oh! That late already! How time flies. These earrings are the perfect size. I'll be back with my necklace to see how they go together."

Picking up her purse from the counter, she headed towards the door; turning, she said, "I've got to see if the table fits the corner. I'll be back after I see whether the mirror is the right size. I know

I want that pair of candlesticks and I'll be back to see how they tie in with my silver tea set."

Looking over at Roger, I saw his mouth come open in obvious wonder. Utterly amazed, as the woman left the shop, Roger came close to me and said, "I can't believe it! She looked and sounded like she was going to buy several . . ." But before he could finish speaking, the door opened and the woman stood halfway in, cheerfully calling out for more information.

"Oh! I forgot to ask. Are you open on Saturdays? I get my hair done and I'll be back after that."

"Yes, we're open on Saturdays," I answered.

"Wonderful," she replied and then left again. Before I could comment to Roger, she re-appeared and again thrust her body partially through the entrance. Smiling broadly, she asked, "How about Sundays? My girlfriend will be in town that day and she loves to go antiquing. We'll be back then, if you're open."

"No! No! Never on Sundays," I barked back, feebly trying not to sound perfectly nasty.

"Well, that's too bad," she said as she started to leave, but the look of disappointment vanished as she continued, "but I'll definitely be back for the earrings on Monday and when I see how the other things fit in, I'll be back for them."

Not saying another word, fearing I would utter harsh words of sarcasm, I restrained myself as I looked at Roger, who was completely befuddled.

Scratching his head and shaking it at the same time, he said, "She sure had me fooled. Didn't you expect her at least to buy a few things? It seemed as if she couldn't live without them."

Now laughing slightly I explained to Roger, "That was a typical example of what we in the trade call a 'bee-back.' They're as common as the 'eye-gotts.' They both come in practically every day. The bee-backs are like bumble bees. With all their oh's and ah's, and hmm's, they buzz around the shop as if sniffing at everything they touch. From their talk and exuberance, one would think they were going to buy you out. They flit from one object to another like a bee, and they wax eloquently over nearly everything they're attracted to. If money was honey, their hives would be empty. Instead of just saying, 'Thanks for letting us look,' which is all they usually do, most of them leave and say, 'I'll be back,' which we hope they won't. Don't get me wrong, Roger, many bee-backs buy, but you'd better have a lot of patience and let them buzz around happily whenever they come into the shop. You can't escape them in this business."

"Whew!" Roger whistled. "I don't think I could take that every day. Between the eye-gotts and the bee-backs, they'd drive me crazy." Pausing to get himself together, he continued, "Enough of that for today!" adding, as he went for the door, "I'll be back!"

* *

A few days later, Arlene, our sales-lady, was having a conversation with Roger (who was now coming in a few times a week to do small chores and favors for us) about the eye-gotts and the bee-backs. Arlene was citing examples of the types of customers who come in daily, and they were laughing about it.

The phone rang, and Arlene called out that it was for me. After the conversation, I joined them, saying to Roger, "There's a woman coming here in about a half hour that you must stay to see. She's from the 'I got rocks' type of customers that we get. Here's your chance to meet one of them."

Letting it sink in for a moment, I gave him time to think what I meant. "Do you mean," he asked, "that they're crazy and have rocks in their head, or something like that?"

"No, Roger," I smiled, "you're not even close—far from it. Just the opposite. You know Florida is a land of wealthy widows. You and I are still alive, so your wife Regina hasn't had a chance to collect 'rocks' yet." Sensing his increasing bewilderment, I continued,

"Guys our age can and do drop dead anytime, and their widows come parading into the shop. Many are decked out, loaded with jewelry, often wearing flashy displays of diamonds. There may be no other place in the country where one can see a single, widowed woman wearing more diamonds at one time then here. These are the fruits of labor and love, the accumulation of one, two or three husbands' gifts to them. Many wear several rings at a time, a collection of precious stones, or 'rocks,' if you will."

"I get it," Roger said, "but I gave Regina one diamond when we were married and she's very happy with that. She's not the type to go around collecting jewelry, anyway."

"That's what you think, Roger. Not yet maybe," I replied, "but widows and widowers move very fast around here. Who knows? Once you're gone, it could be only a matter of weeks before some lonely old gent snatches her away, adorns her with his first and even second wives' diamonds on her fingers; and with what you gave her, she will have a good start on her collection of rocks."

Before he could reply, I continued, "Rocks, Roger, are what the jewelers call these diamonds the women wear when they come into their stores. They are eager to buy them, of course, and many are being sold. Last week a woman came in and I complimented her on her fine array of diamond rings on her fingers. She said, 'This is nothing! I have bracelets, earrings, broaches and various other pieces stored in the vault from my other two husbands. And besides, my sister died and I inherited some of hers.' "

"Florida is not just a great retirement place of pleasures and sunshine," I added, "but it is also the final resting place for millions of ears, wrists, necks, bosoms and fingers that boast an untold wealth of antique and modern pieces of jewelry in diamonds, rubies, emeralds, sapphires, gold and gems of every description. For every two-carat diamond that hits you in the eye worn by the lady sitting next to you in a restaurant, there's probably a lot more in her bank vault or dresser drawer."

As Roger listened intently, I handed him the morning's newspaper and said, "Look here, it's a full page ad to buy jewelry, silver, gold, etc. And there are more of them all the time. They are getting to be as common as the advertising for medical care, health insurance, nursing homes, cemetery plots, funeral parlors, early-bird dinners and every imaginable service catering to senior citizens."

While recovering my breath, I smiled and let this spiel sink in Roger's head. I relished his frown as he said, "I noticed that!"

"Everyone is after us, Roger," I jumped in. "Dead or alive, you're valuable. The gold teeth in your mouth can be yanked out and weighed for scrap value. The gold rings on your fingers can be pulled off the minute you no longer look so good."

Abruptly getting up from his chair, he laughed, saying, "I'm going to keep my teeth in my mouth, my wife isn't going to start collecting rocks, and I don't want an early-bird funeral."

As he started to leave, adequately ruffled, the lady who had phoned about her diamonds was coming into the shop. "Don't go yet, Roger," I said, "you'll enjoy this."

Within a couple of minutes, Roger was within earshot of her conversation as she began, "My brother died recently and I got his wife's . . ."

"Oh! I Love New York"

CHAPTER 19

Because I am in and out of the shop every day, I needed the assistance of a saleslady, Arlene. She had worked at Shelby's, but her services there were no longer needed, thus she came to work for us full time.

One day when Roger was assisting me while Arlene was out to lunch, he said to me, "You're really lucky to have Arlene working for you. Where did she learn about antiques? She told me she had been a model in New York, and she'd had a dress shop in Los Angeles. When did you teach her the business?"

I replied with a smile, "I'm glad she impressed you, but she's learning about the business just working alongside me and with the aid of the various experts who are available around here. This shop is run mainly on words. I go out to buy the merchandise, then we, together, identify, label and put price tags on everything. We have what a lot of businesses don't have, a salesperson who will talk to you. This is where Arlene is at her best."

I went on to explain to him that in the antique business, whether its shows or shops, the relationship between a customer and the dealer can be bewildering. In some shops or booths the dealer springs up to greet the customer; at others, one would have to search amid the mounds of trifles and treasures for his attention. The dealer could be resting, reading, eating or even napping—lacking any enthusiasm. Perhaps, if you're lucky, a nod of his head will acknowledge your presence.

You may even enter a booth at an antique show and feel like you are interrupting something sacrosanct. In one booth there might be two or three dealers engaged in a lively conversation about how good or bad business is, or merely trading gossip. Completely ignoring you, they can make you feel as if you were intruding, so you tip-toe through their stall of antique wares, then leave without a word being exchanged.

One may frequently enter a show or shop and the dealer will notice you looking at an item but never greet you. Asking to see a piece of jewelry, it is handed to you with the remark: "It's 14 karat gold," and no more is said. Or, the awakening dealer may saunter forth and say, "That's a nice cut-glass bowl you're looking at." Then backs off, waiting for you to say, "I'll take it! Wrap it up!"

On the other hand, what happens more often when one enters a booth or shop and asks to see something—maybe a ring—the dealer will hand it to you, saying, "That's a Victorian ring, over a hundred years old. It came from the Broadhurst estate, and was once worn by the Countess of Circumventia. It's one-of-a-kind; you'll never see another like it. We were lucky to get it. My wife just loves it and we sort of hate to sell it, but we can't keep everything we like."

Timidly, you may reply, "Oh! I just thought it was very pretty and was admiring it." You are totally unprepared for the history lesson; or for the dealer removing the ring from your hand—though gently—and then giving you a look you'll soon not forget, slamming shut the jewelry case and disappearing in a hurry.

If anything, in our shop we aim for benign neglect, which requires less effort and often produces better results.

* *

Upon entering Purnie's Antiques, one sees a desk near the front door. Sitting there is our saleslady, Arlene, either on the phone or ready to greet a customer.

A petite blond, Arlene has often been compared to looking like Debbie Reynolds. She maintains a stylish appearance and speaks in a soft voice. Her personality leads to a unique style of conducting business. What she may lack in expertise, she makes up for in her ability to put strangers at ease. Many customers and browsers are tourists from around the globe, and she gets pleasure engaging them in a discussion of their travels.

When I'm in the shop and within hearing, it amazes me to learn how many people, including Arlene, within a short time reveal many chapters of their history. Arlene could draw them into an adventurous exchange of words, usually with no connection to antiques, while they browse or examine an object. What seems like an hour later, she tells me that she's sold an expensive bracelet or wrangled a very promising house call for me to make later.

I often wondered if it works better to be sociable and talk one's way into results, or to be just another antique "expert." But I have come to realize how many lonely people there are in the world, and that she had the patience to be friendly to them all.

Being a person of few words myself, during business hours (unless among friends engaged in one of our many impromptu social exchanges), I find it best during Arlene's "selling technique" to retreat to the backroom, my haven. While this goes on, I can ignore as much of the frontal activity as I wish, until someone comes into the shop that requires my services.

Once, a gentleman in his mid-forties, seeing an elaborately-carved Oriental table in the front window, came into the shop to examine it. Arlene approached him with a few pleasantries, offering him what information she had on it.

Keeping his attention, after asking him "Where are you from?" and "What do you do?", I heard something about complexions, skin and something called Retina-A.

Calling me from the back room, she introduced me to him; he was a dermatologist. Seated at the desk, she was holding his business card in one hand and jotting down some related information.

I heard her telling him what products she was using and asking his advice. There were words like collagens, surgery, creams, cosmetics and age factors, but no words at all pertaining to the Oriental table mentioned, what seemed to me, an eternity ago. Then a couple of silver dealers came in and required my attention. In this busy interval, and in an attempt to expedite a sale for Arlene, I called out a few words to the dermatologist, "That's a lovely and unique table you're buying."

There are but few times when Arlene doesn't interject her own personal experiences in her talks with customers. Her world travels always seemed to connect with someone else's experiences. Just mention a name or place, and presto "I knew about ..." would roll off her tongue.

To cite a typical reaction when a person is asked where he/she is from:

Arlene: Oh, really, I'm from New York. Where in New York?

Customer: East 89th Street.

Arlene: Oh! I love New York. I lived in Tudor City for years. I miss it so.

Waxing eloquently, she pours forth a wondrous litany of moments, people, places and events. The New York of the 1950's and earlier: the 1939 World's Fair, she worked there briefly as a young girl—Eleanor Holmes and Johnny Weissmuller. She knew Leo Durocher and Horace Stoneham, men big in baseball. She had frequented the Waldorf, Club 21, Sardi's, Lindy's for cheesecake, been to endless parties and fun-filled bars where celebrities lingered.

These are not tall tales of imagination or exaggeration. Is a photograph of herself and Buster Crabbe good enough evidence? Name someone else, and she's ready, time after time:

To Customer #1: Oh! You're from Greenwich? I was born in Port Chester, New York, next door. I know that area well. We had a home in Connecticut. Just above Stamford.

To Customer #2: You're from Toronto? I love that city. I was married there to my first husband.

To Customer #3: Where do you live in California? I lived there in the 1950's for a while. Had my own boutique in Hollywood. It was wonderful!

To Customer #4: You're going to India? My husband took me there on our honeymoon. It was part of a trip around the world. Don't miss the Taj Mahal!

To Customer #5: You have a Great Dane? Oh! How I miss not being able to have a dog in our condo. We had a Great Dane back in Connecticut. I started a gourmet dog food company before anyone else, but then . . .

To Customer #6: Where in Germany do you live? My grandmother came from Alsace-Lorraine. She was part German.

To Customer #7: Oh! Paris. I was there last year on vacation. I'm part French. In what part of Paris do you live?

To Customer #8: Yes! These pearls do have a fine lustre. We were in Japan on our honeymoon and we learned a lot about fine pearls and what to look for. My husband let me pick out my own. We were able to match a strand perfectly.

To Customer #9: You're right! It's terrible the way the Indians were treated in this country. I have a friend who . . . . !

Customer #10 to Arlene: I used to be a Ziegfeld girl. Now I'm giving away my age.

To Customer #10: Oh! I was a model in New York. I knew a lot of the celebrities. I've been mentioned in the Daily News and The Mirror by Lee Mortimer, Dorothy Killgalen and Walter Winchell. We always went to 21 and the Stork Club. I was introduced to the Maharajah of Baroda.

To Customer #11: I knew Miami Beach in the 1950's too. Women in furs and diamonds strolling along Lincoln Road every night. We saw Dean Martin and Jerry Lewis poolside at the Roney Plaza. Sophie Tucker and Martha Raye were performing. There was so much excitement and glamour down there then. I'm glad I was around for those wonderful days.

* *

Hollywood stars! We've seen a photograph of her and Walter Brennan, with Jeff Hunter, Neville Brand and Sherry North, all leaning against a corral while taking a break from a Western film being produced.

At first, I thought I would never get used to all of these diversions from business. They were endless and retold with amazing zest and energy, as if it all happened only yesterday. Nevertheless, it is her unique style of conducting business. She has had many a lonely person forgetting their troubles, and inspiring them to recite their fondest memories.

Hearing of her frequent worldly experiences, countered by those of her customers, had me very often shaking my head in doubt and amusement. But it resulted in many sales, of course, and produced opportunities for purchasing more antiques.

I was determined, however, to put her to the test, to discover places where she might never have been, or known anyone living there. It was a serious challenge.

One day, in a discussion on World War II, I mentioned that I had been in boot camp in the Marines and was stationed at Parris Island, South Carolina. I assumed she was living in New York during the war years; although she had once mentioned being married to a military man, I knew none of the details.

"Oh!" Arlene enlightened me, "my husband and I spent several months at that base during the war. He was a Naval officer and was sent there to recuperate from combat duty in the Pacific. I know the area well." So much for that: tell it to the Marines!

Then I recalled that a group of us had taken a trip to Italy and Poland in 1980. It was in August, following Lech Walesa's climbing of the gates at the Gdansk shipyard and when the Solidarity movement was the major topic of the times. At last I knew I could find a place that would leave her nonplused. I would have bet anything!

"When we were in Poland, Arlene," I began slowly, "we made a special point to see the death camps at Auschwitz. As you know, it's a place never to be forgotten, and we had a rather thorough look at it all. It was terrible!"

Looking at her casually but closely, I felt quite safe that she knew no one personally who had been there, and, for a change, she would be asking me questions, instead of making contributory statements. For a few blank moments, she said nothing, but was thinking intently. Suddenly I remembered she always claimed her ancestry was composed of several nationalities; uncertainty began to creep into my mind.

Looking up, finally, after a time, she said, "It was horrible! Just the other day there was a program on TV about the Holocaust. One of my best friends in New York had an uncle in Auschwitz, if I recall, or was it Treblinka? He managed to survive, but she told me all the dreadful things that happened to the rest of his family, who didn't make it."

There's got to be someplace, I thought, desperately. Even if I have to invent something. I said to her, "Jane and I are thinking of taking a cruise around South America. Have you ever been to Tierra del Fuego? Around Cape Horn?"

Trying to keep a taunting grin from my face, I looked at her; her face revealed nothing. At last! Success. Just as I was about to congratulate myself on finally stumping her, the shop door opened and an attractive, dark-complected woman entered. Arlene looked up, leaped from her chair excitedly, and burst forth, "Anna-Marie! When did you get back from Chile?"

Retreating to the back room, I picked up the New York Times travel section, rather hopelessly, and rifled through it. I felt a slight glimmer of enthusiasm when I came across the article "What's Doing In Katmandu!" That's it! I've always wanted a Himalayan trip and here it was. Mt. Everest. Could she top this? Surely I could mention this in the shop and hopefully get no reply from Arlene, no association at all.

Waiting for Anna-Marie to leave, I felt slightly exalted. Then, another gnawing thought entered my mind. She could possibly know someone who knew the British explorer Sir Edmund Hillary, or had been to New Zealand, where he was born. She could also be part English.

No! There were too many possibilities. Give up, I thought. Maybe some day.

Sometimes when these tales of grandiose experiences overwhelm me and I don't want to be reminded of my own varied adventures—good or bad—I mockingly throw up my arms to Arlene and ask, "How did you and I end up like this?" Sweeping my arms outward, I continued, "The people we knew, the great times we had, and here we are surrounded by knick-knacks, trinkets, bric-a-brac, some treasures, all covered by a layer or two of dust. Is this it? Is this all we've got to show for it? Lump us with the rest of the antique dealers; do we end up in the trash heap of history?"

Her spirit flared. I'd hit home! "Not for me, kiddo," she replied, "maybe you're all washed up, but I've got plenty of things I'm still going to do!"

Looking out at the bench as I pondered her last words, two of my mid-eighties customers are enthusiastically discussing their travel plans for the long, hot, summer. Just then Arlene spots a well-known "eye-gott" coming towards the shop and says, "Oh! It's five minutes to noon. Lunch-time!" Hurrying out, she turns and smiles, saying, "Good luck! I'll bee-back!"

Names For The Games

CHAPTER 20

A fascinating facet of the antique profession is revealed in the titles dealers select for their establishments. While helping my brother at my first antique show in New York City back in 1946, I strolled the aisles of the show and was intrigued by the business titles given to individual booths. It was all new to me then.

Seeing dealers at shows only twice a year, we didn't bother to learn each others' first or last names. We came to be known by our booth titles. Some of them were clever, or catchy and witty; others were funny without trying to be, some definitely misleading.

Curious, comical or thought-provoking, booth titles are often carry-overs from a dealer's antique shop. So, whenever a dealer comes into our shop, as many do regularly over the years, we tend to recognize him only by his business name. Or we may have a secret pet name for him, one that may reflect the way he conducts business.

For instance, upon returning from a house call one morning, I asked Arlene if any dealers had been in while I was gone. "Oh! Let's see," she reflected, "LAST CHANCE ANTIQUES was in and they bought a couple of things." Rolling her eyes in thought, she continued, "PRECIOUS MOMENTS ANTIQUES was in and they just snooped around as usual, asking prices on everything and not buying anything. They were especially annoying and irksome today." Our private name for them was AGONIZING MOMENTS ANTIQUES.

We find amusement in labeling certain dealers, and suppose they have a favorite name for us, entwining business methods with personalities.

Take, for example, a husband and wife who never make a decision without consulting the other. Our name for them is BALL AND CHAIN ANTIQUES, belying their real name, something like FREEMAN'S GALLERIES.

Then there's an exceptionally listless antique dealer who has the legal misnomer of something like BUSY BEE ANTIQUES, but is known around as MENZA-MORTE ANTIQUES. Still another pair of dealers are referred to as GARAGE SALE ANTIQUES, because of their large volume of just junk.

* *

It is extremely difficult to find a piece of cut glass that has been around for 75 years or more and still be in perfect condition. On house calls, most private sellers believe their glass to be in excellent shape, unless obviously flawed. However, during their ownership of it, a maid or a family member, even themselves, may have chipped or cracked it without realizing it. Consequently, when we purchase from a private party, who believes it to be perfect, the item must be scrutinized very closely for flaws and shown to the owner. This, of course, affects value, and should be brought to a potential buyer's attention by the dealer when he sells it. Much can be repaired, of course, but at an additional expense.

A married couple seen at many local shows and antique shops are experts and specialists in the cut glass field, and are constantly searching for more fine pieces. The wife, charming and sparkling with energy, reflects her merchandise. In search of fine crystal, she may engage the dealer in conversation at his shop or booth, while the husband, asking permission first, is busy examining the crystal.

Whenever they come into my shop, I don't recall ever showing the husband a piece of cut glass where he didn't at first manage to find the tiniest chip or flaw. Using a magnifying glass, he will "discover" flaws where others couldn't.

We expect this and go through the same routine with them each time. "You won't find anything wrong with that piece, Ben," I say to him, as he picks up a brilliantly-faceted water pitcher. I stand back, knowing full well what to expect. He can't wait to grasp it. Going to the brightest light, taking off his glasses, he turns it at every conceivable angle. Up, away, over, under, now squinting, frowning, his mustache quivering, then, as if at an appointed signal, a slight smile will appear on his face, and he proudly proclaiming, "You're wrong, Henry. Look, right here! And there! See them?" as he points to something so minute I could only see them by standing on my head with a pair of binoculars.

The words are always the same. "This has to be repaired; you can't sell this as perfect. We have to have them ground down. What you're asking is unrealistic. What do you really want?" he concludes happily. (The tiny flaws, to him, have become tantamount to major cracks, but I would expect nothing less from him.)

Smiling sweetly, his wife says nothing, but comes over, knowing that Ben has done his job as expected; the entire procedure is an exact replica of all their visits. If we agree to their terms, and they purchase this piece, the same item will be exhibited in their gallery and priced much higher, without any "repairs," of course, for sale the very next day!

Whoever notices them first as they approach our shop or booth warns the others, "Oh! Oh! Get ready. Here comes 'Chips' and his wife." Their official name is something like CRYSTAL CLEAR ANTIQUES, but to many dealers in the area they are vigorously referred to as PAIN-IN-THE-GLASS ANTIQUES.

A quite different dealer would stop by many of the shops in the area a few times each year. He had a regular route, checking several dealers on his swing through town. Quite elusive in nature, drab in dress for this resort area, he never offers any information about himself, but we know better than to ask.

He called himself The Undertaker—permitting himself a bit of humor. Entering the shop without any advance notice, without much of a salutation, he would ask, "What do you have that you want to get rid of?" With him he has a rather large briefcase filled with cash and working tools. "I'll buy any dead-beat merchandise, any of your mistakes," he offers. Mainly he is interested in jewelry and silver objects. Buying those agreed upon, he tosses them into his vehicle and vanishes.

Practically all dealers at one time or another have some stock they are stuck with and would be glad to get their original investment back, or even less. Enter The Undertaker! His implements are acid for testing the items of silver and gold, and scales for weighing their basic scrap value. The dealer must expect to get the lowest possible price in getting rid of their "dogs" to The Undertaker.

Eager to oblige, always grim, he conveys the feeling that he is rendering a big favor just by taking these items off a dealer's hands. What he didn't provide for this undertaking is the flowers and music as the "dead" merchandise is hauled away. To some dealers he is referred to as the Ghost, since he appears and fades so rapidly.

One dealer, training a new helper, nearly suffered a heart attack when, upon returning to his shop from a very urgent house call, was greeted with the words, "You just missed The Undertaker, but I sold him those two bags of scrap silver under the table in the back room." Rushing to look under the table, the dealer's heart pounded furiously. Gone!

By an oversight, he had forgotten to tell the new helper that he had set a bag of valuable Victorian silver under the same table, which he'd purchased only the night before in a hasty deal. Usually when The Undertaker purchased any scrap silver from his regular customers—as in this case—he merely weighed the bag without checking its contents, and leaves. There were two bags of silver under the table and the helper assumed they were both "scrap." Feeling his knees getting weaker, the dealer said nothing to the helper but dashed to the nearest phone.

"Has The Undertaker been to your place yet, Al?" he asks. No luck! Dejectedly he makes two or three more phone calls. In the end, he can't track him down. The Undertaker is covering too much territory. As he slumps into a chair, he could only visualize his Victorian silver crushed at the bottom of a week's accumulation of "dead" merchandise at The Undertaker's warehouse—never to be identified and retrieved.

* *

In the Fifties and Sixties, many antique dealers transported their merchandise around in station wagons. It was also a great way to advertise their business, especially when exhibiting at antique shows.

On both sides of the vehicle, they liberally painted their eye-catching titles and the types of antiques they dealt with. By their unique printing, any dealer pulling into the show's parking lot could tell who had come to the show. Dealers' vehicles stood out brilliantly: MYRA TINKLEPAUGH'S ANTIQUES; ADA GOODSPEED'S ANTIQUES; BELL, BOOK & CANDLE ANTIQUES. These vehicles would later be seen in hotel and motel parking lots in the vicinity, announcing to the world what the possible treasures were within. They were like tattoos, proudly designed and displayed.

As crime became rampant and a way of life, the names disappeared from most of these vehicles. Dealers were compelled to invent inconspicuous ways to transport their merchandise. The last thing they wanted anyone to know was what they carried in their car, truck or station wagon. It became a complete reversal of the past. The vogue was now to be as low profile as possible. Dealers, after the show, became aware that they might be followed in their vehicles.

The major worry was that their vehicles might be broken into, things stolen or they even held up at gun-point. Dealers were followed to restaurants after the show and burglarized while dining. Motel rooms and parking lots were places to be mugged.

One dealer devised his own system to detract from his image as an antique dealer. He bought a large truck that was once used by a wholesale Chinese food company, with blazing red Chinese lettering on both sides. If one were from Beijing, the characters would be easy to read. Now, he was more relaxed hauling his antiques about the country. That's using your noodle!

Although the advertising has vanished from most of these vehicles, they still attach a lot of importance to the names they select for their venture, as they seek to become even more noteworthy. There are still CALICO CAT ANTIQUES or DEN OF ANTIQUITIES and plenty of BIRD-IN-THE-HAND ANTIQUES to keep alive the homespun and pure American flavor of the antique field. In these days of flourishing antique dealers, with real or assumed sophistication, new titles are always popping up.

As an attempt at conversation or mere friendliness, it wasn't too long ago that I could ask a dealer, "Where is your shop located?" Today, instead of a cordial reply, one is likely to have a business card thrust into the hand, announcing AURORA BOREALIS GALLERY or something quite as celestial. Suddenly, the word "shop" seems too insignificant, and the card changed to read JASMINE AND JAMES UPPINGTON, LTD. Thus is the word "shop" falling by the wayside, along with many catchy phrases, rhymes and riddles that once had adorned the dealers' vehicles and booth signs.

The yoke of the old antique peddler is being cast aside for more prestigious titles that go along with an affluent society's more discriminating collectors. So, too, have prices risen.

ATTIC AND CELLAR ANTIQUES suddenly became HAMPTON GALLERIES. What was once PRINTS AND PAUPER BOOKS (antique book dealers), is now named OLDE LITERATURE EMPORIUM. Where once dealers flocked to MAD MAGPIE ANTIQUES in a tiny hamlet in the Finger Lakes section of New York State, they now enter THE GENESEE GALLERIES.

Some name their shops for prominent people or streets or historical events. Where one nearly broke his/her neck muddling through the relics at BROKEN ARROW ANTIQUES along the Susquehanna River near Horseheads, New York, today they might be frostily greeted by the same owner standing beneath a sign reading SOUTHERN TIER SALON—OBJECTS D'ART.

What was once relished for its surprises and adventures, JAKE'S UNIQUE JUNQUE,—a complete disarray and shambles of a shop where nearly anything might be found, wallowing in disorder, dust and discovery—has now been cleaned up, scrubbed, overhauled, prices raised and re-baptized GRAND BOULEVARD ARCADE.

Not too far away is JEWELS MAGNIFIQUE, which was once called the THREE GOLDEN BALLS PAWNSHOP. Its owners are two dealers from Brooklyn who have since added a French flavor. Having tucked their acid bottles and gold-weighing devices under the counter, they have now splashed themselves with "Obsession," and laid out their jewelry in lavish, brilliantly-lighted, velvet-lined showcases. If one listens carefully, one can still detect a Fulton Street accent, but the manners are impeccably European and the atmosphere and prices are definitely cosmopolitan.

On a recent trip to the countryside of upstate New York (once a great place to chance upon antique jewelry bargains), I made a special trip to check out an old farmhouse antique shop, once called THE CROWING ROOSTER ANTIQUES.

In earlier days, half their wares were in the barn, the rest filled every nook and cranny of the house. It had been at least fifteen years since I'd visited that part of the state and as I approached the Victorian farmhouse in the near dusk of a very late September day—the setting sun igniting the trees in a blaze of color—I had an empty feeling deep within me that there was no way the circumstances could still be the same.

Sure enough, greeting my eyes was a huge, elegantly-painted sign as I approached the large house. But what had once been THE

CROWING ROOSTER (undoubtedly having crowed at his last dawn), was now a different sign, boasting the lofty title of THE MANSION ANTIQUES CENTER.

Talk about sunset years! Appropriately, the sun was just then sinking below the purple clusters of grapes and the sudden grip of cooler autumn air grasping my senses, caused far too many memories to rush into my mind.

Here I was, a much older antique dealer in a new station wagon, who remembered the many times years ago when I approached this same entrance, but always in a convertible, often with the top down. There was no need for a station wagon then. Dealing only in antique jewelry, my business was contained within the trunk of my car.

Walking along the long porch, finally getting to the bell (which was electronically wired—not a hint of times past, when all types of farm implements and gadgets were obviously strewn about the yard), I rang it, half hoping that no one would answer. Then I could ride away, recalling it as it used to be.

A man older than myself, with a gray, pointed beard, opened the door and said, "Sorry, we're closed!" Behind him stood an elderly lady, firmly holding beside her a full-grown German shepherd, ears pointed intently and looking into her face for instructions.

"Is that you, Bill? Is that you, Liz? Remember me—Henry Purnie?" I asked.

Studying me closely, squinting and standing back while his wife took the dog out into another room, he finally grasped my hand and shoulder and huskily cried out, "Well, I'll be!"

After several moments of disbelief as the three of us assured each other of our identity, all those exciting days of business that we had done together suddenly came back to me.

Not only was the old cock still crowing, they told me over refreshments, but their son and his wife had joined them in business and had developed the homestead into a major country antiques center. Dealers still came from everywhere and the "pickings" were still good for them, as they had become so well established. It was still the old story of buying and selling at the best price.

As I drove back to Florida a few days later, all this coming to mind, I felt assured that while the game was still much the same, the names had noticeably changed.

I recalled again, that when I exhibited at antique shows over all those years, how often I'd failed to call the dealers by name. I had read only the sign above the booth and that's who they were. For years at the Miami Beach antique show, the two dealers across from me were named simply MY WIFE AND I ANTIQUES. When they reported that they had had a successful show, I was happy that MY WIFE AND I were pleased.

Today, more dealers are simply using their full names, leaving catchy, tricky and amusing titles to posterity. But if there is a resurgence in eye-catching names, I might drop PURNIE'S ANTIQUES and call myself WHAT'S YOUR BEST PRICE ANTIQUES?

"The Sleeper"

CHAPTER 21

Antique dealers are always buying from one another, to the extent that one wonders if anything is ever sold at retail.

Nevertheless, sales eventually trickle down to the retailer, where one may expect to get the top price. But many dealers go through life and never get the maximum value. One such wholesale dealer is known hereabouts as Turnover Ted, for his immediate disposal of merchandise at a small profit.

Certainly, everyone is out to get stock at the right price. Some of us, like myself, buy very little from dealers. Instead, we direct our efforts at getting merchandise from private homes and individuals. No matter what source a dealer uses to increase his stock, it seems the minute he buys something there's a dealer ready to pounce on it, especially in a shop.

Here's where one of the most important words in a dealer's vocabulary makes its appearance. In the movie industry, a "sleeper" might be the film that got a bad review, yet the public overwhelmingly approved and patronized it, making it a success. The same could be said of a book or work of art, a sporting event or practically anything that seemed of little importance, initially, then develops into something striking or noticeable.

In the antique world, a "sleeper" is not the dealer who emerges from behind mounds of bric-a-brac and jammed aisles of lamps, furniture and over-crowded tables of antiques; who eases himself up from a chair with bags under the eyes and slowly puts down a magazine as he emerges unsmiling and mutters, "Can I help you?" No! This description which so often fits the antique dealer, is not the "sleeper" that is regularly referred to in the antique trade.

A sleeper is an antique or collectible object that is discovered quite unexpectedly by someone recognizing its value which was not at first apparent. The finder's eyes light up. He sees it not only as a bargain but as an object grossly underpriced and far more valuable than the price portrays.

As an astute buyer, he grabs it! Having a price tag on it, once it is in his hands, and until he lets go of it, it's his. What runs through his mind is that the owner doesn't know what it is, what it's worth. That he, the buyer, must seize the moment and the item, and not let go until he makes his decision. If it's valuable, his hands may quiver, but his face must show no emotion, and, above all, he must control his voice.

The first few seconds he is grasping it firmly in his hands are the most crucial. The least said, now, the better; he might ask to look at something else, momentarily, but without letting go of the sleeper.

Heart palpitating, he's spent years learning to mask his emotions and giving the bland look that's so commonly encountered—none of which came easily. If one thinks a doctor's internship difficult, move over for the antique dealer. Both take pride in the results.

In their search for antiques, all dealers are on the alert for their next sleeper. It could come when least expected. It does appear sooner or later, whether it be an item of exceptional value or merely something to make a particular day a bit more exciting.

A dealer can get into the business precisely that way. He happens upon a single antique item or an entire lot that so overwhelms him with the profit he's made that he becomes immediately hooked. Most dealers have adjusted to the idea that a real sleeper is more of a rarity than a frequent experience. He's quite happy just to buy merchandise regularly at a fair price, hoping to make a reasonable profit.

However, in my experience, some dealers appear to buy only a sleeper. They enter an antique shop and never buy anything otherwise. It makes one wonder where they get their merchandise. Of course, the answer to that is that there are some dealers who purchase only at rock-bottom prices, constantly searching at shows and shops, using every method known to the trade, but mainly attrition. If they don't find a sleeper, they get the closest thing to one; we sometimes sell to this type of dealer out of sheer exhaustion.

More gas is wasted, more rubber burned, and more territory covered in anxious seeking by these dealers who are in perpetual search for the Holy Grail of the antique business—the sleeper.

Is there a dealer alive who hasn't sold something too hastily and lost out to another dealer, making him feel good for a long time? When a smooth dealer latches on to an exceptional sleeper, he may still ask for "your best price," just to create an air of nonchalance, being true to form. There are certain dealers who check our stock regularly, rarely buying anything. When that happens, we feel we've not made a sale, but more likely a mistake.

When we were still exhibiting antique jewelry exclusively, we had in our stock then a very heavy silver necklace with an egg-shaped locket. As is true of much antique jewelry, this item had no marks whatsoever. They were not required by the countries of origin at that time. Although it was picked up and examined by many dealers during the course of the year, it was always returned to display. No one wanted it! Finally, to get rid of it, we sold it very cheaply to a dealer, happy to have it sold and gone.

At the next show, the dealer who had bought it from us came to our booth and showed us an exquisite gold Victorian locket and chain, a much desired item and a marvel to behold. "Here's the necklace I bought from you, Henry, at the Hamburg, New York antique show," he gloated. "What do you think of it?" Not recognizing it at all, I simply shrugged my shoulders.

Hastily, he added, "This is the silver necklace you sold me. When I first saw it, I had a funny feeling about it. When you weren't looking, I scratched it with my pen-knife. It was yellow underneath so

I had a hunch someone wanted a silver necklace and had it plated. Now look at her! Isn't she a beauty?" Smiling broadly, he walked away, not waiting for my reply. That was a well-deserved sleeper.

One summer, a noted parsimonious watch dealer approached me at my booth at the Hyannis, Cape Cod antique show and said, "Henry, here's a $50 bonus for that large silver pocket watch I bought from you last year. Let me know if you get any more like it." Word later trickled down through the show that it turned out to be an early American watch by a famous maker. Worth thousands. I had sold it to him for $150. I was the sleeper!

The Promoters

CHAPTER 22

I was pleasantly surprised by an unexpected visitor recently. She had at one time represented the VIPs of antique shows: the promoters. Now in her late eighties, she and her husband had sponsored many highly successful antique shows in the Northeast in the Fifties and Sixties. Having seen one of our large ads for buying antiques, she stopped to chat about old times, thrilled that there was someone still around who remembered her. Now retired, she savored the hour-long conversation over the trials and tribulations she'd weathered over the years, as well as the great pleasures of the antique business.

All antique shows are sponsored or produced by someone or by an organization. Many of the most successful ones are the creation of individuals who devote an enormous amount of time to these ventures. Loving the task, they are in a special class.

If there's a tougher breed than the antique dealer himself, it's the tenacious antique show promoter. Not only can they be financially quite successful at this, but some aspire to a level of prestige that seems to rank above that of mere mortals. It has always been this way, and the dealers don't seem to mind perpetuating this image. They, the promoters, are the leaders; if their shows are prosperous and satisfying, let them be "generals." It's an important part of the game.

How does one spot a promoter at an antique show? I met my first of this breed at the New York Armory Antique Show on 34th Street in 1946. Two women and one man, together they seemed quite unapproachable at first, almost always secluded in their office. This was a surprisingly small cubicle, near the entrance to the show, with windows from which they looked out upon everything that they controlled. From this office emanated the strict rules governing the conduct of the dealers and the show.

The old Madison Square Garden show, held a month before, and just a few blocks away, was the major competitor to the Armory show. Some dealers did exhibit at both shows, if their stock and stamina could endure it. Soon there were other promoters sniffing out the air, out on Long Island and in the suburbs. Dealers were aligning their loyalty and preference for certain show promoters, who in turn sought out dealer allegiance, thus setting the stage for the furious battles to come later.

* *

Some show promoters had a distinctive style, easy to remember. One such promoter, a married couple, had in short time developed several shows in the smaller cities throughout Florida and had no trouble getting the influx of winter dealers to exhibit with them.

Back in the Sixties, these small shows were a source for buying antiques and jewelry from local residents, generally retired, who were glad to have the opportunity to dispose of their antiques.

Although the promoters were antique dealers themselves, they did not exhibit in their own shows. Instead, as I was to observe while exhibiting at one of their shows, they both sat at a table near the inside entrance to be first at the sellers. Selling admission tickets there, they observed first-hand all those who were bringing in bags and boxes of antiques to sell to the dealers.

"Anything in that bag ya' wanna' sell?" was the forthright and down-to-earth approach of the male promoter. Getting affirmations, "Set everything here on this table," was the next invitation. Since my booth was nearest the entrance—as jewelry, silver and antiques were spread out there in plain view—we saw how obvious it was that they had a great thing going.

Taking the choicest things for themselves, stuffing everything else hurriedly back into their original bags or boxes, one of them would say, "There are probably some dealers inside who will be glad to buy these other items."

After observing from our vantage point the promoters' tactics all day, followed by eager responses like, "Yes, we'll sell these; we have no further use for them," I questioned the fairness of these antique show promoters. The exhibitors, paying their booth rent to the promoters, should have the same opportunity of buying from private individuals bringing antiques into the show. Something should be done!

On the second day of the show, while the public was filling up the parking lot, I left my helper in our booth and went outside. I looked for those people with bags and approached them, asking, "Do you have any old jewelry to sell? I have a booth inside but I'd like to take a look here, if you don't mind." I immediately handed them my business card which brought me favorable responses, besides working them for follow-up house calls when they came to our booth inside. I liked this method of approaching better—discovering my own way of "promoting" at these particular shows.

* *

The gold and silver rush of 1980 had spawned ever more antique shows. With all the dealers doing a land-office business, anyone with a little guts, with some venturesome cash, or a brainstorm notion for a new antique show, appeared on the scene.

An antique exhibitor at a show would frequently be approached by a suave and enthusiastic looking gentleman, often accompanied by a charming lady. Both, with briefcases under their arms, waiting until an exhibitor was free before introducing themselves.

"Hello, Mr. Eagerdeeler. My name is Douglas Dirigible and this is my business associate, Helena Helium. We're expanding to have more antique shows in this area." Handing the dealer a

gold-embossed business card with the logo of an erupting vol-
cano, the name read: VOLATILE PROMOTIONS, INC. "We're
sponsoring some new shows all around the country and your stock
looks like it would be an enhancement to our highly selective
antique shows," Mr. Dirigible states.

Handing the exhibitor a list of these shows, which his companion provides, he gets his attention. "Our newest show is in
Waterloo," he continues, "right here in your own state. The per
capita income of that city is $50,000. We will have massive TV and
radio advertising. (The word "massive" is a favorite word of many
of the show promoters, which often is what the dealers end up
with—not in business, but in headaches.) "Our show will be ideally
located," he continues, "right smack on the new Howling Winds
Turnpike, a 16-lane expressway." (Try to get off and on!) "Our booth
rentals are reasonable," he concludes. He then quotes some figures
on costs that makes the promoter of the current show appear a
Santa Claus in comparison. The dealers were already squawking at
the high costs.

To those dealers interested (new ones coming into the profession
all the time), he goes over the list, saying "If you hurry, I have a few
choice corner booths available at these extravaganzas"—he circles
ten or twelve of them. The newly retired couple (glad to get away
from Sinking Sun Condominium for a few days), are thrilled at this
information.

"Look this list over", the promoter suggests, "and we'll be back
this way to sign you up for the shows you want to do."

The promoters then walk slowly down the aisle, smiling while
sizing up other prospects. Stopping at another booth and beginning his initial pitch, the dealer interrupts him, saying, "Thanks
anyway, but we did four shows last month. We've been on the road
so much I forgot where we live."

"Well, may I leave some discount admission cards for some of
our shows coming up?"

"Yeah! I guess that'll be okay."

The promoter motions to his companion, who pulls out a thick stack of their antique show advertisement cards and leaves then on a corner of the table. Walking randomly through the show,they get permission from several other dealers to do likewise.

Customers walking into the booths picking them up are invited to attend the forthcoming spectacles: ANTIQUE EXPOSITION/ FIRST SHOW EVER IN THE EVERGLADES/UNLIMITED DEALERS! Also: SUPER OUTDOOR ANTIQUE SHOW IN THE ORANGE BOWL IN AUGUST. Plus: NORTH AMER-ICA'S HIGHEST SHOW/THE ALL-NEW MT. McKINLEY ANTIQUE MARATHON. These events have several new dealers making excited inquiries from each other. Why not try something totally different!

There was one show in particular where the new promoter had done an especially good job of trail-blazing. It was a rather slow-paced show and some of the dealers were wandering about, doing the usual speculating among themselves as to why this was so.

Sam and Nancy, seated opposite each other at the entrance to their booth, are reading a newspaper. A couple walked in, the husband moves towards a large cut glass bowl. Noticing that his wife was attracted to a nearby neatly-arranged stack of discount admission cards for future shows, Nancy called out to her, "Oh! Help yourself to any of those cards. We're going to be exhibiting at some of them ourselves." Stepping towards the woman, she continued, "The one you have in your hand is for Cleveland in November. That's one of our best shows." The woman calls over to her husband (who turned away from the punch bowl which he had been studying intently), to join her. The three of them, as they picked up various cards, became engrossed in discussing future shows.

Then "Oh Charles, look!" the wife exclaimed, "they're having an antique show next spring in Cuddesbeck. That's not too far from us."

"That's a new one for us, too," Sam volunteered, dropping his newspaper and entering the discussion. "The promoter just left and we signed up for it. It's supposed to be a very good area for antiques." They discussed this forthcoming show very enthusiastically before the couple left with several cards in their hands, at which Nancy and Sam smiled, pleased with the conversation.

As the couple wandered into the next booth, the man said to his wife, "There was a cut glass punch bowl which could fit in very nicely with our collection. I meant to call your attention to it but you were busy. Let's go back!" The wife hesitated and said, "They'll be up in our area this spring; we can catch them then."

Back at the booth, Nancy walked across the aisle to Sylvia's booth and asked, "Are things slow for you, too? We've sold very little so far. I can't understand it; this show was always one of our best." Before she receives a reply, she sees another couple enter her booth. One of them picked up a couple of show cards and says, "I see they have a show in Atlanta next month. Where is this new auditorium?"

Smiling, Nancy replied, "That's a first for us, too." Then she called out to Sam, who put the newspaper down and came over. "Sam! Can you give these people directions to that auditorium in Atlanta?"

* *

Many of these new shows soon disappeared as fast as they'd been contrived. The more successful a show was in a particular area, the more of a target it became for the new promoter. The trend was, if one antique show was very successful, why not move into the same territory? And better yet, why not have it three weeks earlier and get the jump on them? Exhibitors! There were plenty of them. The best shows had long waiting lists of exhibitors and some of the younger dealers were tired of waiting for the older dealers to die so they could take their place.

Paying their admission fee,many a visiting promoter, with brief cases, show cards, floor plans and contracts would roam the exhibition halls of well-established antique shows and recruit dealers for future shows. In turn, dealers looked for the excitement of trying something different—limbering up the bones of many an older dealer.

Observing the raid going on right before their eyes, the residing promoters became alarmed at this effort to move in on their territory, and took measures to protect it. As far back as 1950, we witnessed antique shows that were considered to be sacrosanct, eyed enviously and finally emulated. Now nothing seemed inviolable in the soaring and roaring 1980's.

Some promoters adopted very strict defensive measures to guard their domains. Of these, some were ludicrous and provided laughs for everyone except the promoter trying to protect his show from the encroaching promoters. The original promoter let it be known outright to all "that if you exhibit with VOLATILE PROMO-TIONS SHOWS or any other promoter coming into the area, you will be prohibited from exhibiting at this show in the future."

That was enough to keep most of the dealers faithful, but there were new dealers entering the field every day, appearing as ambitious retirees, as restless academic dropouts, bored couples, or those tired of their long-time professions and trades.

What followed was that a few original promoters began writing contracts that had some interesting clauses. Like: Said dealer may not exhibit in any antique show within a 50-mile radius of this one, or any other antique show held within three months of the same. Etc.

Another example of capitalism in action came from promoters who already had several highly successful antique shows to their credit and desired to expand their empires. They had a captured list of exhibitors whom they could corral into these new ventures.

As they envisioned their names (beyond Sawgrass County) emblazoned on the antique show marquees throughout the nation, they became more intimate and friendly with the exhibitors. At a dealer's booth, the promoter would enter and in a pleasant and jovial manner say, "Hi Cuthbert, how's the show going?"

Since this is the promoter's best show, for himself as well as the dealers, Cuthbert smiles weakly and replies, "Oh! Fine, Mr. Allmyne."

Drawing up a chair, the promoter says, "You always do well. Cuth; you've been at it a long time. Everyone knows you."

Pausing momentarily, Mr. Allmyne continues, as he gives Cuthbert a friendly pat on the back while smiling radiantly at Cuthbert's wife, who is busy wrapping sales, "We've been lucky to get a couple of new shows lined up and I thought you should be among the first to know."

Armed with contracts and maps, he lays some of them on the counter and says, "I have a great corner booth for you at a new auditorium we were fortunate to get in Anchorage, Alaska, in October. That's three full months before our Florida shows. We have the exclusive rights. Magnificent scenery, fall foliage." Cuthbert gulps, as Mr. Allmyne continues, "And the other show is in September on the Outer Banks of Cape Hatteras, North Carolina. No promoter had ever tried this location and we are very excited about it. We can do the deposits for these today."

Waiting for a reply from the stunned Cuthhert, the promoter rises and says, "I know you're very busy now, but look these contracts over and I'll be back later. You've always been one of our best dealers."

Later, discussing this with Cuthbert, another exhibitor tells him that he too was made an offer that you can't refuse from the promoter. "We already do three of his shows that are lousy just to keep a few of his good ones," the dealer complains, "but what can we do?"

Having had decades of experience with promoters all over the country, I find that they generally have the interests of the dealer in mind. But, some of them lose sight of this in their march towards prominence—nay—immortality, forgetting they are very much in need of the exhibitor to survive.

"What'ya Mean!
It's Been Appraised For
Lots More!"

CHAPTER 23

There is no other aspect of the antique business that is more controversial than the appraisal, be it written or verbally given. Buying and selling being the backbone of the antique profession, the word appraisal enters the picture daily.

Generally, antiques can be identified for what they are and value placed upon them with little difficulty. However, there are some items that present a challenge as to their true identity and actual worth. Disagreements in appraisals occur often enough where they frequently may have to be given as an opinion.

Serious errors happen in appraisals involving objects worth millions or just a few dollars. No matter how authoritative the appraisal, how reliable the dealer or prestigious the auction house or gallery, mistakes occur. Be it human error, done knowingly or innocently, with the many tricks of the trade, errors will always be made.

It was brought out in the media just a few years ago that an "Imperial-Russian Easter Egg," purchased for over a million dollars, was very controversial as to its authenticity. Lawsuits followed, appraisals were retracted and excuses offered by many an expert in the field. If top authorities make major errors in judging important antiques, imagine what happens in everyday dealings in antiques of much smaller value. It is no surprise to any antique dealer that two written appraisals, whether a single, specific object or of an entire household of antiques, can have very different appraisals. This happens all too often.

Fun indeed! Oral appraisals are the life-blood of the antique trade, its dynamics. One dealer's quote could be your fortune or catastrophe. One can find people out there daily, running from dealer to dealer, getting all kinds of opinions, prices, estimates, appraisals on everything imaginable.

We ourselves are not in the appraisal business, but we do give written guarantees of what we sell and, if asked, give both a high and low value, as the case may be, of the items in question.

Appraisers may charge a flat commission, or by the hour, as in the contents of an entire household, by each item or whatever is agreeable to both parties. The higher value of an item can mean a higher cost in the appraisal, itself. Some people may want a high appraisal, some may want to keep it low. There are all kinds of reasons to evaluate antiques.

The over-valued appraisal is the one we encounter most often, especially on jewelry and silver. When a private party is selling us any of these items, they may present a written appraisal for insurance purposes. These are usually based on the present "replacement" value (what they would spend to replace it at current prices). Because the appraiser charged a proportionate fee, or because the party so desired it, many written appraisals are set too high, often ridiculously so. While it may have the owner feeling richer, it does present a problem when an item is sold.

A man recently brought in a diamond ring which he wanted to sell. Since we advertise to buy jewelry and antiques, we do not hesitate to make an offer. When I offered him $2200 for his ring, he jumped back with a flushed face and drew out appraisal papers. Although the ring was accurately described, it had the ring's replacement value of $7500, which left him sputtering and stammering. In an attempt to arrest his rising anger, I politely informed him that a very high appraisal was common and that he was given top replacement value. That didn't prevent him from leaving in a huff.

For instance, try buying an expensive piece of jewelry from a reputable jewelry house and return the next day to see what they might offer you for it. It's the same with a new car; once you've driven it off the lot, the value plunges downward instantly. People understand this when we explain it to them. In the case of diamonds, especially, many people were or are led to believe the cliche: "Diamonds are a good investment." They can be, but only if purchased at the "right price."

This also applies to antiques of all types, where appraisals are concerned. Many people seem to have great faith in their original written appraisal and carry appraisal papers with them from dealer to dealer, year after year, trying to fetch a price close to what's typed on the papers. The power of the printed word!

Whenever appraisal papers are shown to a dealer, he usually finds himself in a situation where he may have to defend his offer— and sometimes himself.

The prevailing misconception is that everything has to go up in value. Actually, diamonds, silver and gold jewelry were a lot higher in 1980, during the gold and silver rush. But not all antiques continually go up in value. Some have lost their popularity (pocket watches generally); yet, paradoxically, antique silver is bringing higher prices today than when it was worth ten times more based on weight in 1980. Appraisal papers drawn at that time would not be appropriate today.

We've encountered some interesting situations where people had antiques to sell and, in the process of negotiating, produced appraisal papers that, in themselves, looked like antiques.

In one instance, a gentleman who had been an Episcopalian missionary in China during the 1930's, handed us several sheets of wonderfully handwritten descriptions of various Oriental objects of art. Each item was lovingly listed, beautifully described in elegant script, and its monetary value affixed aside it. The prices, of course, were shockingly low by today's standards and a delight to behold.

"To be sure," the gentleman said, "my wife and I didn't pay those prices. We knew a lot of people and traveled to many obscure villages. Bought very reasonably, we had them appraised when we returned to this country in 1938. I guess they would be worth considerably more now."

True. And as was often the case when we did encounter yellow, parchment-like appraisal papers—forty years and older—the objects were sold because the time was now appropriate. Having enjoyed them a great part of their lives, money was not the issue and the sellers were closing out a long-gone marvelous era. Fortunately, they came to us to finish out that period.

"Oh! It Can Easily Be Fixed!"

CHAPTER 24

People who have antiques to sell are often advised not to take the first offer, but to get two or three bids or appraisals. This is especially advisable where they inherit valuable objects and know little or nothing about them and have no papers of evaluation or provenance.

This is particularly true in Florida with its large population of older people. The settling of estates, large or small, is big business and the competition for all classifications of antiques is fierce, as shown by ads in papers, television and radio.

An elderly, distinguished couple entered our shop one day. The man began the conversation, "Mr. Purnie, we were sent here by a jeweler who said you specialize in antique jewelry. Would you look at something we have?" The gentleman then pulled out a small packet wrapped in several tissues, held together with rubber bands. The woman then added, "This is my mother's French enamel lapel watch. We were offered a thousand dollars for it a long time ago."

Without seeing it, the price sounded reasonable. They were scarce these days, and still a good collector's item. After unwrapping it from the yellow, tattered tissues and about to open the original velvet-lined box, the man warned me, "Be careful! The front cover of the watch is off; but that's nothing, it can easily be fixed."

One of them carefully removed the watch from its fitted velvet case and put it on a tray I had there for such purposes. True, the front cover was completely off its hinge. I turned it over to inspect the other side as the woman interceded, "Some of the enameling is chipped but it can be re-enameled and no one will ever notice the repair."

Listening to all being said, I could see it was a particularly beautiful watch with fine miniature paintings on both covers, encircled by small rose diamonds. A bargain for the price mentioned. As I was about to examine it closer, the woman pointed out to me, "Some of the rose diamonds are missing, but another jeweler who looked at it said they could be easily replaced."

Might as well open up the back, I thought, and look at the movement to see who made it. Could be a famous maker! Trying to open the inner lid, I spotted nicks where others had tried to open it but had apparently scratched it quite noticeably, probably with a pen knife. Opening the back cover, that too was loose and didn't protect the works properly. Just as I was about to see if the watch worked, the woman warned me, "Don't wind it up; the main spring is broken but we were told that, too, could be repaired."

All facts out in the open, there were at least six major faults with the watch but I was being assured by the owners that I was looking at a gorgeous and valuable antique piece. They were obviously waiting for my ohs and ahs. Instead, I wondered if they had heard my inner groans and murmurs of despair over an object of beauty now rendered hopelessly useless.

As it turned out, they had recently taken it to three jewelers, before being advised to take it to an antique jewelry dealer who would appreciate it and would "pay you more for it." Waiting for my reaction, the man then asked, "What's it worth to you?"

"Were there any offers at all?" I inquired.

"Two of them said they would pay us for the gold value, about $150, but we certainly wouldn't sell it for that."

All I could say was, "At one time, this piece was a very fine watch, made about 1880 by Henri Capt, a nice old key-winder. In its present condition, we have the remains of a good old Swiss watch, once very desirable (of more use to The Undertaker, I thought), not worth more than its gold value and some spare parts. A delicate item like this should have been handled properly, but some jewelry dealers were only interested in whether an object is gold or not. Certainly they were careless in inspecting it. Someone ripped the back cover off, and there were several chips in the enamel. Very difficult to mend. And though the rose diamonds may be replaced, the overall condition would require too much work to make it desirable again, not to mention the expense. I just don't think I would have any use for it. I'm very sorry."

By then, the couple was exasperated, frustrated and probably certain that all jewelers and antique dealers were crooks and phonies. If only they had taken the original offer, before its hand-to-hand mutilation by other appraisers and jewelry buyers had damaged it beyond repair.

Many antiques, jewelry included, brought into our shop have been subjected to excessive handling through inexperienced scrutiny, all with the notion of getting various appraisals. It's okay for the public to match one dealer against another, but it's better to sell certain antiques before they are broken or mangled from over-handling.

Prime examples are fine porcelain and art glass. Much of it in private ownership will be chipped or flawed at some point, however minute the defect. That's the first thing we have to point out to a prospective buyer and what we must detect when purchasing from private sellers. Anyone possessing such items should examine them very closely; most likely they will find a noticeable fault in what they would have otherwise bet was in perfect condition.

"No! You won't find any chips or cracks in our crystal. I took special care of it myself all these years" is one of the most oft-repeated statements we hear in homes where we are purchasing.

After looking over the piece, seconds later, we regretfully have to point out the defects and stand back for the genuine expression of surprise. "That can't be! Where? I never saw that before."

After absorbing this bit of bad news, the follow up is often, "Oh well! Who cares about a few chips. You can't notice them. It's still a lovely vase." Other frequent comments are: "No one's that fussy!"

Or: "That can be ground down." Or: "If I liked it, that wouldn't bother me if I were buying it."

I don't usually bother to suggest to them that if the tables were turned and I were attempting to sell the identical item to them from my shop, in their eyes, these little blemishes would suddenly become major imperfections.

That's where the phrase "as is" makes its unfortunate entrance in the antique profession. In buying and selling, it stands!

By Dawn's Early Light

CHAPTER 25

Few things are more important to an antique dealer than being the first to see antiques as they come up for sale. How he might be first on the scene gives the dealer more heart palpitations and emotional joy, or distress, than just about any other action in his life.

For instance, at the opening of any antique show, the first several people in line to buy are the dealers. However, if it's a very large show, the first four score or more are nearly certain to be all dealers.

Regular customers to our shop check our merchandise as often as once daily to once a week. Certain ones can sniff out anything "newly-arrived", before it can even be price-tagged. Some know our stock better than we do.

When an antique dealer walks into our shop and another antique dealer is there, although they have never set eyes upon each other, they instinctively recognize that they have mutual interests. Should they know each other, there is a greeting of sorts, but inwardly they are far less than casual. Their composure will stiffen, their facial expressions become masklike, and a smile, should it come, can be measured by the speed of light.

The encounter here becomes even more interesting if we are wrapping purchases for one dealer when the other dealer enters. The new arrival, barely acknowledging our presence, gives a penetrating look at what is going on, even hoping to catch a glimpse of what was just sold, then he vanishes. While many a dealer will stay and conduct business, of course, this one has conveyed the message that he's just missed out on first chance at our most recent acquisitions and has lost all interest.

To be confronted with a house full of antique dealers at a private estate sale is the equivalent to attending a good wrestling match. It was in the house of a local ninety-year-old bachelor—once a reclusive man of means—where a sale of special interest to dealers would be held.

For this event Sarah and her husband Matthew arose before 4 A.M. and not only brewed two pots of coffee, but ate a hearty breakfast to gird themselves for the day's onslaught. No doubt, such a scene was being duplicated in the kitchens of many other dealers that morning.

From total darkness into dawn's early light, dealers streamed forth from their station wagons, vans and trucks, Toyotas and Mercedes, all aiming to be there "first." Hurrying into line as close to the front entrance as possible, holding their position, looking forward to seeing how many were ahead and glancing backwards to see how the crowds were stacking up, they knew things were going to be as hectic as they'd anticipated. The dealers grudgingly acknowledged each other's presence, finding it difficult to even say good morning. To find a smile under these circumstances would certainly be rare and quite unlikely.

Daylight soon had gathered enough strength to reveal the dealers' faces to each other. (Darn! There's Ruby and Henry Flashman ahead of us in line. I thought their daughter was getting married today.) She did!

The longer the line becomes, the greater is the anxiety and stomach churnings, and heavy was the time to ponder your fellow antique dealers' ability to live on and crop up ahead of you everywhere. (I thought PAMPERED PAST ANTIQUES was lately very sick but there he is. Looking awfully gaunt and anemic, he should be in the hospital, or at least home in bed. And there's that new young dealer from Dania. He grabs everything! How did he learn the business so fast? It's going to be a madhouse today!)

The waiting becomes excruciating until the doors finally opened and the dealers push and shove towards the entrance. Those who were permitted to enter first split and stampede in all directions. Others were held back until there was a semblance of order. It is important to lay one's hands on any available object that one is interested in; but if that isn't possible, seize anything: silver, crystal, art, china, jewelry, rugs, statues or whatever is close.

If you are empty-handed within just a few minutes, what is unbearable is the sight of other dealers getting everything and you nothing—a miserable vision of dollars flying past you.

(Hurry! Grab something! Look! There's FIRST CHANCE ANTIQUES and they've already got their arms full. One of them looks like he's clutching a big box of silver. He could fall with that load—he had a hernia operation recently. His partner has a big cut-glass punch bowl he's struggling with. Why are they smiling so? And there's Linda Allabout; she's already toting two bags full of something and heading into the next room. And there's her husband, that puny thing, struggling with some heavy Oriental rugs. He could have a heart attack. What people!)

An exceptional flurry of activity is heard coming from the main living room, excited chatter emitting throughout the area. A large oil painting has been snatched off a living room wall by a dealer standing sock-footed on a sofa.

As the remarks about his audacity spread, the man is pushing towards the back door before the agonizing eyes and gaping mouths of several dealers, with the picture turned inward and the price tag of $1200 hidden. Panting heavily, he struggles to keep the antique frame from hitting anything. Thrusting a fistful of money into the hands of one of the appointed cashiers, he dashes out the door and past the line of still-waiting dealers, whose eyes strain to catch the blur-of-a-dealer lugging an ungainly heavy object. Struggling to reach his large van, he is yelling to his partner—running behind him—to hurry and unlock the door.

Later, an art dealer told me he had seen the painting and knew it to be very good; but he'd missed out himself, by being blocked by two ladies who were inspecting some antique linens. "Wiped out by rags!" he said.

Now the rush to buy becomes more furious. The dealers know that

among things yanked at (pulled, tugged, lifted and carried away excitedly towards the cashiers), there are "sleepers" to be had. As objects of
every description are being happily hauled away by dealers, their
smiles are being countered with the groans and unhappy looks of
those who are less fortunate. Thus did a swarm of human locusts
speedily lay bare the floors and walls of a once venerable dwelling.

Near the exit were two dealers dejectedly seated on one of the
few pieces of furniture left. "Sarah," the man said with exasperation
to his wife, "why didn't you wake me up at two o'clock instead of
three? We coulda' had that painting. The guy that got it was only
four people ahead of us in line."

With an exhausted and resigned look, Sarah replied, "Matthew,
what are you talking about? Are you crazy? You know we don't buy
paintings. What do you know about them?"

Soon a rumor spread that a $50,000 painting had been sold for
practically nothing. (Months later, the information seeped back
that the painting had been re-sold for $25,000; but it was too late
for the dealers to feel only half as bad.)

Antique dealers have an uncanny ability to survive prolonged
years in the business, but many pay the price: dark circles and bags
under the eyes, attributed to being over-used and underslept. One
of their eye-wearying practices is to never blink. If two of them are
competing for the same item, they often manage to stare each other
down. Their constant search for merchandise and the situations surrounding their procurement gives the dealer a perpetual look of
alertness, until he succumbs to weariness as the battle is finally won.

On the other hand, some dealers seem never to suffer these
maladies of the complexion and countenance; they look very well,
indeed, at all times. There are even some who appear to never make
mistakes and are the envy of other dealers. They seem to have a for-
mula for maintaining a healthy look, one that reflects composure
and confidence under the worst of circumstances. They literally
make other dealers less fortunate look like victims, while they enjoy
the crest and ebbs of a tumultuous trade.

I Beat Liberace To That
House Call, But . . .

CHAPTER 26

What would probably be one of the best house calls that a dealer could ever hope for, I merely blinked at and bypassed.

It was in the early Sixties and I was to exhibit at a first time antique show in a new building in Atlanta. It being near Christmas, ahead of the scheduled show time, I thought I would visit my sister Edith, her husband and their four children in Pensacola. Never having been there, a distance farther southward, it could be an adventure.

Unlike South Florida, of course, I found the stay in northwest Florida a pleasant and invigorating interlude. We toured the towns and beaches and I literally got a taste of the old South. My sister's husband was a native of Mississippi and we had many stimulating conversations regarding old-time controversies and customs. Billboard signs still remained along some of the highways in the South that read: IMPEACH EARL WARREN. He was then Supreme Court Justice, serving during the struggles of the Civil Rights movement. So there was never a dull mealtime.

One evening, we were to visit two of their long-time friends, but not before her husband was to cook a deep-South dish called "gumbo." From the corner of one eye, from dawn to dinner-time, I watched apprehensively the ingredients being popped into this huge, simmering pot—okra, spices, seafood and various chunks of undefined seasonings and trimmings. Although it sent out an appetizing aroma, I was more the thin-bullion and good-old New York style chicken soup kind of guy—a finicky one from way back. I approached the dinner table cautiously.

The kids ranged in age from five to thirteen years or so, and they were entertained by this strange uncle from the North, as much as I was intrigued to be there. I made sure I sat between two of them and kept busy in animated conversation. Where I knew I could somehow get myself through the meal if I could surreptitiously chuck some of the mysterious chunks that were floating or mired down in my generous bowl of gumbo into theirs. Laughing, hand-gesturing to distract their attention from the table, I managed to do this without being caught. The dessert was fine and the kids walked away from the table stuffed.

After dinner, we all packed into the family station wagon and went to see these "interesting ladies" I had heard so much about. We drove directly into the heart of the city and came upon an old house, the front lawn fenced in, a sign clearly reading: MUSEUM. Privately owned, it was a museum-by-appointment only residence, but always open to friends. The ladies were very proud of the contents of their home and used the title, MUSEUM, as one might honor something noble—deservedly so, as I soon discovered.

Since the exterior of the wood-framed house offered no hint of its contents, I was totally amazed upon entering to find there: huge crystal chandeliers, sofas and long benches in velvet and damask; one of several mirrors stood floor-to ceiling high, and wide, in a ten-inch ornate gold frame. These furnishings were an antique dealer's paradise; few would enter and not be awe-stricken with delight.

At the time, unfortunately, I didn't appreciate what treasures were unfolded before my eyes, truly deserving of the best in museums. I still had a one-track mind centered on antique jewelry, and the ladies had none of that available.

The women, Ada Wilson and her daughter, Julia, were accomplished and vivacious personalities, indeed, and quite entertaining. My sister and her husband had become their very good friends, the husband frequently being called on to do a chore of a technical or domestic nature. Their home being practically downtown, Ada had been well-known in the city and respected for her own paintings as well as her historical interests in the county.

It was about this time (I found out later) that they had been thinking of breaking up their museum. My sister's husband had even taken a trip to Washington, D.C. with Mrs. Wilson, regarding the disposal of a valuable oil painting she had in her possession. At the time I was there, I had observed the amassed variety of antiques only with mild interest; my attention was diverted to the furnishings filling the rooms and the furnace heat made the air stifling and musty. The time seemed ripe for these magnificent antiques to be removed to new ownership. Ada, advancing to an age of diminishing interest in antiques, knew she needed to find someone interested in them. I was in the right place but at the wrong time.

Later, as we all gathered about an old piano where Mrs. Wilson played Christmas carols, they bounced off the sparkling crystal, giving the ambiance of a far earlier era. Later yet, we were served a "treat,": Julia made some of her own special pralines, which she passed around generously. They were "awfully sweet, sticky and very Southern," I thought. I managed to eat one, but rolled the rest into a handkerchief and smuggled them into my suit-coat pocket. This was my day for squirreling away pleasures of the palate.

Mrs. Wilson being exceeding loquacious, we listened to tales of her grand travels around the world with her husband, and their collecting these lavish antiques that were shipped home, now set in a wood-framed 19th century house in a small Southern city surrounded by palmettos and palm trees, sand and Southern accents. I perceived myself as on a luxurious miniature trip of old Europe. It had been a long evening, mind and sight boggling with treasures I didn't fully appreciate, and it was becoming increasingly more confining. When the hymn "It Came Upon A Midnight Clear" rose for the second time, I knew I needed some fresh air.

A few years later, after Edith had moved from Pensacola, the subject of Mrs. Wilson had come up one day. She related to me the time Ada had attended a concert downtown given by the late pianist, Liberace. Ada, becoming entirely enamored of him, later went backstage to meet him personally. From there an invitation to see her "museum" was readily and eagerly accepted. For Liberace, an avid antique collector (seen at many antique shows), the personal invitation to her home could only be a wonderfully surprising and exhilarating event. Here was a grand collection of antiques, acquired over time from their European settings, and here was one of the world's most charming men (in the eyes of millions of women) with this feast of treasures about to be laid out before him.

As my sister reported, by Ada's breathless wording to Edith and her husband, "he loved EVERYTHING in my home." After a few visits there the ultimate "house call" was consummated. As told by antique dealers in the area, years later, we heard that it had been the "talk of the town."

The disposal of Mrs. Wilson's antiques drew a lot of attention since she was a highly respected member of the community and her "museum" locally popular. The contents of the house were loaded into three large vans, for which it was said she received twelve thousand dollars. Neighbors watched as elegant and ornate antiques were removed from the residence.

Sparkling crystal chandeliers, large, gold-framed mirrors, and velvet chairs and other elaborately designed items of furniture were now to be displayed and used on the other side of the continent, in the possession of one of the world's most famous entertainers. Included was a Louis XV desk that had belonged to the last Tsar of Russia, Nicholas II. On it was signed a famous treaty during his father's reign and was regarded as the most fabulous piece of the entire collection and held to be priceless. All of this once spread before me, waiting for the "right" person to come along and perpetuate its destiny.

Now, thirty years later, not only do I have a far greater appreciation and knowledge of antiques, but in the event that another "private museum" comes my way, I'm far better prepared. I have attacked my piano and produced a rendition of "Clair De Lune" and a few other such melodies that might capture the heart of a hard-of-hearing widow coming into my social life. There is no doubt that Liberace had beat me and everyone else to that house call, even though I had been there first. In the lexicon of the music student, my "flats" had allowed for Liberace's "sharps."

GONE
GONE
GONE
GOING
GOING!

Oriental Rugs And Not A Prayer Of A Chance!

CHAPTER 27

People who knew me when I was an antique jewelry dealer only would often ask: "How did you ever get into the general line of antiques, Henry? You never bothered with them before."

"Mistakes! Mistakes!" I would reply.

During the twelve years after my trip to Pensacola and my visit to Mrs. Wilson's museum, I still had not taken time to learn and appreciate other antiques. There was still plenty of antique jewelry around then, and I felt no need to get involved in a field so diversified, requiring hauling cumbersome items to shows. People who dealt in these antiques seemed to be forever wrapping and unwrapping them; even silver was too heavy and bulky to bother with. I could easily transport myself, my jewelry, and supplies in the trunk of my convertible, driving with ease to any part of the country.

Crystal and china break too easily. There were always loud and sporadic crashes at antique shows, other dealers running to witness the disaster.

Not only was it easier to be a jewelry dealer, from the viewpoint of manual work involved, there was a certain superiority to it—false though it may be. At an antique show our boast was that we could be the last ones to set up, and the first ones out. Over the decades, as other dealers saw how fast we could do both, they would say to us, "You people are so lucky." To which we would smile and smugly reply, "We planned it that way!"

That complacent world came to a disastrous end for me when I conducted my own personal auction in 1975. In my business dealings, I never attended auctions; there was no need to—too time consuming. I was under the impression, however, that auctions were the best way to dispose of merchandise in a hurry while getting the best price, people biding one against the other. Instead, it inadvertently evolved into a day-long house call, including "sleepers," for those who attended the auction.

When my mother passed away that year there was no need for my wife and I to remain in a house (too large for us) that I had inherited in agreement with my siblings in Utica, New York. Thirty years of significant pleasure-seeking having come to an end, our plans were long overdue—to open an antique jewelry shop in Florida. Real estate then—as antiques in general—would not rise dramatically in value until a few years later.

Initially, some of the antiques in our family home were distributed to family and friends, but most remained, allowing us to "draw a large crowd" to our auction, or so we thought. Unaware of their current value, we assumed there would be plenty of ordinary people who would pay substantially for select antiques, so we relied upon the auctioneer to get top prices.

The Saturday on that late fall day was pleasant for upstate New York. It could just as easily have been miserable. It wasn't long before we were informed of several other auctions of importance within fifty miles of us, which kept the anticipated crowd down to less than we had hoped for. Less competition, of course, meant fewer and lower bids. We didn't realize this until we observed that the dealers in attendance were mumbling and nudging each other. Some made hasty phone calls; there were smiles among partners. After the first few items were sold, we saw too late that we were at the mercy of circumstances. Items placed out on the front porch, an ideal spot, had bids coming sharp and short—much too short— because we didn't have the right crowd there. It became a heyday for the dealers, and for us, an estate sale gone awry.

My friend Ted, who was in the crowd, seeing what was going on nearby, told me to look across the street. A small group of people, undoubtedly dealers, were clustered on the sidewalk having an auction among themselves for rugs just purchased from us. At that, we no longer wondered why our many old Oriental rugs had been auctioned off so quickly, sold early in the daylong sale. Those who bought retreated early with their bargains.

That evening, seeing the house emptied completely of its contents, I felt as if a steamroller had passed over me. In this bleakest of moments, the realization that I was an unappreciative boor, if not a complete numskull, gripped me intensely. I kept all of this to myself, largely; there was no one else to blame, although I did feel that some of my antique dealer acquaintances might have warned me of the pitfalls that do occur.

Later, an inexplicable sense of resignation finally grasped me. With a near-vacant house that looked like my head felt, I shrugged my shoulders and accepted this self-wrought fate. However, without my realizing it then, I began to see myself in a new role as an antique dealer. For as time passed, it was as if a huge curtain had suddenly opened, allowing me to see all antiques in a different perspective. No longer were they merely a blur of beauty too burdensome to give them the attention they were due.

In ensuing days, as I looked at old Oriental rugs, I took note of their color, weave, age, size and beauty, and within a short period of time, a new vista began to open. Recalling a bronze statue of Mercury that once stood in our family hallway, all but neglected by me, I now realized that the wings and deftness of feet and agility of body were as appealing and just as artistically created as the carved Victorian onyx pin-and earring set I held in my hand. The intricately carved Chinese teakwood table, with its elephant legs and ivory tusks, surely was as desirable as any elegantly designed, heavy, antique pocket watch with its three shades of gold. Recalling a tall crystal vase we'd had at home, so deeply and sharply faceted, it was certainly no less beautiful than a gold bracelet in my jewelry case, with the diamonds refracting light in all directions in their brilliant dispersion of colors.

Mistakes usually being the great teachers they are, it was not long after that auction that I began my quest for antiques of all types. And I slowly began to fill my newly-acquired condo with select antiques, starting off with one antique Persian rug. In the long run, that auction has become a watershed in my life, but not merely from a financial angle.

Throughout the many years at our present antique shop, many tales of woe had been told by customers who had had similar experiences. Anyone looking at our display of Oriental rugs, a frequent comment is: "Oh! You should have seen the antique Oriental rugs in our home in New Jersey! It makes me sick! We gave them away for nothing."

"Look at that cut glass," her friend points out, "we had so much of it. I wonder where it all went!"

Eyes afar, countless memories are revived by customers nearly every day, all receding into the past, of treasures once owned and barely appreciated, and whimsically or mysteriously dispersed. Along with the "eye-gotts" and the "bee-backs" there are probably just as many "we-hads."

Some Lawyers Make Good
Antique Dealers

CHAPTER 28

While watching a rerun of "Sanford & Son" on TV recently, which certainly is not an unrelated program for an antique dealer, I was amused with their portrayal of the antique dealer. The male dealer fluttered about the shop using a high-pitched voice, old Fred Sanford muttering something like "acey-deucy," and the canned laughter arising loudly from the background.

I've seen other movie and TV programs where the male antique dealer is depicted in like manner, usually with an English accent, even when the location is Brooklyn or Atlanta.

The notion that dealers were gay was widespread in the Fifties and Sixties, when there were far fewer dealers or antique shows and shops. When we first exhibited at shows, there seemed to be a greater proportion of dealers who were gay, a terminology not yet widely used then nor having its present day meaning. Undoubtedly, they were among the first to recognize an interesting and profitable profession for themselves.

People envied their astuteness. In those earlier years the single, male antique dealers were often lumped together, as were ballet dancers, hairdressers and interior decorators, as being homosexual. Since then, times have certainly changed. There are still many gay people in the antique business, of course, as in all other professions, but they are now recognized, as are all others, for their failures or for their talents and successes.

The married couples, the "mom and pop" antique show exhibitors and shop owners, still comprise a good share of the antique world, as they always have.

However, the difference today is that one can wander through an antique show or shop and find it difficult to categorize the dealers. The boom in antiques—money, travel, excitement—has changed that. Fact is, there are more fascinating, weird and interesting characters in the make-up of the antique dealer today than ever before, sexual preference being the least of considerations.

And women! Today they represent the show promoters, shop owners—the top banana running the antique booth. In dual operation with another person, they may be friends, partners or lovers, among which there may be doctors, lawyers, dentists, disgruntled computer technicians, plumbers, ex-industrial workers or school-marms.

We have been on many house calls where a lawyer has final disposition of an estate, including all of its antiques. He may call in one, two or three antique dealers to give him an estimate or appraisal. Some dealers seek feverishly to obtain these connections with lawyers and banks, hoping to be the first called to purchase the estate. For some dealers, a call from a lawyer to help settle an estate is the equivalent of a baseball player being called up from the minors to play in the majors.

When called, the dealers give freely of or charge for their service; what they hope for is a chance to buy some or all of the antiques. This is a wonderful opportunity for the lawyer to learn about antiques, especially if he gets two or three "estimates" or "appraisals" from the eager dealers.

The lawyer may observe the excitement of the dealer as he is led to a table covered with antique silver. He notices the dealer's hand if it trembles slightly as he scrutinizes some diamonds, and calmly watches as the dealer anxiously jots down the names of the artists of the various oil paintings hanging about the walls. Hmnn! Very interesting! The lawyer's secretary may be on assignment at the estate and takes notes; prices are jotted down and the dealer is thanked profusely. "We'll get in touch with you," the lawyer thanks him, and "you've been very helpful."

To himself, the lawyer may think: Fascinating people, these antique dealers. Their work is so interesting. Let's set this painting aside. Wouldn't that French bronze clock and matching candlesticks look wonderful in my office!

On a recent house call an elderly lady explained to me that she had inherited some of her brother's antiques and it was now her duty to dispose of them. In Florida, there are an amazing number of older people who have plenty of antiques of their own, yet finding themselves falling heir to more from a deceased relative.

Noticing a tall, bronze Tiffany lamp, I inquired about it. "No! That's one of my things," she replied, "but the lawyer taking care of the estate wants it." Fair enough! She then went on to show me what was for sale, and we easily reached an agreement. I inquired about antique jewelry, and she replied, "I do have a lot of it, but it's all taken care of in my will."

"May I see some of it anyway?" I asked. "It's always interesting to see antique jewelry since so much of it has disappeared." Returning from her bedroom, she brought back several old, yellowish envelopes. Each one had a name scrawled upon it; she emptied them on the table. Among the lot were several desirable and highly salable items.

As I admired them, she asked what they were worth. When I replied, she was amazed, as well as might be, since "these things have been put away for years and years." Making her an offer on two items, "in case you ever consider selling them," she mused, then said that her relatives were not closely related and live in Indiana, adding, "Most of my things are going to friends, many I haven't seen in years, but they are in the will." In deep thought, she went on, "I don't even remember some of these people, or just barely so. Why don't I just sell you three or four pieces?" Fine!

Paying her in hundred dollar bills, she was further delighted and said, "This is something new to me. I haven't ever thought about selling anything."

From this encounter developed a relationship that would last into her final two years. She would phone me every three months or so and have more envelopes ready for me on the table. She soon began to sell her other antiques. A silver pair of candlesticks would have a name on the underside: "For Abigail Cunningham from Minnie." A painting: the heir's name on the back, and so on. Over the months she was having fun taking the labels off various antiques and selling them, though she certainly didn't need the money.

The pleasure and surprise to her was that these items could be turned into cash and that everything did not have to be turned over to heirs and friends.

On a succeeding visit there one day, a deep look of consternation came to her face. "I've been thinking," she said, "my lawyer knows I was going to give away all my things to different people after I'm gone. Do you think I will get into trouble if he finds out about my selling them? Everything had someone's name on it and now a lot of it is gone. What will they think . . . ?" she trailed off.

Glancing over at the impressive Tiffany lamp that was "spoken for" by her attorney, I replied, "I don't think either you or your lawyer need be overly concerned about anything you wish to sell, Mrs. Hollenback."

She was one of the luckier ones who discovered that it made sense to sell. It gave her joy to dispose of her antiques while she was still able to, once she again realized that everything belonged to her anyway. As many of the wealthier people get older and make no provisions for passing on their antiques, should they suddenly become incapacitated, things could "disappear." With the influx into their residence of many individuals, such as, attendants, visitors, accountants, friends, neighbors, relatives, lawyers and antique dealers, the estate may not be recognizable when it comes time for its settlement.

At a recent estate sale, a neighbor who had known the lifestyle of the deceased was one of the first admitted to the apartment. Looking about, she was aghast, "Where's Mrs. Eyegott's diamond and sapphire bracelet? All that's here in this sale is costume jewelry. Where's her large silver tea set? She had two lovely oil paintings in the living room. They're gone and the sale has just started." Concluding with, "I knew this house when she was alive; what's left here looks like a garage sale!"

Mourning Marie

CHAPTER 29

Florida, with its density of older people, its congested area and pleasant weather, provides the best conditions for garage sales. Some newspapers have a listing of them longer than the Help Wanted section. Also, there is apt to be a number of antiques inadvertently included in garage sales, thus the high incidence of antique dealers cruising the area, seeking them.

As everyone knows, getting there "first" is the magic word. People are aware that a garage sale advertised in the newspapers can expect "early birds." A garage sale advertised for the weekend is likely to have a dealer pulling into the neighborhood or cruising by slowly sooner than the owner wants.

One can spot the addicts—the regulars—at garage sales by the magnifying glass suspended from the neck or gripped tightly in hand. They hone in on all objects, looking for sterling marks on silver and karat stamps on any yellow metal. Well-known, upper-class antique dealers meeting their peers at these sales, shy from the other to escape recognition or blushingly stammer something like, "We were just riding by when the sign GARAGE SALE on a telephone pole caught our eye." But, both suspected that this was how the other got a good share of his or her merchandise.

Caught in the act of shuffling through trifles? So what! One dealer was smart enough to name her antique shop THE GARAGE SALE, resting in peace and prosperity thereafter with no apologies.

One of our shop regulars, privately called "Garage Sale George," appears with a perpetually wistful look on his face. Many years ago he bought a Patek-Philippe pocket watch at a garage sale for $10. It had been thrown in with some costume jewelry and a dealer later gave him a fantastic price for it. Since then, he's spent endless weekends raking through untold tons of garage sales goodies and junk, hoping to make another killing. His bumper sticker reads WE BRAKE FOR GARAGE SALES; his eyes have a constant garage-sale glaze or daze, and his weekends are lost forever.

Shrewder than many others and devoting to it even more time as she glides over a three-county area, is the notorious garage sale eagle (some call her a buzzard), referred to as "Mourning Marie." Each week, clutching every tabloid that advertises forthcoming garage sales, she can read in minutes a list of items in the hundreds and pick out the ones most likely to have antiques for sale.

Early in the week, she has her list of prospects, and is off and running. Pulling into a driveway or in front of a house in her impressive, late-model dark blue station wagon, and dressed almost totally in black, she will ring the doorbell. Something like this will follow:

"I want to apologize for disturbing you, but I happened to see your garage sale ad for this coming weekend. My mother in Minneapolis passed away yesterday and I have to fly out to the funeral tomorrow." (Or brother, sister, uncle, aunt, father, even husband, if the house looks exceptionally well-stocked with antiques.) "I know it's a terrible imposition," she continues, "but I had to be in the area anyway, and wonder if I may just peek at a few things you'll be selling?" A handkerchief is dabbed at a sniffle, a presumed tear is hastily dried, and the homeowner quite likely might answer, "Well, I suppose that will be all right," as his wife steps to one side.

Entering, Marie's eyes change instantly from fallen sparrow to that of a sudden soaring eagle, catching everything in one fell swoop. "What a lovely home. We once had to sell everything, too, when we moved. Circumstances require these things from all of us sooner or later. Are you moving?"

"We're thinking about it," is the reply. "That's why we thought to start out with a garage sale and clear out a lot of small things. We have the garage set up for that, if you'll come with us."

Marie stalls and walks slowly as she passes through the rooms saying, "Do you mind if I admire your things?" Before they can reply, she points to a pair of elaborate antique candlesticks and asks, "Will those be for sale later?"

"We weren't thinking of selling anything in this room, yet; we wouldn't know what to ask. Would you be interested?"

Masking a complacent smile, she now makes a generous offer, and is not surprised when the couple falters only slightly and turn to each other and say, "Might as well, we have to start somewhere sooner or later."

"That's a rather interesting painting on the wall and I know someone who would be delighted to have that pair of urns," Marie smiles sweetly. Before the owners are aware of her aims, she is removing objects from shelves and walls, inspecting them closely. Placing several choice items on a table, after politely asking permission, she skillfully convinces them that this is probably as good a time as any to dispose of some of their antiques. They agree!

Finally getting to the garage, she picks the cream of the crop from the garage sale items, all marked, some very cheap, including a few sleepers. Sales completed, the owners offer her newspapers and bags in which to carry everything out.

"I just happen to have some boxes in my wagon for some of the heavier items," Marie volunteers, as things are rapidly wrapped. She insists they not help her, and expertly clears the table in minutes.

With a most grateful and kindly expression, Marie turns to the couple and says, "I really appreciate your allowing me to come in early. I would have loved coming here this weekend, but I can't, of course. I'm sure your sale will be very successful." The couple beam appreciatively.

Loading up her wagon carefully, the owners marvel at her efficiency and again express sorrow over the death of a loved one.

In sight of the owners, she dabs at her face with a white handkerchief as she pulls away from the curb. Around the corner, she
heads for the nearest coffee shop for a relaxing moment following
the success of her self-created estate sale purchases.

She will sit down and pull out her list of other prospects, still
having time to kill-another-bird-with-one stone this morning. Not
too far away is another home advertising a sale for the coming
weekend. Now she must recall: At that last house, who did I say
died in my family?

"Don't Wipe All The Gold Away"

CHAPTER 30

Recently, on a brilliant, winter Sunday morning, we took a ride up to the Delray Beach "ANTIQUE MARKET." This is a covered mall that swarms with tourists in the season. We went there only for the ride; on my day off, I avoid business like a plague.

Squinting my eyes as we strolled about, I did a double take at a figure sitting beside a long station wagon near the entrance to the market. It had to be! "Gwendolyn! Is it you?" Grasping Jane by the arm, I hurried over to the wagon as this lady with a hat pulled over her eyes looked up at us, blinking in the sun and smiling slightly, wondering what this was all about.

The years were kind to her. I recalled instantly when I first met her in Chicago at the Conrad Hilton Antique Show. "It's me," I hastily added, giving her my name and extending my hand. After exchanging mutual amazement in seeing the other after so many years, I introduced her to Jane. As we talked, I recalled her as dealing in the finest of art glass and antique dolls—long before many dealers did the latter.

Her presence here only confirmed my notion that dealers never want to give up the business. Comfortably seated in the shade, a table of bric-a-brac spread before her, contact with the public was what her life was all about. It didn't matter what she was selling or, in fact, if she sold anything at all. She was one to derive sustenance from her communication with people, a dealer's lifeline, even though it was a far cry from her elegant display at antique shows many years previous.

She had been a very successful antique dealer, having an especially keen eye for the exceptional in her select line of antiques. She had to be in her nineties now—as it was soon revealed. As her eyes twinkled, I was sure none of what was happening now mattered except as a link to times past. She enjoyed thoroughly speaking of incidents long past, of no importance to anyone now except us. If only for a few moments!

Gwendolyn had been smart enough to buy property in Florida in the late Forties, when there were more alligators, mosquitoes and sand fleas here than people. Indeed, just a few yards away from where we now were standing, was a large parcel of property she once owned. On it stood a motel, built in the Thirties.

Back then, when she also owned property in Maine, she had exhorted my brother and I to purchase this motel and the land it was on. Her price was $10,000.

"Henry," she smiled pleasantly, "you and Vin should have bought my motel then. I heard that the last time that property was sold, the price was well over a million dollars."

In 1951, my brother could have easily bought the property. But neither of us had any interest in flagging down passing winter tourists to our motel rooms.

The main route then from the Northeast into Florida was Highway 301, which was straddled with many small cabins that were built in the Thirties and Forties.

Gwendolyn's motel in Delray Beach back then was on U.S. Highway 1, the main route through eastern Florida. Surrounded by boondocks, palmetto trees, swaying palms and prickly bushes, it was a pinpoint of civilization on the way to the town of Ft. Lauderdale and, 40 miles further south, to Miami. "Henry," she reminisced, "we used to sit under a palm tree outside the motel, waiting for a car to approach, then waving them down to stop here instead of going farther on. We got overnight customers that way, and served them fresh-squeezed orange juice in the morning. The tourists from the frozen North loved it and we had fun. As time passed. we accommodated many antique dealers who made our place their regular winter headquarters."

Being a pioneer in another respect, just a year or so later she had approached me at the Ft. Lauderdale Womens' Club Antique Show and asked, "Henry, how would you like to exhibit in my 'flea market' in Maine this coming August?" What's this, I thought. Last year she was trying to sell us a motel, this year she's got a new scheme.

At that time, most people, myself included, would be hard pressed to guess that the term "flea-market" didn't have something to do with itching and scratching, or something unpalatable. No such exhibit as flea markets were around as yet, that we knew of. It was only when Americans started traveling to London and Paris in large numbers after World War II and returning to tell tales of shopping in the streets of those cities that the term became popular.

"I have this property on the coast of Maine," Gwendolyn had related enthusiastically, "and I'm getting up a group of dealers to come up there in August and set up their antiques outside for the weekend. There are a lot of tourists and you should do very well. It's never been done there and I think people will love to come out in the fresh air to buy antiques. It should be wonderful—right on the ocean. Like a vacation. I can rent rooms cheaply to some of the dealers."

That summer, arriving a day early at the "Flea Market" site, where I was lodged at one of Gwendolyn's cabins, small but cozy, I exalted first in the sun and then the pounding of the ocean. Looking about, I thought this could only be the best of both worlds—Maine in the summer and Florida in the winter. Selling antique jewelry for a living could provide this and more. That evening, several dealers picked out their locations and arranged their tables for the next day. All they had left to do was put out their merchandise at the crack of dawn.

Before sunrise the next morning, dealers moved about hurriedly, setting up folding tables, draping them. Out came sparkling crystal, many pieces of gleaming sterling silver, antique furniture, lamps, porcelain and bric-a-brac. All were genuine antiques of an era before "collectibles."

It was particularly easy for me to set up. A couple of folding tables, draped, jewelry grouped together, and I was in business. Most of my jewelry was pinned to satin or velvet covered display boards, easy for customers to see the jewelry, to handle and try on: Victorian earrings, cameos, rings and many more items. For jewelry more valuable, a small glass case held them locked away but visible. A mirror was provided for viewing the items on.

Ready for business, customers attracted by a large sign reading— FLEA MARKET—were filling the parking area along both sides of the highway and walking in, curious to learn what this was all about. At the same time, the entire area suddenly became engulfed in fog. White, thick, wet and misty vapor swirled through the air, rendering dealers and merchandise alike nearly invisible. A cool dampness swept in with the rolling clouds of moisture and any would-be customers disappeared from view—afraid to walk about lest they stumble into some antiques.

"Oh! Don't worry about this," explained Gwendolyn, as she cautiously but cheerfully went from dealer to dealer. She assured them that "this will burn off in a little while. You'll see, it's very normal for this time of year up here."

Nature took its course, but not immediately. Not for a couple of hours would the much-awaited blue sky appear through patches of now fast-dissipating puffs of haze. Gloom dissolved with it and customers and dealers alike were seen and heard in a frenzy of activity. Scanning the entire premises, I saw dealers wiping moisture off glass and china and sterling silver and rapidly drying off furniture with heavy towels.

Being enveloped for a couple of hours in total humidity, when I looked down at my display boards of jewelry, horror suddenly gripped me. The boards, held together with paste and cloth, were soaked through, discolored and shriveled. They looked miserable! While solid gold jewelry presents no problem, except to wipe them dry, the gold-filled items had suffered quite visibly. Covered as they are in a layer of gold over a base metal—many pieces further worn down by use over a period of 75 years or more—these appeared to have a reddish, wet rust coming to the surface. Or were peeling! Picking up a few pieces to dry with a cloth, some of the "rust" actually came off on the towel. In haste I had to dry them lest they became permanently affected.

When a fellow dealer came by to see what was happening, he laughed, "Henry, don't wipe all the gold away, or you won't have anything left to sell."

This terrific scenery blended with salt air and sea spray was my initiation into flea markets. If I were to keep them up, I'd choose my elements more carefully.

Along Cornfields And
Skyscrapers

CHAPTER 31

The race was on for antique show promoters to get dealers to spread their wares under God's unlimited skies. Where? In their own backyards! Mother Earth would be their auditorium and showcase.

"Just imagine," said John Morford to his son, "if we can get 100 antique dealers on that green, open field, right next to where the corn is growing, we could have a big show. Have them on a summer Saturday when people are out riding around with nothing to do. We could fill it up with antiques."

Looking along the Mohawk River into the corn-tasseled fields opposite his antique shop in Fonda, New York, John Jr. and his dad visualized carloads of tourists parked along both sides of the highway coming to the show. They would pour out of their cars and down over the grass and mud, through cow chips and dandelions, and gather about the dealers who had spread out their wares under billowy summer clouds. The fresh air would fill their lungs; the cow barns, dirt, grass, rain, the sun and even the diesel fumes from the barges chugging upon what was once part of the old Erie Canal would give them a distinct flavor of the countryside. City folks would love it!

Dad said to his son, "Let the dealers bring their own folding tables; we'll charge them a few bucks to set up for the day, sell a lot of hot dogs, hamburgers and soda, and sit back and enjoy ourselves. You know how they crowd into all those indoor shows down in New York City and even over in Schenectady. There's a lot of dealers in upstate New York who would think it a great change to sell out in the open and not have the expenses or confinement of an indoor show. Very informal, nobody has to dress up. Look at all the tourists who would come into this area from the Borscht Belt down in the Catskills. Maybe even Eddie Fisher! A lot of celebrities entertain there all summer. People ride subways all week long; then for fresh air come up here to see green grass and leaves, cows, ducks and live chickens—not just those made into soup. We can't miss!"

Johnny had no trouble convincing my brother and I that this was a great idea. We had previously set up in a couple other outdoor flea markets and this area should be perfect for one. And only 40 miles from home!

All the city haggling we were accustomed to would be happily done out here in the open. Where pale-faced Americans could wander on the very same soil where Mohawk Indians had roamed. Talk about heritage! Tourists from the island of Manhattan would be strolling on hallowed ground, buying trinkets of gold and silver. Someone might even stumble upon some Indian bones and arrowheads.

On that beautiful sunny Saturday, before setting up our own merchandise, Vin and I went scampering about for possible sleepers. In no time I found a large, solid gold Victorian necklace with an egg-shaped locket for $25. It was in a box of costume jewelry, selling for gold-filled. I had little trouble reselling it to a tourist from Long Island minutes later for $100. In a flash, she had it around her throat, covering what time had unflatteringly exposed, and loving "flea markets."

Word spread rapidly about the success of these first antique flea markets in the cornfields; the next summer there were flyers announcing new flea markets and mother nature found new tenants. All of which became a source of supplementary income for many antique dealers and noted for their great "fun."

Two flea markets that began in the Fifties grew in prominence, expanding and enduring to this day. They actually became famous.

The first of them was "Gordon Reid's Auction Acres" in Brimfield, Mass. When we first exhibited there, it was a one day affair—Saturday.

Jackie (my future wife) and I would leave Utica, New York at 4 A.M. and arrive at the field in Massachusetts about 8 A.M., a distance of 200 miles. Gordon Reid would reserve us a spot near the flagpole, a choice location. The show would close about sundown and we would either drive back to Utica or go on to New York City to exhibit there the next day.

"Auction Acres," as Reid's show was called, became so widely known and popular that it soon developed into a two-day show. Dealers began arriving a day or two ahead, buying and selling: at night, with flashlights; by day, there in the rain and mud or in the broiling sun. This was held three times a year.

Over the years it continued—snowballing! By the Seventies, other promoters had branched out and surrounded Auction Acres, capitalizing on Gordon Reid's initiative, foresight and pioneering spirit. Each show soon consumed the best part of a week, bringing dealers from all over the country.

Flea markets spilled into adjacent areas and became famous in the antique world. Three times a year, thousands of people converge on these flea markets. For many today, it is a thrice-yearly "must-do" event. A pilgrimage!

Several years after we had participated in this show, when they were only a one-day affair, I was in Cocoa Beach, Florida, for an antique show in the ballroom of a motel. Relaxing in my room after setting up that afternoon, I answered the phone to a familiar voice bellowing out cheerfully, "Henry! How the heck are you? This is Gordon Reid. I saw your name in the lobby, on the list of exhibitors for the show here tomorrow. We're just passing through and staying overnight. Why don't you come down to the bar for a drink?"

Joining him, he said, "I'm just having a coke. Why don't you have a Manhattan or something?" We chatted about the old shows and had a few laughs. He had made his mark in the antique world through flea markets. By his ingenuity, a stretch of Massachusetts became famous for its antique flea markets; he put the area on a tourist map. His pattern was one many promoters would follow: setting up huge antique flea markets in cornfields, in city parking lots or along dusty roads and muddy highways all over the country. It was he who provided the source for so much excitement and thrills for so many people. His "Auction Acres" might rightfully be called the "mother of outdoor antique shows."

Another pioneering promoter of antique flea markets in the late Fifties was Nate Mager, who was already noted for his exciting annual antique show and sale at old Madison Square Garden every February. He found his own "field" there, in downtown Manhattan at 26th Street and 6th Avenue, nestled among the skyscrapers. For several Sundays in the summer, we would exhibit at this new outdoor flea market. It opened at 1 P.M., closed at 7 P.M. It drew huge crowds of New Yorkers—who could hardly be expected to stir much before noon on Sundays. As a novelty and with great bargains to be had at an outdoor show in downtown Manhattan, it rapidly became very popular, existing to this day. It was great for selling; buyers flocked to us. Noting that we were from "way upstate" they looked for sleepers, crowding our booth from opening to closing.

Occasionally, on Saturdays, we would exhibit at Gordon Reid's show in Brimfield; then after 6 P.M., drive to New York City and an overnight at a friend's apartment in Queens. Having time for some carousing, the next day we would sleep late and still get over to Nate Mager's "26th Street Flea Market" to set up for the show. Business was always good! Packing again at 7 P.M., the 250-mile drive back to Utica was virtually nonstop. Jackie would sleep most of the way back—deservedly so—since she had a regular job to face early Monday morning.

Ordinarily, we would leave Utica early Sunday morning and drive to the "26th Street Flea Market," work all day, and return that night. Our last trip there, it rained incessantly once we got to New York. Impossible to open up, we went into a restaurant nearby, waiting out the rain—which never ceased. It turned out to be a 500-mile round-trip for a deli sandwich and a beer. Who else but an antique dealer would do this?

As the years advanced, we gave up all outdoor flea markets, to which we had also taken our accumulations of costume jewelry, often bought very cheaply in lots with antique jewelry. We often recalled with amazement what we once had thrown out on a bargain table for only a few dollars, now was being featured at antique shows and in shops as quite valuable. Such jewelry as silver and marcasite, costume jewelry with names like Miriam Haskell, Hobe, Eisenberg and other "signed" pieces were displayed openly on our bargain tables with little regard. (Today these names and other old original costume jewelry items are largely sought after and command premium prices.)

It's in the nature of women to rush to a bargain table—jewelry especially—even if they originally intended to buy something more expensive. No matter how much in disarray the pile of jewelry appears at a glance, or how elegant a lady is dressed, she cannot resist diving headlong into a table of low-priced jewelry, especially if other women are flocked about it. Searching excitedly, they will wrap an old rhinestone necklace around a perfumed throat, shove a pair of pierced earrings (even drawing blood) through the ears; or snap on two or three bracelets around their wrists, and a ring or two on her fingers. Because it's "second-hand" and "cheap," it would make her day.

Gold In The Cellar

CHAPTER 32

In 1969, my brother Vin passed away. Afflicted with cancer, his demise left an enormous void in our household—our father having departed in 1964. This great old thirteen-room home, once the pride of Vin's life, was now left to just my mother and myself, for which we were required to hire a live-in housekeeper to care for her. I was at the time exhibiting extensively at antique shows and was away most of the week.

When Vin was alive, being a bit eccentric, he had a habit of stuffing envelopes with cash and putting them aside, for whatever reason, such as having ready cash for someone he was expecting to come to the house to sell him some jewelry, which happened frequently. It would be convenient to reach behind a nearby picture on the wall or beneath a sofa cushion (where he was reading) and pull out the ready cash. At times the cleaning lady or a visiting sister (in the process of extra housekeeping), would find one of these envelopes. "Vin, I found this between two pillows in that old chair that no one uses," was an occasional statement, received with a casual "Thank you," as if expected. (He would at times forget about them.) Rewards would come later, in some form.

After his death, my brother Joe and I became the executors of his estate. Remembering his many money-tucking practices, we thoroughly cleared out the rooms, cellar to attic. The big house, filled with antiques in every nook and cranny, had a somber, Victorian atmosphere. In time, some in our large family of relatives, young and old, considered the house genuinely "spooky." A couple of my sisters would never sleep there, making sure that circumstances would not

315

require it. Quite likely for the reason that this house had no experiences tied to our childhood days.

Somewhere up in age, the three-story house of clapboard siding would make all kinds of nocturnal sounds, especially in winter. While the oil furnace hummed from the cellar at top capacity when icy Canadian blasts reached down and embraced every house in upstate New York, "things" seemed to creak and rattle in rooms and on stairways. Outside, the tall trees there had sounds of their own as the winds howled and whistled through them, causing branches to brush against the house and windows to whine, doors to rattle.

Throughout the house for everyone to admire stood several pieces of statuary in various postures, large figures and figurines darkly bronzed or of porcelain, an arm, leg, bust, gracefully extended in action. Guarding the staircase stood a pair of five-foot high antique Chinese vases of porcelain, dragons encircling their girth. All of which seemed to have a life of their own at night, against a backdrop of drapes and carved Victorian couches and chairs.

For those of us who were living there or had lived there, thirty years of large-family comings and goings—including in-laws and nieces and nephews—had been a natural and enjoyable part of our adult lives. But, by night, visiting family members often felt something else come alive there. For that reason, I sometimes relished perpetuating the myth. A relative could hardly expect to be there on a Halloween night.

After Vin's death, one of my sisters continued coming with her husband for one of their usual family visits on Sunday. By daylight, she enjoyed her visits there. One time they stayed unusually long on a blustery, late October evening. While her husband was downstairs chatting with another visitor, she was upstairs helping me gather a few last pictures from our deceased brother's room. Superstitions continued to run rampant in that time; she was still fascinated by the "spirits" roaming the house, but apprehensively.

"There's something very strange here, Helen, but I have to tell you and see what you think," I said, putting a finger to my lips, and directing my sister's attention towards a window. "Since Vin died, this window closest to the bed, where his head rested, a slight breeze comes into the room, the curtains moving ever so gently, although the window is never open. It happens anytime ...." Before I could finish, she took to the stairs, called out to her husband, "Frank! It's late. Let's get going!" And that's how it was!

My mother, at nearly 87 years of age, was a stooped, gray-haired lady, who made her way about the house with the aid of a walker. Rocking in solitude in a dimly lit room, surrounded by antique objects in this large old house, she might have been a nightly sight that "Psycho's" Anthony Perkins would have appreciated. To accommodate her feebleness and save her from stairways, a living room (of two) downstairs was converted into a bedroom for her convenience, from which she roamed more freely.

When one night she awoke in the wee hours, she arose and headed for the kitchen. There she turned on a dim light to get a drink of water. In all innocence she had "walkered" towards a man who was trying to pry open the back door. At the sight of her against the shadowy background, a weird, hunched-over indiscernible object moving towards him, the would-be intruder fled noisily into the rainy night. My mother calmly related this strange experience to us in the morning.

My mother had inherited the house and contents and in her generosity, let the family carry away some of the antiques. In turn, I would inherit the house intact, four of us living there for the next six years, including the housekeeper.

Disposal of the cellar's contents after Vin's death was the biggest job. An accumulation of thirty years: tools, heavy boxes of broken antiques, an assortment of scattered objects.

It was to a remote and little-used portion of the cellar (behind a wall stacked with boxes of dusty and discarded household items), where I reached far into a corner and felt something leathery and crinkled. Tugging and pulling out a very heavy black traveling bag—something a railroad man would have used in the Forties—I finally worked it out into full sight.

Because my brother had been methodical in making out his will and assigning possessions as he saw fit, Joe and I were joyfully shocked when we drew forth the bag into some light and hastily opened it. "What's in it?" was on both our minds, but Joe asked the question, as we peered into the fully opened bag.

"GOLD!" we said simultaneously. Solid gold pocket watch cases and covers. Bent, broken and twisted, they were nevertheless gold! Examining them, most were marked 14 and 18 karat.

Although Vin had managed to repair or make useful a good many pieces of broken old jewelry, certain watch cases were unsuitable, had to be scrapped. The movements were gone, and the cases were easy items to save if one were hoarding scrap gold. They were heavy, their value easy to determine.

Vin and I, both, collected a lot of scrap gold in the course of buying antique jewelry, and usually sold a packet or two on a monthly basis to a refinery in New York. Obviously, he had had a little fun in the squirreling away of this secret cache.

He had often said to me, back in the early Sixties, "Hank! I know gold is going to double in value someday—to $70 an ounce. You'll see!" The people I knew in the jewelry business harbored no such thoughts, nor were they hoarding any gold.

Grinning widely over a sackful of heavy yellow metal, Joe and I examined several of the bent and battered watch cases, seeing them only as scrap; but the phrase, "as good as gold," never had a truer meaning.

Turning to Joe, I said, "I'll separate this according to karat, then weigh it and see what we have." In a couple of days, when I had that pleasant chore completed, the final tally came to a value over $12,000, at $35 per ounce. My mother, to whom it rightfully belonged, said we should use it for home expenses, including the salary of her housekeeper. A nice financial assistance it surely had become.

Planning to send it out in small packets over a lengthy period of time, I suggested to Joe, who was far more prudent than I in saving money, "Joe! Why don't you just buy the whole lot as an investment and be done with it? Suppose gold doubles in value some day? You should let some moths fly out of your wallet!" Laughing, he replied, "I've got other places to invest money if I want to. Let's just go ahead and keep sending it out in batches."

In 1980, when he and his wife were visiting us in Florida, we scanned the ocean off our balcony as we chatted about the outrageously dramatic rise in the price of gold and silver that was then taking place. Gold at the moment was about $800 an ounce. "Well, Joe," I said, "you don't have to be a genius to figure out that at today's gold prices we'd both let a quarter-of-a-million dollars slip through our hands when we emptied that black bag of gold from the cellar."

That night, while we were drift-fishing in the ocean, he caught the largest fish and won the $65 pool. Not bad! Not bad at all!

Five Days Only—
Millions To Spend!

CHAPTER 33

"It looks like the good old gold-and-silver rush days back in 1980," exclaimed a jewelry dealer who spent the winters in Florida and visited our shop frequently. He pointed to a full page ad in the morning's paper: WANTED TO BUY ... SILVER ... COINS ... JEWELRY ... GOLD ... DIAMONDS ... WRIST-WATCHES ... ANTIQUES ... etc.

"You're right, Bob," I agreed, "except, if you'll notice, everybody is now advertising for ANTIQUES, which is the big switch. All the precious metals dealers have rushed into buying antiques. Full page ads are running all over the country again. Their stress is for gold, silver and diamonds, but they are expanding into every field, including Collectibles, Costume Jewelry, Paintings, Glass—anything to get the public's attention."

Dealers from other states report that they've noticed the appearance of itinerant buyers in their area again, taking out full page newspaper ads and conducting business from local motels and hotels.

Nowhere more than in Florida, perhaps, where many buyers with million-dollar spending power for these items are as common as advertising for medical care, health insurance, cemetery plots, crematoriums, doctors, churches, dentists, restaurants, lawyers; down to early-bird dinners, $1 movie theatres, false teeth, face-lifts, escort services, and implants of every type.

Everyone seems to be after the old folks' gems, heirlooms, even bodies, or parts thereof. The competition is fierce for everything from gold teeth (still in one's mouth), to the bones in their bodies (living or deceased). All the "WE BUYS" are after the "EYE-GOTTS!"

"I'll bet a full page ad like that cost $10,000," said Bob, "then they have to rent a buying room and motel rooms for their associates. That's a lot of overhead, but it must be paying off or they wouldn't be doing it."

Another customer volunteered a measure of information: that he had taken a wrist watch into one of the buyers who offered him $75 for it. "I couldn't understand that," he said angrily. "They had this big ad telling how much they would pay for men's old wrist watches. They had pictures of watches—watches they were paying thousands of dollars for. They offered me $75 for mine, which looked just like some shown in the paper. I told them I would rather throw it away!"

"Well," Bob replied, "if you'll notice in this ad, they advertise they pay from $100 up to $50,000 for certain watches. That's the point! They're looking for the rare ones or special makes and models. Everything is advertised "UP TO." The range is incredible and it's true that rare items will bring big prices. They have to catch the public's eye with a huge, splashy ad. A lot of people come in during those five days so there's apt to be a lot of sleepers with all the stuff that's brought in. They probably pay much the same as any dealer, but imagine the variety and volume."

This conversation prompted another customer to enter the conversation. Antique shops are like that! There may be four or five total strangers browsing, but if a topic is controversial or especially interesting, they often feel free to contribute their ideas.

"Up where I come from," a newcomer said, "we have people who come into town and take out these big ads, like here. One advertised that 'no one could pay more' than they would. I couldn't understand that. Was there a law that said only they could pay more? It sounded good to us, so my wife and I took some things down, jewelry and silver. They looked it over, weighed it, and made us an offer. Turns out that we had a better offer from a local dealer a few weeks earlier. So I reminded them about their ad claiming they would 'pay more than anyone else.' He mumbled something about the objects having to be 'certain types.'"

"So you end up shopping around for the best price after all," said another customer.

"No matter who you go to, you have to take a chance on them being honest with you," said another.

"It stands to reason, the bigger the ad, the more the expenses and the cheaper they have to buy," another suggested. "We answered an ad once where they advertised for people to trade in their valuables in the bank for a Mercedes or Lincoln Continental—whatever it was. We had some diamonds we inherited and when the man told us what he would pay, we laughed at him and left. Heck! His offer wouldn't buy much more than a new set of tires. How do you know who to believe?"

"It's all impulse," said the first customer. "People are impressed with these big ads and they're overwhelmed and tempted to sell. It's human nature. A big showy ad draws a lot of people. We got rid of a lot of silver, but we knew what it was worth and the offer was fair."

"That's the answer," piped up another. "If you know what you're selling, you'll get a better price."

"If you're happy with the offer, what the heck's the difference?" said another.

"What do you think?" was the question directed at me.

"Well, we do a lot of advertising locally to buy," I replied, "and we try to make what we think is a fair offer. The more salable an item is, the higher the price a dealer will pay for it. A lot of mediocre antiques, jewelry and silver are not that easy to sell, so our offer may not satisfy the seller. We can't make everyone happy. Sometimes we pay more than they were offered elsewhere and they sell to us. It works the other way too; they may have gotten a better offer at another place and are not satisfied with our price.

Don't forget, too, when you're dealing with antiques, you're often dealing with sentiment. It's hard to put a price on that. But in today's highly competitive market, dealers don't like to lose the opportunity to buy from private people, so they have to be careful in their transactions with the public. All dealers have their systems of buying."

As the conversation continued and these people, myself included, seemed to be enjoying this idle-time-turned-fruitful, I went on to tell them of the various methods I had encountered in my business experiences.

Firstly, any dealers who advertise that they give "free estimates" or "free appraisals," as we do, are obligated to do so promptly.

However, when a dealer is approached by someone with items to sell, with no solicitation on his part, there may be other procedures.

One of the original systems that I rarely encounter today is where the potential buyer tells the seller after examining the merchandise: "I will make you an offer, but once you leave here, or refuse it, then my offer is no longer any good." A one-shot deal—rolling the dice.

Another method used is to say to the seller: "I'm interested in buying your items, but I would prefer you get an appraisal or another offer first, then I'll make mine."

We still know dealers who will never make an offer on anything. They insist the seller put a price on their items. This is a big gamble in a highly competitive market and one we've never employed.

Even some of the big ads in the newspapers advise people to "Bring us your last offer. We will top it!" That remains to be seen, after the seller has "shown his hand."

Back in 1946 and for years thereafter, it was interesting to see the long lines at the "APPRAISERS" booth at old Madison Square Garden Antique Show & Sale. They were strategically located near the entrance and were well advertised in the newspapers in advance: WE WILL APPRAISE YOUR ANTIQUES AND JEWELRY

FOR $1 PER ITEM. What a wonderful gimmick and service to the public. People stood in lines outside in the freezing late February winds, clutching their heirlooms under their arms, waiting for the doors to open. There would be three or four specialists who eagerly and, no doubt, expertly identified whatever was brought in. After the verbal appraisal, there would be many who would inquire: "Where can I sell these items?" Such sales could be accommodated right then and there, or referred to an associate or local dealer. Since then, dealers have progressively invented their own methods of buying.

No matter the language, whether it's called an "appraisal," an "estimate," or an "offer"—whether it is "INSTANT CASH," or "IMMEDIATE CASH," or "MILLIONS IN CASH," the seller can take his pick and shop around in an expanding field of buyers.

However, when a person is looking for too many offers, the objects might eventually show the wear and tear from too much exposure and too many dealers handling them, and thus risk losing their value, appeal and desirability. Even antique dealers have their limits!

"How Much Did You Say
They're Worth?"

CHAPTER 34

We sometimes have to go to a potential seller's bank to purchase their jewelry, which is understandable and encouraged. A gentleman stopping at our shop inquired if we would be interested in purchasing any diamond jewelry; if so, would I pick him up at his home.

"I'll stop by promptly at 9 o'clock tomorrow," I happily told him.

"What's that?" he asked, cupping his ear. I reiterated; he nodded and left.

At the bank, we took his safe deposit box into a cubicle, a small one with an open top. In the box were three good-sized European-cut diamond rings, and a diamond and sapphire bracelet, styles popular in the 1920's. Inspecting them with my loupe, I noted there were many flaws and characteristics needing explanation.

When I made my offer, he, tinkering with his hearing aid, replied, "What 'd ya say?" Again, this time getting closer to his ear, I shouted even louder. Obviously confused, pausing momentarily, he finally replied in a loud voice, "I was planning on getting at least three thousand dollars more." Success! I got through!

"Mr. Everhardt," I continued, shouting yet louder (embarrassed but helpless). "the reason I can't offer you that much more is because of various flaws in some of the stones. They are beautiful, but they will only bring a certain price, and I have to point them out to my customers."

Looking at me quizzically, he replied, "I don't know what you're saying." By this time his hearing aid was ringing and buzzing and he was getting exasperated. It was awfully quiet in the bank.

"How much are you offering?" he shouted once more, putting his face right into mine. I knew all the people in the bank were waiting to hear my answer—some perhaps with offers to top mine. I could hear a humming-bird's feather drop; I had visions of everyone being frozen in their tracks, like the old E.F. Hutton ads.

In desperation, not daring to answer, I took a large piece of paper from my valise and hastily printed: CAN WE PUT THESE BACK INTO THE VAULT AND GO TO YOUR HOUSE TO DISCUSS THE PRICE?

"Oh! Oh, sure," he finally nodded, although he appeared still not to know what this was all about. His home being but a five minute drive away, arriving there, I guided him towards the center of the house, away from any windows. After he adjusted his hearing aid, I shouted loudly, using a pad and pencil to clarify everything. He smiled, satisfied with my explanations some minutes later. When I noticed a couple of neighbors standing on the sidewalk on the way out, I just waved, wondering if they were in on the final deal. Everything turned out fine. Our business completed.

Back at the bank, I paid him in cash, as he requested. Hoping to produce a smile in parting, I said, "This was just a quiet little matter between us, Mr. Everhardt."

"What 'd ya say?" he frowned in a friendly way.

I had purchased several antiques from a man whose wife died recently. A day or two later when he came into our shop and recognized some of the silver items, he was not concerned about the price tag (we had doubled the amount paid him); he seemed uneasy, nevertheless, saying, "My daughter and son-in-law are visiting me next week. She loves to go into antique shops and she might just walk in here and recognize that silver set."

Since the set was rather large and placed prominently in the center of the shop, I understood his concern. "If you like, I can put it away for a couple of weeks or so," I volunteered.

Occasions arise, when, after purchasing something, there comes a frantic phone call, "Mr. Purnie! Remember those gold beads I sold yesterday? Can I buy them back? My daughter hit the roof when she came home from work."

"Of course," is the reply, but the request would have to be quite soon after, else they could be resold. Although this happened infrequently, I found it good business to return it, however painful at times.

Years ago at an antique show, a woman stopped at my booth and asked me to come out to her home to purchase some jewelry. Included in the package deal was a large, dragonfly brooch, which was part of her collection of costume jewelry.

As was customary when on a week-long business trip, I would collect everything newly purchased into sacks and toss it all in the trunk of my car. Back home for the weekend, I would sort, polish or repair the items. Coming upon the bag of costume jewelry with the dragonfly, I hastily inspected it and was about to place it with flea market items when something caught my eye.

Examining it under bright lights, the "costume jewelry" brooch reflected a suspicious glint. Upon closer inspection, I discovered it to be a Georgian silver and gold brooch, with small rose diamonds—not glass—and a cabochon-cut ruby. Hastily dipping it into a jewelry cleaner, it came out sparkling, looking like it was ready to fly away into heavenly spheres.

This was the sleeper of the year, upon which I put a high price tag, not really caring to sell it. Because of the price, it wasn't snapped up; as the months rolled by, I even forgot about it, knowing it looked good in my display.

A year later, I was exhibiting in the same city where I had purchased it. That, too, had slipped my mind. During the course of the show, a woman asked to see the brooch. As she looked at it intently, noticing the price tag, she calmly said to me, "You probably don't remember me, but you came out to my house last year and bought some jewelry. I don't recall you paying anything near the price you're asking for this brooch." Flustered, I mumbled something like "I can't remember it," meaning it was undoubtedly so.

I expected her to scream out in accusation, and possibly say, "You gypped me!" or something similar. But before I could gather a suitable reply to explain my "discovery" among the costume jewelry bought from her, she just smiled sardonically and said, "I guess that will teach me a lesson," and walked away. It was a very awkward moment I couldn't easily forget, and I simply took the brooch out of stock and set it aside for my private collection.

I knew I would never forget her face nor the incident, but, getting it out of my sight would at least remove the visual accuser.

Many years later, while exhibiting at a Florida show, where I had moved, the same woman appeared at my booth. She asked if I recalled her, and I could truthfully say that I didn't. She then brought the incident to my mind and by now I could pass it off more comfortably as "an experience that occasionally happens."

She was now retired, but lived in the area. Noticing that I was no longer dealing in antique jewelry exclusively, she totally stunned me when she asked, "Do you buy other antiques, too?" When I answered a feeble "Yes," she explained that her husband had passed away and she was about to dispose of her antiques.

Over the next several months, I bought an assortment of things from her, including antique jewelry. I went out of my way to make certain not to buy anything as a sleeper. I was happy to get the merchandise but more impressed with her attitude about the past. A lady of class!

At least four times a year I called at her home, even getting on a first name basis. One day, when she phoned me to come out to buy more antiques, I went to the bank and dug into my private stock. I took out the dragonfly brooch—I had even forgotten what it looked like.

But I knew where it belonged! Greeting her at the door, without saying another word, I took her hand and firmly placed the brooch into it. Looking down at it, she barely smiled, but there was a twinkle in her eye. She said nothing, not even thanks, which would not have meant anything in this situation. She went into the bedroom to put it away.

There was never a word of discussion about it. Its value, beauty, loss and resurrection had been taken in stride. Certain things just happen in the antique business.

Stickpins And Jingling Pockets

CHAPTER 35

Although all antique dealers have experiences they will never forget, some dare never to reveal certain ones, or only many years later, when they believe the parties involved are deceased. Meanwhile, they keep them in the hidden recesses of their minds. And there are some who immediately tell all, bragging about their exploits. Some of their experiences may be gloriously fantastic, while others border on the evil and the subconscious harbors them forever.

The techniques employed by dealers when they buy from the public or from each other can range from the amusingly innocuous to forms of trickery, but all have their special attributes. Boldness is not the least of them.

This audacity was evident at a show in which I recently participated. One dealer went about a booth appraising another dealer's stock of antique silver, making him an offer of over $50,000. Within an hour, the deal was consummated and the items hauled away. For dealers at antique shows to sell out their booths, or portions of it, is not surprising. It is done frequently.

It was in Ogdensburg, New York, in the early Fifties, when I first witnessed a dealer's buying out the contents of an entire house. I was exhibiting at a show there when a woman approached my booth saying, "I have several pieces of jewelry similar to yours that I would be interested in selling." An appointment was made for early next morning.

At the time I was to enter that elegant old Victorian home on a golden fall day, with a view of the St. Lawrence River, I was not interested one iota in the antiques that gave grace to her rooms. Barely would I notice the early morning sun as it filtered in fall's splendor of color through the red and yellow leaves, nor would I take any particular notice of the intricate, handsome furniture or the glistening of silver and the richness of the rugs and bronzes.

What I did notice before entering the home was the new, large station wagon parked in the driveway, with an antique dealer's name splashed across both sides.

When the woman appeared to my ringing of her doorbell, she seemed slightly flustered as she beckoned me inside. With apology, she told me that an antique dealer was already there looking into other antiques, but since I was only interested in jewelry, she'd set that aside for me.

She took me to a room where she had a large box of various jewelry; among them was a long velvet roll of assorted stickpins, all handsome samples of a past era. There were pearls, moon-stones, opals, small diamonds and other gems mounted upon dragons, wishbones, enameled flowers and figures of people and animals. "My husband always wore a stickpin in his tie to work," she smiled. "Look these over while I continue with the other man, if you don't mind."

As I arranged everything on a marble-top table, a gruff voice was heard coming from the dining room. Through the French glass doors, I made out the figure of an antique dealer, someone from the area I lived. He was exhibiting at the same show I was. From antique dealers I'd heard that he had been advised by his doctor to find a hobby that was less stressful than his present occupation. He had a leonine appearance, his head supporting a massive crop of wavy white hair. Wearing a three-piece suit, he re-lit a fat cigar, then strolled about the room pointing out items of interest, appearing anything but stressed.

Stopping at certain objects, he picked them up; inspecting them closely but hurriedly, he bellowed forth, "$20 for that lamp, $2 for that silver bowl, $25 each for those two paintings on the wall, $12 for that pair of urns, $10 for that rug," and so on. However, many items in cabinets or hanging on walls were simply: a dollar for this, a dollar for that, another dollar for this, and so on. The woman politely asked him to slow down, as she couldn't write down the information fast enough. The $1 items covered several pages.

As he moved about, the dealer constantly jingled something from a pants pocket, while the other hand bought out the estate. I later learned that he always carried a pocketful of gold coins which he liked to feel and clank against each other. There's something warm even about a cold, gold coin that probably served to calm him and encourage authority. It didn't matter that the coins might get scratched, only that he jostled them soothingly, their weight adding to his pleasure. His doctor told him to relax.

She obviously approved each price that was dictated. It was as if he was doing the lady a favor; his demeanor already suggested that, but in a business-like fashion which implied there was no alternative.

What a lesson in buying! What a business! I thought: To sell at an antique show one day, and the next morning you're called out to someone's home and you've immediately replaced your merchandise at much cheaper prices.

Pulling out a fat roll of bills, he looked quite impressive as he paid her. Indeed, he had practically emptied the house. I heard him make arrangements over the phone for a large truck.

When it came my turn to name prices, learning from him, I bought without hesitation. Starting at "$1 each for the stickpins," the lady simply nodded her head in agreement as we went by each item. The rest was easy. I knew I could resell the stickpins for $2 to $5 each. This early experience had certainly convinced me that I was pursuing the right career.

Forty years after my first house call, buying antiques from homes is still my main source of supply. Since then, a thousand changes have taken place, other than the value of the objects. Dealers are intensely engaged in battles of wit and maneuver of the mind with the general public. They both love the haggling. To their credit, the public has become ever more sophisticated; they know how to bring the dealers around, who devise yet more tricks to challenge them.

By their browsing through antique shows year after year, many people have acquired an expertise to rival the dealers. Upon entering a home, the owner may recite a history of their antiques to the dealer, rightly or wrongly so. The owner is no longer necessarily the underdog.

The most common delusion a seller may offer is, "You're the first dealer I've called in to look at these things." Second to it is, "We have no idea what we want for them." These are legitimate counterattacks to the methods employed by the dealers; a game people have learned to play on equal terms.

A dealer may enter a home today and look about and notice books on antiques. Its owner may very well be able to quote exact prices on many items, as listed in a book. They may even expect higher prices than the book values, assuming that all antiques go up in value—even overnight!

Today there are books on every conceivable antique and collectible. They're sold at antique shows and book stores, new subjects ever forthcoming.

There has been an entire new field in just "Memorabilia"— interesting new phrases concocted that end in "bilia." Most of these collectibles are items that have acquired a status of nostalgia, from the turn of the century to the present day.

At an antique show today, sooner or later a dealer will be asked by a collector: Do you have any "Railroad Memorabilia" or "Sewing Memorabilia." Also "Movie Memorabilia" and "Baseball Memorabilia," and so on.

Practically any subject (cowboys to old guitars to old photographs), that brings back memories of recent years, can be classified as "bilia" and develop a surprising value of its own. It wouldn't surprise me if a movement came up in the antique trade today that is collecting information about the sexual antics of our ancestors and things related, under the title of "Risquebilia." And the tricks of the dealers themselves in a category labeled "Dealerbilia."

Armed with books on every imaginable topic and prices gathered from all the antique shows in the country, the public has become a powerful challenger in the business, giving dealers some interesting encounters.

It pays to use everyday psychology when dealing with antiques. The ways are many and a few of the skills are worth knowing. A dealer can at times get people to sell their antiques by the negative approach, suggesting, "Don't sell them!" hastily adding, "Don't you have children or grandchildren to pass them on to?" This usually evokes a few responses, along with appropriate facial expressions: (1) We've already given them enough! (2) They don't appreciate things like that! (3) They'd probably sell them anyway! (4) They'd rather have the money! (5) They don't want to polish any silver! (6) We have no children! Or—they say nothing—perhaps a faint smirk appears to release unpleasant memories and incidences of the past. However, telling them with emphasis "not to sell" may have the effect that brings the mind into a mental fist, and thinking, "Why should he tell me what to do?" One way or another, it nudges them into thinking about their antiques, and perhaps of their disposal.

When people decide to sell their antiques and call in a dealer, more is involved than just the merchandise. If a person is quite elderly, he may be accompanied by a friend or relative who gives him support and the security of a second opinion. This is fine and certainly recommended.

Two others may be present with the owner, just sitting, saying nothing. One senses that their wish is to keep some of the antiques for themselves. They might even have an intense desire for some of the objects about to be sold. Although the owner may have already given them things, there are still items they are "fond of." They often have the notion that should the owner not get a good price, they were ready to make a better offer.

In this case, to buy wisely, a dealer should "sell" himself first to friends or relatives. Whenever I detect such circumstances, which is frequent, I prefer to quote a price on the objects I surmise they, themselves, would like to possess.

Picking up, say, a sterling silver pitcher, I would tell the owner, "I can offer you $250 for this, but if anyone you know should want it, it's okay by me." By then, the "anyone you know" is fidgeting a bit. Had I made an offer of $150 for it, the "anyone" might have jumped up and eagerly said, "Well! I'll give you that for it, Mrs. Eyegott." But with the offer made being high, she lets it pass. I again select a few choice pieces and offer prices as high as I care to go; again the companions are stymied, expecting low bids. After a bit of such maneuvering the friends relax and decide they don't need any more antiques after all.

Another fairly common situation arises where relatives arrive in town to sell the contents of the home, obviously the heirs. Apprehensive about getting the right price from an unknown dealer, they may ask for an estimate—something they can think about (and possibly call in another dealer the same afternoon).

By picking the most desirable items and offering a high price, the dealer (even surprising himself at times) gains their confidence and cooperation. Jotting down every sale made, they are soon going from room to room, pulling out drawers, emptying closets and clearing cupboards. "How about this?" they ask. Some even help to pack the things. Adding up what the antiques are bringing them— plus the condo, cash, stocks, bonds and whatever assets may be there, the heirs are immensely pleased and relaxed in the day's accomplishments. "Great-Aunt Sylvia was so wonderful," one says, "it's too bad we couldn't get down here to see her more often."

A dealer's favorite ploy, when buying from a private home, is to discover first what the owner definitely does not want to sell. Such as, when an owner points to a pair of silver candlesticks and says to the dealer, "I wouldn't sell these for anything, but if I wanted to, what would they be worth?" Taking them in hand, admiring them, the dealer may reply, "These are exceptionally lovely. Don't ever take less than $1200 from any dealer." (His offer might have been $500.) He then continues walking about the house, appraising objects not for sale, at very high prices. Feeling good about the high value of the items on which they got a free appraisal, the owners are now eager to let the dealer purchase the rest of the antiques. Since these are not as important to them, the dealer can usually buy the rest at reasonable prices, the owners thanking him profusely over the whole deal as they help him to pack.

On the way out, the owner points to a painting that the dealer wouldn't want in his shop and asks for a last minute "evaluation." Obligingly, the dealer gives it some attention and says, "Very nice! Don't ever take less ..."

Another house call, another situation. After a dealer has made a few other purchases, he may be excited about several antiques the owner "will not consider selling at all." Eyeing a valuable painting, the dealer may use lavish words like, "Oh! If you would only sell me that painting! I'd love to have it hanging next to my grand piano; it would fit in so nicely. Would you consider selling it for $ ...?" Or he might see a diamond bracelet and say, "My wife has always wanted one just like that. It would make her so happy. Could you possibly consider selling it for $ . . .?" The owners are often impressed and swayed by this personal touch to the objects' future and "know they will have an appreciative owner."

"Well, okay," the owner surrenders, "you might as well take them too, if they mean that much to you." The next morning, the painting and the bracelet are tagged with a price, packed into the dealer's van and are on their way to the next antique show. The new owners beam happily in anticipation of exceptionally profitable sales and an enhancement of their booth.

In hopes of being subtle in doing so, dealers endeavor to get as much help from the owners as possible. At the next home, he's looking at several antiques he'd been called in to purchase. Trying to analyze the owners at the same time, he asks himself: What would they expect for some of these exceptional pieces? or have they any idea of their value? He doesn't want to bid either too high—one can always go up in price but you can't come down—or ridiculously low. Conjuring up a ploy, the dealer might ask the owner, "What did you say your silver tea service was appraised for?" The owner hesitates, turns to his wife and replies, "Well, we've never had it appraised, did we, Maude?"

Nice try! The owner could have come up with a figure to make it easier for the dealer but he caught the maneuver. In fact, they've had one written appraisal and two verbal offers from other dealers. Everyone's entitled to play games.

A couple of phrases dealers use when buying are: "Oh! Isn't that a shame!" and "Too bad!"

An enthusiastic owner fetches from his bedroom his deceased wife's diamond ring he might sell. He hands it to the dealer, its two-carat diamond set in a platinum, filagree mounting. With his jeweler's loupe, the dealer scrutinizes the ring, soon shaking his head. "Well," he says, "it's too bad that it's an old mine-diamond." The owner looks perplexed, and fearing something dreadful, asks, "What does that mean?"

Frowning, the dealer replies, "The diamond has a high dome and it is not cut right to let in maximum brilliance; it's an old-fashioned European cut. That makes it less valuable than a round, brilliant-cut diamond of the same size." The owner absorbs all this, looking somewhat dejected as the dealer continues, "You'd lose a good percentage of the stone when it's cut down. Too bad!"

"Does that mean you wouldn't buy it?" the owner asks apprehensively. "Well, yes, I would buy it, but . . ..," the dealer hesitates, paving the way for a low price. What he doesn't tell the owner is that although it's true that "old-mine diamonds" usually are not equal in value proportionately, they are very salable, and widely sought for their age and beauty. It's "too bad" he doesn't tell the owner that.

The seller next brings out a complete set of lovely ornate silver, a service for twelve, with several extra serving pieces. A delight to behold, it's about 75 years old and quite fancy. The dealer picks up one or two pieces, and instead of expressions of admiration the owner expects to hear, the dealer might say, "Oh! Isn't that a shame!" Stunned, the owner looks about him, not knowing what the dealer is referring to, and asks, "What's the matter?"

"There are monograms on every piece. Those are much harder to sell, unless you find someone with the same initials," the dealer says sadly, shaking his head at the same time. What had once been inscribed in a manner of family pride, of beauty and pleasure, is now treated as a scourge. The owner is downcast momentarily. Then, with a sudden hope brightening his eyes, he asks, "Well, can't the initials be removed?" To which the dealer hesitates, reflecting little encouragement, but finally concedes, "Yes, but that's expensive and it depends how deeply they're cut into the silver."

Easing his way into a much lower price, what the dealer neglects to mention is that he may know someone with those initials who would buy the set in a minute. Also, that the silver set was so beautifully designed that the initials wouldn't matter that much, nor was it all that expensive to have them removed. And lastly, whoever buys the set from him would have to cope with the problem, should there be one.

Sometimes a reverse situation arises in house calls. Left to settle an estate, the heirs fly to a ritzy condo in Florida, overlooking the ocean. Surveying the magnificent view, they contemplate the contents of the apartment that are now theirs to sell. Call in an antique dealer! The yellow pages list many who make house calls.

The dealer, barely avoiding an accident in his speedy response to the house call phoned in from "Top Of The Dome Towers," breathlessly enters the apartment and prepares his eyes for an antique feast.

"My aunt loved Oriental objects," one heir says. Looking about, the dealer needs only to pick up a few pieces to see that the apartment is indeed fully stocked with Oriental items, but all were imports of recent vintage. The market has been flooded with them for many years now; the apartment's contents could be mistaken for a shop in downtown Hong Kong today. It doesn't take long to ascertain that the oldest thing in the house is the dealer himself.

Mustering up sufficient politeness, he explains that even though there are a lot of expensive Oriental objects, they were classed as "contemporary" and of no value to him. He points out that what they have here apparently are things that were purchased for their beauty and appeal, and not for their age. Then the dealer, hoping to salvage something from this excursion into futility, asks, "Do you have any jewelry that was left to you?"

"Well, yes," an heir replies, "but we thought we would keep that. They traveled all over the world; they were quite wealthy and I know my Uncle Leonard bought my Aunt Clarrisa anything she wanted. We should have it appraised by a jeweler before doing anything with it."

Although the dealer may bristle at the last remark—his business card they have on the table clearly states that he also deals in jewelry—his eyes glisten. "As long as I'm here, could you show me a few pieces? I can set a value on them, if you like," he states, trying to calm his anticipations. Fetching out eight or nine boxes from a bedroom, with a pleasant smile, the female heir carefully unwraps several pieces, waiting for the dealer's admiration.

Picking up every piece and quickly dropping it back into its box, as if fearing contamination for even handling something so inferior, the dealer may barely be able to restrain his frustration as each item turns out to be costume jewelry. A collection of baubles of very little value, many were souvenir pieces of places visited, made of glass, brass, white metal, rhinestones and other man-made substances.

When he tells this to the heirs in crisp tones, they are taken aback in total shock. One heir says, "I can't believe Uncle Leonard would buy anything that wasn't valuable. They had a lot of money. How about this platinum diamond and sapphire bracelet?" she asks, as she pulls it carefully from her purse.

"It's blue and white glass and chromium-plated," says the exasperated dealer, nearly tripping over his valise in an attempt to scramble for an exit.

People have different ideas of what "old" means when talking about their antiques. They read our signs in the shop window or our newspaper ads and come in to say, "We see that you buy old rugs. We have some; would you be interested in coming out to the house to look at them?"

"How old are they?" I ask.

"We bought them new over twenty years ago." We explain that they should be at least from the 1920's period.

Recently a man came into the shop with a pocket watch he wanted to sell. I made him an offer which had caused him literally to jump in rage. "Don't you pay anything for its age value? This is an antique!" he nearly screamed.

"Yes! I know!" I replied, "it's about ninety years old and I considered that and its gold value and a couple of other things."

"Well," he snarled, "my grandfather owned it and he died at ninety-seven, and it was passed on to my father, who died at seventy-two, and I'm fifty-five and I've had it for ten years. It's got to be over 200 years old and you're telling me it's worth only $250?"

American pocket watches have a serial number on the movement which indicates the year it was made. I looked it up for him in a book and showed him the exact year in which it was made. Like a lot of people might do, he had totaled the ages of everyone who had previously owned the watch, thus arriving, as people do, at how "old" all their antiques are.

There are instances, however, when even dealers sell their merchandise where the age factor is ambiguous, even re-created.

In the early Seventies, a fad existed for authentic American Indian Jewelry—silver and turquoise, the older the better. Hand crafted, there were heavy necklaces, bracelets, rings and assorted, beautifully-designed jewelry, from the Thirties upwards, often signed by the artist.

Aside from their commanding top price, the demand for nearly anything in American-Indian jewelry (the term "Native-American" not used then) became voluminous, which flooded the market with good, not so good, and quite bad items. Ranging from one thousand dollars and upwards for the best necklaces, the temptation was too great not to imitate.

One old-time dealer who exhibited at many of our antique shows was always among the first to take advantage of a craze. When antique stickpins became popular 25 years ago—every female had to have one in her lapel—he was there with the new, gold-plated imitations. When the demand was for antique cameos, the genuine ones usually being carved from conch shell or onyx, among other natural substances, he was one of the first to feature the man-made composition cameo. Looking like authentic cameos, but molded from cheap compositions, he mixed them with the genuine ones displayed in his jewelry cases.

His booth was purposely jumbled, especially the several jewelry cases he displayed, to give the customer the impression that this was the ideal place to find a sleeper. Planned that way, and unlike most dealers, he gave no guarantees of what he was selling.

In their eagerness to join the trends, customers flocked around his booth; he seemed to have a fair abundance of what was popular at the time. "How old is this cameo?" a customer may ask, pointing to one in the case.

In the frenzied atmosphere, the dealer replies hastily, "I just bought a lot of this from a very old lady. She had to be ninety-five. What else can I tell you?"

His prices were very negotiable, so if people did not get the genuine article, they had fun bargaining with him while he mumbled and stumbled about the booth, chomping on an unlit cigar, dressed as a country peddler. Jovial, robust and extremely loquacious, he knew how to "put on a show" in his booth. Most people who bought jewelry and antiques from him did not expect total veracity about their purchases. But most went away smiling!

When the turquoise fad first erupted, he was strongly suspected of buying a lot of new Native-American jewelry and burying it into the ground. Later he exhumed it all, dipping them into acids to give them an appearance of oxidation, then scattered them among his cases. They sold fast! Who took time to ask many questions?

Among those not fooled, seeming to have the market cornered, were two sisters who paraded about the shows, each wearing pounds of authentic old Indian jewelry. Having deep tans, their throats, wrists, ears, waists, arms and fingers were all laden in heavy silver jewelry. As they walked up and down the aisles, they literally clanked as they looked to add to their collections, if possible, but mainly to show the world their treasures. Hardly having any bare flesh left to cover, the silver did a wonderfully expensive job of concealing their wrinkles.

Some dealers' manners are so superficial—if not outright naive—it's embarrassing to be in their presence. We know a pair of highly successful dealers (working together) who stop by a few times a year. They don't have a shop, but their exhibits at the antique shows are among the best. Their rule is to never give discounts—so they say.

Stopping by their booth one day, I overheard one of them tell a customer, "We don't spend a lot of our time hunting down antiques to sell them cheaply just for you. This isn't a flea market!"

When they come to our shop, they rarely ask for discounts. However, since our business is largely tailored for dealers' business, we're always prepared to do so.

One of them will pick up an object, look it over and ask, "How much is this, Henry?" Quoting him a dealer's price, he usually ponders a bit, but still retains the item, an indication that he wants to buy it. Expecting this, I offer to take the article from his hand, pretend to perhaps re-evaluate it, then lower the price even more. After which he would say, "Okay! Put that aside for me." This goes on for several items; never does he ask for the lowest price, but he actually does better by not doing so. This is a tacit act we both follow; doing so for too many years to change now.

But we didn't need to, until recently. Times making their changes, it seems that one of the partners has a grandson who has recently joined their firm. Exceedingly knowledgeable about antiques, as many of the younger dealers have become, he was now accompanying them on buying trips.

When the dealer and his grandson recently came into the shop for the first time, I was impressed with the youth's grasp of the business. And that the senior dealer with whom I had been doing business for years, was now asking the young dealer his opinion about most things they considered purchasing.

Picking up an item, the older dealer asked him, "Do you think we can sell this, Jeff?" The grandson, looking over the item carefully and with admiration, asks the price. At my reply he frowned slightly, hesitated and said something like, "We had one of those recently; it didn't move very fast."

At that, the older one said, "Still, I think it will sell. Leave it out for a few minutes, Henry." After an accumulation of several items that were pending a decision, they came to me to go over prices.

When I quoted my lowest prices on each item, the grandson said, (knowing the senior dealer wanted all of them), "Well, we won't get rich on it, but that's okay. We'll make something!"

My ears burned at this retort; I felt the older dealer might be wincing within as much as I was. We both refrained from making a comment, but I knew this was a conduct not to be repeated in the future.

As they left, I called out to them with a smile towards the grandson. "Nice meeting you. I know you won't 'get rich' on the things you bought, but I'll always be happy to help you get there."

As expected, on their next appearance several months later, there was absolutely no repetition of such drama on the part of the grandson.

Over the span of years in the antique profession, even though there may have been dramatic changes in the field, some things remain the same, fortunately. The sleeper is alive and doing well.

In the April 1991 issue of Arts & Antiques, a leading story was told about a dealer who picked up a souvenir spoon at a flea market for $20. The dealer who sold it said he didn't think it was silver, but the buyer had "good feelings" about it.

After much "dogged research," it turned out to be a rare, early-American silver spoon. With diligent effort its authenticity was determined, for which the new owner was offered $20,000 but turned it down. With the spoon picture on the cover of the magazine, incentive increased for dealers as for people in general, who hustled off to flea markets—through fields of mud and rain or of sunshine—and to scour through garage sales, antique shops and shows or wherever else "old stuff" was being sold.

Shortly after this article appeared, a man came into our shop armed with three books on silver spoons and headed for our silver cases. Asking to see our coin silver spoons (we had several), he methodically proceeded to examine each one. Opening one book after the other, with a smirk, he was completely oblivious to us as he "looked up" each spoon. Knowing what to look for, he silently but emphatically rejected each one. Still saying nothing, he gathered his books, shook his head lightly and retained his private thoughts. As he neared the door—without a word of thanks—I called out to him, "Did you happen to hear about the guy who bought a silver spoon for $20 and it turned out to be worth at least $20,000.?" To which he didn't so much as turn back for the smile on my face.

Another sleeper found that commanded the attention of all newspapers that day, happened more recently, where someone bought at a flea market a picture in an old frame, paying $4 for it. Behind the picture they later discovered an original print of the Declaration of Independence. Its estimated worth was over a million dollars.

Harder for some of us older dealers to adjust to was that stage in our business that had taken on what is called "COLLECTIBLES." Probably never heard of thirty years ago or more, I can't remember when they first appeared. The term is used prominently in describing objects not necessarily "old" or legally "antiques," but nonetheless may be very valuable. And very popular!

Major auction houses have exclusive sales on "Collectibles," where each year other such objects have created enough interest to be included in that ever-expanding market.

One very particular,if not snobbish, antique dealer who frequents our shop refuses to handle anything that comes under that classification. He haughtily describes those people who deal in them as "dealers who have run out of antiques and buy and sell anything that's more than a couple of months old."

I well remember when there was so much antique jewelry that we wouldn't be bothered with anything else.

When we first opened our shop in Pompano Beach, we made a house call where we were compelled to buy everything. Included was a collection of over fifty Hummels. This was our first fling at very popular "collectibles."

Collectively, these "kids" looked cute enough, and there aren't too many people who don't like kids. But my difficulty was the concentration on their identifying marks—the clue to their value—for which I purchased a current book. Simple enough, everything seemed to be centered upon a bumble bee.

Bottoms up, I looked for their identification marks and was confronted with bees: half-bees, small bees, full bees, old bees, and all kinds of bees centered in the letter V. I was stung and numb with ennui.

Our wish was to sell them fast. Putting the fifty Hummels in a glass showcase in the front window, they drew more attention than some recently acquired fine Nineteenth century porcelain figurines, which was distressing to me.

People coming in to examine them looked for the bees. Even bee-backs were attracted to them. I understood that the Hummels had to be handled to determine their value, but in the juggling and inspection of them, some became chipped—no one mentioning it.

People apparently find them so lovable that some are stolen. Easy to drop into a purse or a pocket and easier yet to resell to those handling "collectibles," we lost a few.

Loved or despised, either reaction is common. We've been on house calls where we bought valuable antiques and heard the words, "But the Hummels are not for sale." Such a remark might bring sighs of disappointment to some dealers, but it was music to my ears, playing the "Flight of the Bumble Bee."

Whenever anyone comes into the shop and asks, "Do you buy Hummels?" I tend to jump back as if stung and reply thus" "Well ...Hmnnn ...Aaah!

Dania Forever

CHAPTER 36

In the early 1960's, D.S. Clarke, one of the pioneers of the antique show business in South Florida opened a large antique shop on US #1 (the main business highway) near the south end of Ft. Lauderdale. Already a success in promoting antique shows around the country, Mr. Clarke saw the potential of a permanently established center in that area. Together with his wife and a few employees, his shop there became one of high quality, occupying nearly a city block.

Soon thereafter, more dealers congregated to the same location, renting all surrounding available stores; their shops lined both sides of the street for a few blocks, with free parking in front of the stores. When their business immediately flourished in that location, other dealers soon rushed to join the community.

When space was no longer available, they looked to the next community down from Ft. Lauderdale, the small city of Dania. At the time, there were many vacant stores available, also on US #1 and on parallel side streets. Opportunity awaiting the opportunist, within a few months everything was rented and a sign erected at the town's entrance which proclaimed: DANIA! THE ANTIQUES CENTER OF THE SOUTH!

At the time, I was residing in Ft. Lauderdale for the winter, while we exhibited at three antique shows. Noting the feverish activity, we too rented a very small store and erected a sign painted: ANTIQUE JEWELRY.

The first winter there, the crowds were spectacular. Cars honked through traffic jams, side streets overflowed with people and more cars hunted parking places. All the shops had a continuous flow of people weaving in and out of them. Buyers came from everywhere, sellers from the surrounding areas; eye-gotts and bee-backs galore, plus tourists and the curious.

The antique business was indeed coming into its own and making a big impression. The quality and variety of merchandise was excellent, which gave further encouragement to collectors and out-of-state dealers.

Most stores had a back room which several dealers converted into a social area after business hours. Going a step further, a few even made them into living quarters. A small range and a refrigerator, a bed and a few cooking utensils, a curtain or drape to separate business from the living area, a lavatory, a shower stall, soap, toothpaste, and a place for the bird, dog or cat, was more than enough to call "home."

In the early morning, brooms were seen whisking both sides of the street as dealers neatly prepared for the day's invasion of people. In a community spirit, shops often took turns having a cocktail hour after a hectic day with the public. Drapes, curtains and shades would be drawn across storefronts, a "CLOSED" sign signified the beginning of night-life. Several stores developed rather elaborate entertaining quarters and would be magnificently decorated with antiques that were otherwise for sale during business hours. The silver used for dining from that night might have a price tag on it; the Victorian lamps that made the evening so pleasant and cozy were all plainly tagged with their price, as were the couch and chairs that you sat upon. Beautiful oil paintings hung nearby were identified and labeled; and the sparkling crystal punch bowl centered on the table might even have a "SOLD" sign on it.

That first winter was one of fun and festivities, mixed with business exploding with activity. This air of happy economic flurry and congeniality prevailed for a few seasons, but as the congestion from street traffic and pedestrians multiplied, all storefront parking had to be banned, which caused the carnival atmosphere to be lost. For many dealers, the antique business had never been so much fun!

Today, Dania retains its reputation as a convenient one stop antique shopping center, drawing many international customers as well. But most of its original dealers had moved on, of course. Still, a recent newspaper article had proclaimed Dania as being the "Antique Capital of the South," with about 200 dealers. Without checking the facts, that many would seem a sufficient number for a "candles and cocktail party" after hours, as in the "old" days. And the assurance of a prosperous future.

Part III

Walking Canes
And
Hurricanes

Hurricane Andrew

CHAPTER 37

O ur shop-front bench was not only a source to remind us of the past—bringing us the elderly, with or without canes—and giving us an outpost for promoting business, but it was a basis for much laughter. Humor being a natural and important part of our business, this is our style, one that makes the day more pleasurable. A smile can be easier gotten from an individual than getting into his pockets, but the first helps the other.

Our day at the antique shop is one with a relaxed atmosphere. One good house call or a large sale affords us leisure moments in between. From where Arlene sits behind a desk, only a glance outward and she's a witness to many activities to which she might be enticed. Taking a break, she might be out there; other times she saunters out to other shops, chatting and chipping away at the work week.

However, when we get a flurry of business and I have need of her back at the shop, by chance I found an effective medium for signaling her. It was a five-foot long, copper and brass antique stagecoach horn, made in England, the type one might use to announce the arrival of the horse-drawn carriage coming from London to Dover.

Needing her instantly, I dash out of the shop and blow it vigorously, sending out blasts in all directions, which resound loudly throughout the area. From high to low it can never be predicted what note may emit from it, only that it draws attention as it reaches the ears of the one being summoned. At the sound, people hesitate in their tracks, look about, then smile in wonder and disbelief at the someone blowing a long, antique horn. When word spread around from known patrons of the shopping center as to what the horn-blowing was about, the usual comment was, "Oh! There's no trouble. That's the guy who owns the antique shop. It's his way of letting his saleslady know she's wanted back at the store."

Soon enough, Arlene would emerge from somewhere, and slightly embarrassed as she returns to the shop, shaking her head in disapproval, yet smiling and saying to anyone nearby, "That's my boss! He's a nut!" At times, when she's expressed her displeasure of this boisterous method of getting her attention, I would remind her that if the horn somehow "got lost" or put out of commission—since it is not for sale—I would not be too happy.

"People out there love this, Arlene, they've never known anything like it. It's a free show and look at the advertising we get out of it. You know how much good merchandise we've gotten by attracting people in the shop (house calls). Don't you remember that great pair of antique bracelets we got last month by blowing this couple into the shop?" I smiled broadly. "It's made you well-known and me infamous; what's wrong with that?"

The Party

One day in early 1992 a couple came into the shop. Pursuing her usual inquires into their backgrounds, Arlene found someone who knew people in Albuquerque by the same surname as her own. Could they be related? she wondered. In a spontaneous decision she decided to take an early vacation to New Mexico. It soon evolved that they could be cousins. Following a bit of correspondence, this was indeed so, and in the next few months, there was much contact between Arlene and her new-found relatives.

Inspired with this knowledge and the desire to be among relatives, Arlene decided to move out of Florida, after living here for seventeen years, to begin life anew out West. She was at a stage where she needed a change, and the prospect sounded alluring. She seemed to be spiritually and physically directed towards this move, this tremendous challenge. We admired her courage and drive to take on a new venture that people far younger than herself would not consider.

There was no question but that we send her off royally, to gather a group of perhaps thirty people. With a large cake, plenty of good food and drinks, and some singing around the piano, it could make for a jolly party and appropriate farewell.

We scheduled it for a Friday, the 21st of August, at my apartment with its close-in lofty view of the Atlantic Ocean. Included were my two widowed sisters and a niece from Miami, a fifty mile drive away. The party also gave me an opportunity to exhibit some of my private antique collection.

At the same time I had one eye targeted on a "tropical wave" that was brewing a long way off in the Atlantic. Few if any gave it much thought that night. A major hurricane hadn't hit our area of Florida in decades.

As the evening mellowed and I managed to ravage Rachmaninoff, plunder Puccini, violate Verdi and murder Mozart upon piano keys, not to mention the muddling of tunes like "As Time Goes By" and "Melancholy Baby," accompanied by a rambling, resounding mixed chorus, I felt assured that Arlene would not soon forget this party.

My home entertainment having dwindled down in recent years, unexpected compliments came from guests who took note of the antiques and paintings there. I pointed out to more than one person that if it had not been for tooting the horn to hustle Arlene back into the shop, I would never have met some of the people from whom I had acquired a few of these objects of art.

Sufficiently fed and feted, guests all departed, leaving only my family, who were staying for the weekend. Before retiring, I turned on the TV to see "What's going on in the tropics," a once-an-hour update on weather conditions coming off the African coast during the hurricane season.

This being the height of the season and no other hurricane having appeared to date, only the "tropical wave" was being tracked as it came off the African coast. This was a large cloud mass we were following on its path as it built itself up rapidly from a tropical depression into a tropical storm. Before retiring, it had gotten our full attention.

By the next morning, the tropical storm had developed to hurricane strength and was said to be headed due west, directly towards the Bahamas and our heavily populated three-county area.

Preparing dinner for 5 P.M. that evening, Frances, Edith and Kathy were in and out of the TV room that day. Frances, who feared driving in the rain, entered the kitchen to hustle up the meal, exclaiming, "Let's eat and leave. I've been through these things before and with a hurricane, there's going to be a lot of rain before it gets here."

She had in fact been through a couple of hurricanes, having lived in Miami from 1940. She'd often described how all the leaves were stripped from the trees and what a mess was left in its wake. But she hadn't seen anything yet! Little did she or anyone else know what was to come.

The meal was anything but leisurely. Worse yet, there came an intrusion to the anticipated dessert. (Having baked and brought in a blueberry pie for one meal, Edith withdrew to the kitchen to serve up the pie for each of us.) Frances chose that moment to duck into the TV room for the latest check on the hurricane reports. About to take a first bite of the pie, everyone was struck still from the alarm emitting from Frances as she dashed into the dining room, crying out, "That's it! I'm leaving here right now. It's on 'Red Alert.' Let's go!"

Edith, taking the news of the rapidly approaching storm more casually and with fewer comments, was irritated that Frances wanted to leave that minute. The two of them had driven up together. Kathy, my niece, had planned to leave earlier on Sunday evening for work Monday.

During the remaining meal, now being consumed in a highly-strained atmosphere, Frances rose abruptly and said to Edith, "I'm leaving in fifteen minutes. If you want to go with me, fine; I want to get home before dark." Recanting her first statement, after calming down somewhat, she agreed to delay departure for thirty minutes.

I went out on the balcony alone as they, all three, hastily packed. Having a grand view of the ocean from our ninth floor apartment, I could visualize the oncoming storm out there and what havoc it would wreck upon all of us in hi-rise buildings standing proudly along the beach front, north and south, as far as one could see. We had never been tested by a hurricane. Was this the moment of truth? I'm sure the three of them thought about this without mentioning it. They certainly knew that anyone living as close to the ocean as Jane and I would be the first ones advised to evacuate.

Within a half-hour after dinner, Jane and I escorted them to their cars. It was a sunny, pleasant evening and everything appeared perfectly normal. How quickly, how drastically the course of life can change, far too many of us would soon know. The change was on a path just below the horizon.

Jane, having an apartment on the floor below me, had offered to clean up after dinner. We then retired to the TV room to watch the continuous attention paid to this very ominous threat.

The storm, now officially named "Hurricane Andrew," first of the season, was headed straight westward, full-speed towards us. Hurricane warnings were extended from Vero Beach, about 100 miles to the north, to the Florida Keys, far south. Those who entertained any thought that it might change its course, would be vastly mistaken. It was "our turn!" It could be the "Big One!" The question remaining was, who was going to get the worst of it?

The phone rang. It was our friend Ruth, who lived six miles north of us. Alone in her lovely, third-floor condominium, she faced directly upon the Atlantic, very close to the ocean.

"That was Ruth," Jane said. "She was very lucky to get a flight out of here to Chicago and wants to know if we can take her to the airport the first thing in the morning."

I'd often kidded Ruth about her being on the third floor, where from a large balcony, she would certainly have "the best possible view of any hurricane that came pounding ashore." In reply, she would say, "Thanks a lot, kiddo! You can stay here! I'll be gone!" Now, on this rapidly vanishing Saturday night, it was far from a joke.

"I knew that you would have to go the antique shop very early in the morning to put up your storm shutters," Jane said, "so I told her we would call her back, let her know definitely." Within minutes, Ruth phoned back, saying she was fortunate to get a friend in her building to drive her to the airport. Her flight being the last one available, the airport then closing to all traffic.

Out of the present commotion, television pictures of the last days of the Vietnam war entered my mind: of helicopters descending and plucking people from the roof of the embassy. As one 'copter hovered overhead, anyone that could reached out to grasp at other bodies as they were being hauled aboard the aircraft. Some fell off as the planes, thus burdened with refugees, fled the area.

How things had changed within 36 hours; for years, many had remarked on the "big one" that was long overdue in our area.

From a barber's chair the conversation I heard would often center around hurricanes. Someone said, "I wouldn't want to be living in any of those condos on the ocean if they ever get hit directly by a hurricane." Another added, "They've never been through one yet. With all the wind, the flooding, the flying debris, and the storm surge, they could cave right in when the tide hits broadside or the sand beneath them gives away. Nope! I'm glad I live out west a few miles. You can have your ocean front living!" Others sitting around the shop would concur, while those of us living there might shift our thoughts to people living in California, with the ever-present threat of earthquakes, or to people on the Plains, where tornadoes are a way of life. You can't worry too much about it; this comes with the territory. Until it strikes!

"I'm going to be out there at dawn tomorrow," I said to Jane, "to find someone to help me put up all those shutters. It's quite a job and everybody will be running around making their own stores secure."

"If The Ship Sinks, I'm Going Down With It."

On that anything-but-usual Sunday morning, heading for the shop while Jane prepared to evacuate, I cruised the few blocks about the area to see how other business establishments were securing themselves. Our shop faced the ocean, just a block away; and since the Intracoastal waterway was just a block behind us, any storm surge would surely flood the entire area.

By now the media was reporting that the hurricane, increasing in size and speed, was on a direct course for South Florida. Yesterday there were projections that it would not hit until Tuesday; today they were forecasting landfall for the early hours of Monday morning. A day sooner made a lot of difference! The winds were estimated at 150 miles per hour, a major category-4 storm.

Evacuation went as instructed: those living on the beach and seeking refuge from their condos and single-family homes were ordered to go inland. Go west! Anywhere west. Away from the ocean, streets were being rapidly deserted. Roads north were soon bumper-to-bumper on major highways. The early birds, already in Central and North Florida, were snatching up all accommodations available. Motels anywhere west of here, over the Intracoastal and a few miles inland, were taken quickly by carloads of people.

At the shop I hauled out our large shutters. Luckily, Arlene came by to see if I needed help; she scouted the area and was lucky to find a husky young man with the necessary equipment to assist us. Who could wish for anything more?

Arlene, about to move to Albuquerque after seventeen years in Florida, was about to witness a hurricane—wanting to or not. Could there be a more impressive send-off?

Although it was Sunday and our regular maintenance men not expected, they arrived on the scene, to help shop keepers put up their shutters while keeping in mind their own homes to be taken care of when they finished here. Time was winding down with the atmospheric changes coming in.

As we secured our shop's exterior with full-length shutters, from sidewalk to window tops, the ambiance inside took on its own strange appearance. At 10 A.M. in the morning, even with all the lights on, metal shutters blocking out all daylight had the shop taking on the look of night-time. I sat at the desk trying to relax for a few minutes, appraising the situation. But there was little to foresee without previous experience.

So far, all had proceeded rather calmly, but surely there was a measure of anxiety in each person. I thought about all the shops and stores in a three-county area who were taking similar precautions to protect their property and treasures. Most of us, as I, had never experienced a direct path of a hurricane, nor had I one dollar's worth of flood or hurricane insurance for my antiques. With no direct hit for 50 years, few of the shop owners had given much thought to anything like this happening here.

All my jewelry and the best of silver objects now packed into my station wagon to take home, I cleared certain items off the floor, should there be flooding. The rest of the stock would stand or fall; the will was all in the forces of "Andrew."

As I loaded my car, it was still normal outside. Partially blue skies, only now there was a stronger breeze beginning to stir. I made a couple of phone calls from the shop to friends in Utica, New York, describing the eerie feeling rising over the entire area. Telling them this could end up being a great disaster; that there was nothing left to do now but leave. Plenty of warning had been given; the rest was up to each individual.

Nothing further to do concerning the shop, Jane and I had the afternoon to decide whether to ride out the storm in our shuttered apartments, or what? Off and on came swirling rain squalls forewarning those who might disobey evacuation orders. Everyone was being ordered to leave the beach area for their personal safety. Most, it appeared, had done so, as an unfamiliar ghostly desolation was cast over this ordinarily fun-filled stretch of ocean front.

Back at the apartment, we encountered a few of our neighbors loading some emergency supplies into their cars after they had secured their places. By now, whoever hoped to leave would not be able to go far, only away from the ocean, as the highways north were already jammed to capacity.

It was about 1 P.M. when Jane and I rode over to her son's home. We had been invited to stay with him, his wife and two children. But we soon learned that everyone in their area had also been ordered to evacuate. Although they were located about a mile inland from the ocean, it was on a canal that led directly to the ocean. Floods! Winds! High tides! Anything could happen! Looking about, we noticed they had not yet put up any of their shutters for the many windows to be covered.

"Where are Gil and Gilby?" Jane asked.

"You know Gil," her daughter-in-law Patti replied. "he and Gilby are out helping the neighbors put up all their shutters. I don't know when they'll be back." Her daughter, Mandy, was in her room cleaning up just as if it were any normal day.

Jane's son, Gil, being in the construction business and handy with tools, had been out all morning, securing other peoples' homes. "He's not going to leave," said Patti smiling, "but you can still come and stay with us. We're going to ride it out." How many other people had the same mind set could never be determined, but many would have new respect and meaning for that phrase in less than twenty-four hours.

Having made plans to leave my station wagon at a friend's house ten miles inland, we took care of that chore. We now had to decide on what our final action would be; we had Jane's car to use, if necessary.

Returning to our apartment, we saw a few residents of our building still there, disregarding the admonitions of the police and fire departments cruising the area. Knowing that no one could force them to leave, they planned to stay. A few simply had nowhere else to go.

"Let's stay here!" Jane said. "It's getting late in the day and where else can we go anyway?"

"It's okay by me, but what are we going to do with your car?" I asked. Although our apartments had metal shutters on the windows and balconies, any vehicle left behind would most certainly be flooded, if not completely wrecked.

Just then, Jane's phone rang. It was Arlene. Living alone, she had been invited to stay with some mutual friends who lived in Tamarac, an adult community about ten miles inland, certainly far safer. Having already installed herself, she told our friends that we were going to remain in the building. Nancy, who owned the house, got on the phone, "Bring some personal supplies and get yourselves out here immediately," she ordered.

Adding some food and canned water to our personal luggage, we loaded up and within a half hour were on our way down the elevator. We met a neighbor there, a widow, who said with determination that, "no matter what, I'll stay here, even if I go down with the ship!"

Forgetting something, I returned to my apartment; there I took one last look, a studied look around at the curiously quiet, dark and now-forbidding rooms; these rooms and possessions I had lived with and thoroughly enjoyed for fourteen years. Thinking how I had delighted in collecting a lot of valuable antiques and paintings, I was sure my fellow antique dealers were viewing their private possessions with similar feelings, as anyone else about their belongings. My rooms full of treasured objects and a newly-purchased baby-grand piano were all facing an ocean that might soon cause huge violence and destruction to them. And down the street, just three blocks away, my store full of antiques! I pictured a 20 foot storm surge of water sweeping everything away. But getting ourselves out of harm's way came first. The weathermen on TV had been saying: "There's no way this hurricane is not going to hit us directly!" I thought of Hugo, and other storms of the past.

Back down to Jane's car, I met a neighbor who was having words with his wife. He wanted to stay but she insisted they go forty miles south to Miami where she had relatives inland. Some firemen patrolling the area finally convinced them they should leave.

For Jane and me, it was settled. We got into the car and headed out, feeling oddly relieved. There was no confusion to be seen, no panic. Even as we drove over the bridge to the mainland, all was calm as the bridge-tender secured the drawbridge. Looking out the rear-view window at several tall condos, I knew there would be a few individuals in each, weathering out the storm. For everyone, first-hand knowledge of what they might experience just wasn't there, yet they had exciting expectations of the unknown.

With a complete sense of inevitability of a possible calamity, everyone within the same limits suddenly became equal. Along a hundred miles of beach, there was a boundless wealth of homes and condominiums, and within fifteen miles of the ocean, a population of over three million people, all with one main thought: who will get the worst of it? None would know what they might be doing twenty-four hours from now, once the hurricane had forced itself into our lives.

Thousands were in designated shelters, many more like us were invited to stay with friends inland; there was a feeling of safety in numbers. And since at least seventy-five percent of the population had never been through a major hurricane before, there was a feeling of immense excitement. Nothing else mattered for the moment. We were captives!

"At least we get a warning in a hurricane," Jane said on our drive to our friend's home. "In California, an earthquake strikes without warning and in less than a minute or so everything could be gone— possession and lives, both." As we approached the entrances to I-95 and the Florida Turnpike, we were glad we were not on either road. Cars were barely creeping along, all headed northward.

Arriving at Nancy's home, people were still boarding up their homes in this community, with only a few hours of daylight left. Warmly greeted as if it were just another Sunday afternoon, we unloaded our contributions to what we expected would be a few day's stay.

Nancy's friend Ollie was there, a man in his 84th year, who lives in another section of Tamarac, about a mile away. From my home-town in Utica, we'd been friends for over thirty years. He and Nancy were avid card players, and I'd spent many an evening play-ing with them.

Jane, rarely indulging in this kind of pleasure, settled on a couch, and, like most everyone else throughout the region, watched the uninterrupted TV coverage of Hurricane Andrew. Arlene was in another room unpacking a few things; her permanent move to Albuquerque had to be delayed.

After a few hands of Gin-13, Ollie got up and said, "Well, I guess I'll be going before it gets dark."

Not believing what he'd said, I stood up, "What? Where are you going?"

"Home!" he replied.

Ollie was hard of hearing, so I shouted back at him, "What the heck are you going to do at home all alone during the hurricane?" I was so stunned that this was the only comment I could make at the moment.

Since he and Nancy had been close friends for many years, he was accustomed to staying with her.

"Well, I just want to be there if anything happens," he replied.

"Like what?" I immediately countered, still on the defensive.

"If things get shoved around or get out of place or something like that," he calmly replied, putting his cap on. "When I owned the bar way back years ago," he continued, "a hurricane came through and tore my big sign off the building." Apparently, he was recalling the time when he owned a bar and restaurant over twenty-five years ago and had experienced some hurricane damage. So now here was another person who, willing to go it alone, did not want to abandon ship.

I walked out to Nancy; she was shaking her head and said, "I've been trying to convince him to stay but you know how stubborn he is."

"Hey, Ollie," I called out, trying another approach, "this is a big storm and we might need you to push things back in place right here. Since your home is all shuttered up anyway, why go there and sit it out alone? Besides, it's starting to rain now."

He still wasn't convinced, but I wouldn't give in, saying, "Ollie, the reason we came over here is so we could stay up all night during the hurricane and play cards. We won't be able to sleep anyway, and we might have to stay here for a couple of days."

His eyes brightened! There were few things that he loved more than playing cards. I'd known him in another situation similar to this, where out would come a bottle of scotch, a cigar and a couple of decks of cards, and absolutely no thought whatever about not staying up all night. He and I used to frequent many bars in the Sixties in Ft. Lauderdale, especially those that didn't get much action before 10 P.M.

Finally he settled back comfortably, winning the first game easily, after which he got up to stretch a bit. But I noticed Ollie putting on his jacket and cap. Now what? "Where are you going?" I asked him.

"I want to move my car closer to the building, out of the street," he replied. Not moving nearly as fast as he once did, I asked if I could move it for him. The rains had finally begun and so did some swirls of wind. Refusing my request as he stood at the door, he

said, "It'll stop!." But when suddenly it came down harder, he did-
n't budge. "I'll just wait a few minutes," he continued, a picture of
patience.

"Ollie," I laughed, "we might be staying here for three days, waiting. The hurricane has just begun to sweep in."

He didn't reply, only drew back in from the rain and waited. I
went inside and reported this to the others and got the expected
chuckles. Suddenly the squalls eased off, the rain soon stopped, no
doubt part of a forthcoming pattern.

Ollie slowly walked to his car and carefully drove it into the driveway, sandwiching it between two others. "There's going to be a
lot of stuff blowing around," he said, as he looked skyward and
confirmed that it was okay now for things to start up anytime they
wanted.

When Jane came out of the main bathroom, she said to Nancy,
"We forgot to fill the bathtub with water. We're going to need it for
flushing the toilet." Nancy replied, "I didn't forget it. The plug is
too small and it leaks out anyway." Adding, "There's a hardware
store over on Prospect."

We didn't hesitate to meet a need in the idle hours ahead. There
was still a couple of hours before darkness and it took but a few
minutes to get there. Cars were still observed heading for the turnpike. Aside from being outside during a hurricane, the worst possible place to be caught in a frontal assault of 150 mile per hour
winds and rain was in a line of traffic grid-locked on a highway.

There we found a line of last-minute shoppers at the hardware
store. All eyes seemed to be alert with excitement in the impending
threat. There was an air of resignation that Mother Nature would
prevail. Everyone now seemed exceptionally polite and considerate;
on this score, humanity would prevail. The worst of times could
bring out the best in people, and this would soon be proven.

As we waited our turn, three youths, barely in their teens, were
involved in an animated conversation much like that awaiting

Christmas Eve. Anticipating "150 mile per hour winds," they had homes, parents and friends to share this with. In the future they needn't listen to old-timers say, "You don't know the half of it. You've never been in a hurricane." This was a class-4 category, only a step away from the worst. Beat that!

Back at Nancy's house, Jane and I took a walk through the neighborhood. It was now raining only lightly. Weird! We expected torrential rains by now, but Andrew's behavior was less than had been expected—so far. We met a few people strolling about in what seemed to be a pervasive air of "let's get this thing over with!" Strangers smiled and talked and developed a camaraderie under increasing darkness and the sound of an occasional rumble of thunder coming from the east.

About 11 o'clock that Sunday night, after much card playing and the sound of continuous warnings and reports from television, we all went to our respective beds—some make-shift. "This beats any motel," someone called out to Nancy. Sleep came easy enough after an exceptionally long and anxiously busy day. Andrew's landfall was expected near 2 A.M.

I was abruptly awakened! The lights in the kitchen went on and shone in my face. I heard voices and I called out to Jane, who could see what was going on. "It's only 3 o'clock!" she said as she got out of her bed and went into the kitchen. Coming over to me, she said, "You won't believe this, but Nancy is making breakfast for everyone. She says she always gets up at 3 A.M., then goes back to bed." This was an adult community where senior citizens were accused of routines far from normal. Yet we all had expected being awakened by the onslaught of ferocious winds, not the sputtering of bacon and eggs.

Within minutes, all five of us were up. Although we heard winds howling through this structurally well-built house, there was still no hurricane. We opened the front door and could see trees being blown not too strongly in every direction; saw a steady rain, but not exceptionally heavy, and heard some thunder. Turning on the TV, we learned that the hurricane had made landfall.

I looked up at Nancy's wonderfully-sculptured antique Chinese silk rug. It was so large that it hung from one wall, ceiling to floor, and still had a few feet rolled up at the bottom. Her husband had brought it back from China in the Twenties and it was worth thousands. She had an antique French cabinet containing many Oriental ivory objects and still more items of jade and semi-precious stones formed into miniature animals. They were select pieces from the nineteenth century. Was this house—as so many others, I wondered—going to bear up under the hurricane, now presumably upon us? Would the roof come off and expose us and all these beautiful and coveted antiques and furnishings to torrential rains and winds?

Now the lights went out! All power was gone, flashlights came on. Apparently many questions needed answers. Amazingly, we could still chance opening the front door and look out. There was an increasing fury and lightning in the direction of the ocean, where I imagined the pounding surf and high waves rolling into the beach area and up to our condo while flooding everything in the business area only a block away. Would the shutters on the apartment and the antique shop withstand the fierce winds? Would other things blow apart? The crack of thunder and flashes of lightning off in that direction were strengthening that notion.

We were lucky to have had an early breakfast; the only thing left to do was to go back to bed and wait. So far we were safe in this house. Forget the antiques and other possessions! I thought of Jane and knew her mind was on her family, close to the ocean and on a waterway. But she was not the type to mention it now.

Things had to get worse but none of us expressed that thought openly. I suspected and strongly hoped that while we were in the middle of whatever was happening, we were not in danger. Would we be spared again? By all TV appearances, this one had to be the

Big One, but why wasn't it more furious? Although no one was complaining, there were many unanswered questions.

In the next two hours before dawn, we half-dozed and tossed around in our beds, nothing else to do. Although we had no electricity by early daylight, we now knew we had apparently escaped the full impact of Andrew, so we ventured outside and found that the winds and rain had decreased greatly. Looking about, we saw many broken branches, leaves covering cars, but no evidence of anything catastrophic. Was everyone this lucky?

It wasn't long after full daylight had revealed everything on this cloudy, strange Monday morning that the power came back on and our TV set resumed giving sporadic reports from downtown Miami, where the real tragic tale was beginning to unfold to us "safe" ones in Broward County.

When Jane and I decided to cruise around the immediate area and see how everything looked, we got radio reports that immense destruction had struck in South Dade County and the savage-like extent of it was just beginning to unfold and trickle in. But here, there was only light wind damage—some broken windows, a few power lines down, some trees toppled, signs ripped apart—but no houses or buildings suffered any great damage. Except for one or two cars out there, the area was totally deserted. We went back to Nancy's for coffee, freshly made and greatly appreciated.

Jane was relieved when she phoned her son's home and discovered they too had been spared from any catastrophe. We then decided to head for home. The closer we approached the waterfront, the more it was evident that we were indeed fortunate.

Aftermath

From our apartments, one then the other, we opened the shutters; looking out from the heights, we saw mounds of sand drifts and refuse strewn all along the beach-front and into the road just below our condo building, all of which gave evidence that the water had come up that far.

The extent of the total damage elsewhere, however, grew by the minute as TV reported the destruction of Homestead in South Dade County and areas west of Miami. Getting in touch with Edith (France's and Kathy's phones "out"), she was pleased to report that her apartment had escaped any damage (surrounded as in a beehive with other apartments), but she was still shaken by the harsh experience and events unfolding in the aftermath.

Not until a day later, when roads became passable and more phones were restored, could Edith learn and relay to me what had occurred at France's residence. While her house had been somewhat damaged, it was her forest of trees, the biggest of them, that had ferociously toppled over. Crashing all about her, she had spent the three fiercest hours sitting frightened in a tiny closet, praying as she heard each tree being uprooted, thumping to the ground. Luckily, her largest tree, a very old Banyan and one she loved, fell in a direction away from her, sparing her.

Kathy's house was mostly water damaged—roof partially ripped off. She and her family—dog included—spent the few hours in terror, going from room to room.

With their power out for several days, Kathy and Frances would move in and stay with Edith for nearly two weeks.

Over the next few days, it was established that Andrew had caused the most destruction of any natural disaster ever to strike this country, causing losses of well over 20 billion dollars.

President Bush took a trip to South Florida, particularly to Homestead and Florida City, the next afternoon —both largely leveled. Still maintaining its speed of 150 miles per hour, Hurricane Andrew sped on towards Louisiana, where another billion dollars in damages was to be inflicted. While 52 deaths had been attributed to Andrew, and over 60,000 homes destroyed, and 250,000 left homeless, the entire population of South Florida would view all future hurricane seasons with far greater respect and trepidation.

All roads south, thereafter, were heavy with traffic giving aid to those stranded in the worst-hit regions. And although others were advised not to attempt driving into the devastated areas, Jane and I did just that, as many others did in their anxiety to see about family and friends. Unable to see my family yet, we spent the whole day viewing the absolute destruction that we hoped would never happen to us. We, who lived fifty miles north of the hurricane's center, were but a mere speck away as viewed from above—yet spared.

When we opened the shop two days later, less for business than to restore a semblance of normality, the shock of all that had happened to other regions was permeating the air. Friends came in to relate their personal experiences, all of whom had connections to someone in South Florida.

First on the scene was our friend Jim, the eighty-five year old gentleman who lived by himself two blocks from the shop, next to the Intracoastal.

"People kept coming by to tell me to get off the beach," he said, "and I kept telling them I was leaving any minute." He laughed, continuing, "I put up the storm shutters, had a couple of scotches, and went to bed and slept through most of it."

Next, his lady friend Ida came in to report on her family. Her son, a career Air Force man, had a house in Homestead. He, his wife and two children left there to ride out the storm with his mother in Pompano Beach. Lucky they were indeed! Their home had been demolished as were so many others in that city. "I had to laugh," Jim said, "the three-year old boy kept telling everyone, over and over, 'my house broke.'" There were many like them, who could never return to their homes.

Sooner than expected, we had returned to the capricious nature of the antique business. In a little more than a week, it appeared that the vultures were circling the area. There seemed to be more jewelry and antique buyers than ever advertising in the local papers. Ads ran from full page down to the classified lines. Even in a three county area with over three million people, that seemed excessive.

What were people thinking? Were buyers expecting a mass exodus of people from the region and hoped to be on hand when they unloaded their treasures in haste? The fact was, with August and September being the slowest business season in Florida, newspapers were offering big discounts to their advertisers. Taking advantage of it, as we always did, it could easily be misconstrued, just after Andrew, as an act of greed or opportunity in a time of great tragedy. Undoubtedly, many began to look at material things, especially valuable and fragile antiques, as of low priority in the face of a 150 mile per hour hurricane's destructive force about to sweep into their lives.

As antique dealers drifted back to our shop, we heard of a few dealers who had been wiped out entirely. More than one of them had tried to take with them half their shop as the hurricane approached.

One dealer near seventy-nine, more active than ever, who throughout his life had filled his large old home with choice antiques, boarded it up and "remained with the ship." He had chosen to go out in grandiose style, should it be so. And, immediately after the storm, he discussed the idea of selling most of his personal antique treasures and moving into a condominium.

The eye of the hurricane having passed overhead with its fiercest winds, his fine old house had withstood the forces gallantly. But his beautiful, ages-old flora having been ripped apart, had him seeing everything in a new light.

But, two months later he had eased back to normalcy and several months later wouldn't dream of giving up the luxury of his well structured house of the Thirties that had already proven to be "hurricane resistant." Moreover, the flora could be easily replaced.

We soon noticed an influx of new dealers into the shop; some not taking a subtle route, but asking outright: "Are people selling their antiques now, because of the hurricane?" I answered truthfully, "No! Not really!"

The one surprising exception came from one of the steady bench-sitters, who spends at least three hours weekly sitting out there chatting with the regulars. He was never seen without his favorite cane, a most unique antique walking stick. Its head was of amber, carved into a slim-shaped werewolf, with beady red eyes of garnet. It became his conversation piece amongst a "house full of antiques," something he would "never sell." He was one of those who had great fun telling dealers he wouldn't sell any of his antiques, but would "let the kids fight over them."

Since he was so familiar a figure about the shop, I felt as comfortable kidding him about his possessions as he did in tantalizing the dealers about them. I had long since given up on him as a prospective source for procuring any merchandise. Eager and ready sellers were always at hand.

"Look, Mr. Eyegott," I'd often said to him, "I don't want to buy your antiques. Give them to your kids to sell some day. Of course, they won't get offers as good as you would. You know their real value. They'll be in such a hurry to sell the condo and get whatever money from its contents as well, plus everything in the banks, that only a small part of their value will be realized. You know how that is!" That usually produced the desired effect when truth struck. He wiped away his perpetual grin of complacent affluence.

So it was to my amazement one day when he came, not to the bench as was his habit, but directly into the shop. "Henry," he said forthrightly, "my wife and I have decided to move back to the Chicago area; we want you to come over to the house and look at some antiques we are considering selling." His unusual solemnness stunned me, but I hurriedly made an appointment.

Yet more astonishing was the readiness with which he dismissed my suggestion that "they might want to leave the sterling silver to the kids." Brandishing his cane high, the werewolf's head with its bared teeth stressing the point, and he epitomizing the character as I'd often perceived, he blasted back, "Naw! They wouldn't want to polish it anyway."

It was then that his wife muttered, "What, with the hurricanes and all, what's the sense of keeping a lot of things we never use?" So it seemed that Hurricane Andrew had stirred up motivations not anticipated; and who knew when, where, or how his repercussions would affect someone.

Along with purchasing some of his antiques—relatives getting "wind" of their decision to dispose of things and hurrying down in a large van to whisk away the major portion—I was fortunate in buying his trademark, the werewolf walking stick.

Kiddingly, I'd said to him, "We'll miss not seeing you out on the bench after so many years, Mr. Eyegott. You ought to sell me that cane. It'll give me something to remember you by."

"Why not, Henry!" he said, much to my surprise. "I've got others!"

"I'll never sell it, Mr. Eyegott," I assured him, and with those words I emphatically traded places with him. The antics of the antique dealer had surfaced.

When within two weeks after the hurricane many of our regular dealers began appearing, we knew for sure things were back to normal. The swiftness of their return made an incredible impression on me when the dealers we referred to as "Chips" were back on the scene.

Handling a cut glass water pitcher we recently purchased, the husband of the team was already scrutinizing it as closely as ever, if not more so. Into the sunlight that filtered through the window of the shop, he turned the object in every direction. Completely oblivious to others nearby, he squinted his eyes, contorted his body and rubbed his fingers over every single facet until he let out, "There it is! There's a chip right there. It has to be ground down. It's not perfect!" His face beamed with success while his wife bestowed him with her customary smile.

Were things back to normal? Only two weeks after experiencing Andrew's destruction and seeing complete devastation not too far from here, I couldn't believe the return of such trifles. Were the three of us being reduced to chatter about a few invisible chips on a single piece of cut glass? I couldn't say anything; more likely I was numbed in disbelief. Where so many had lost everything, and where we were concerned that it could likely have happened to us, how was I expected to focus my eyes on a couple of tiny flaws in a single crystal piece? For a few moments I couldn't reply, but when I returned to reality, I heard myself uttering, "You're right! It's chipped!"

A little later, two regular dealers came in and went through their usual routine, casual as ever. The wife clutched an oversized binder-checkbook under her arm as customary, showing everyone that she was ready to buy. Walking about the shop, one called to the other when something interesting was found. Two heads together, they went into surreptitious and intense discussion of an object: hushed whispers, passing the item to each other, murmuring. At times I wondered what incredible sleeper they might have discovered, right under my nose.

At last they reached a tacit, mutual agreement. The object having survived every conceivable criteria for its possible purchase, one of them turned to me and asked, "What's your best price on this silver pickle spear, Henry?"

Such important decisions!

Such a business!

Such a life!

The "Upright"

CHAPTER 38

Will wonders never cease! Approaching a half century of dealing in antiques, I thought I had learned every trick of the trade. But, it seemed, new ideas were just waiting to get their grip on me. The antique shop identified for its "bench out front" was to be accompanied by a bench inside.

How coincidental! Only a few days after we had seen the movie "The Piano." I made a house call to purchase some antiques. It was there that my eyes were drawn to a sturdy-looking upright piano.

"Would you play something?" I asked the young man who was selling the home and some of its contents. Surely he would allow me a test of its sound. Off in the living room, there was also a concert Steinway.

Walking over to the upright, his fingers masterfully played some Chopin, such as to be envied by many. Praising his dexterity, I ran my fingers over the keys, noting their exceptional tone, a Baldwin about forty years old. He gestured that I try it, so I did a bit of LaBoheme, mainly to compare it with my baby-grand at home.

"Nice tone and resonance," I commented, in which instant my mind pictured a place for it. Where else but in our antique shop!

"It's for sale," he laconically replied, "but not the Steinway, of course."

But where would I place it? How was I going to squeeze it into our already over-crowded shop would have to be worked out. Yet I knew this was an opportunity to do what I had often thought about for years, and I wondered why I hadn't done it sooner.

Making a hasty agreement over the price, the next day the piano was delivered to our shop. With much re-juggling of antiques and fixtures, we found the ideal location for the oak-finished upright.

A place was found near the side window, not far from the front door, which is open to the outside most of the year. Located as we are at street level, centered in a busy pedestrian area of our shopping center, we easily captured shoppers' attention. Refrains of "Chopsticks" by a young girl would flow out into the ocean breezes. Like the piano in the movie (by the same name) as it stood stranded on a wild beach in New Zealand where it overlooked the Pacific Ocean, if we rolled out our own upright (for whatever reason) just several yards out, so could it also rest under a tropical tree close to the Atlantic Ocean.

Any customer looking interested was invited to perform. Their first reaction, "Nice tone!" was my opinion. Thereafter, the most frequent question was, "How much is the piano?"

My reply to everyone, "Not for sale! But you're welcome to sit down and play."

"I wish I could play," came the common response from most people.

"Well, sing then! Entertain us." To which, if I or anyone else was playing, many bravely rendered a few phrases vocally.

In the initial days we became what seemed like a transition from an antique shop into a miniature concert hall. Where previously the shop had been only a scene of haggling between antique dealers and customers, it now took on the airs of a music hall, as well.

To the strains of a popular Puccini aria I was playing at the piano, a stranger ventured into the shop and in less than two steps of preparation, performed a superb tenor rendition of the piece. With the magnetic range of his voice drifting into the air, like food aromas attract other senses, so did his musical talent allure people and bring them to the open door to see what was going on.

When the singer told us he was visiting from Italy, I said, "Stop by anytime and we'll do something from Pagliacci next." No business was done here in those minutes, but it gave people plenty of smiles.

A German couple walked into the shop one day. His wife was interested in an antique necklace—our saleslady, Flavia, eagerly assisting her. As the man browsed, I encouraged him by word and gesture to perform at the piano whatever he liked. He seemed pleased to exercise his talents, to be briefly relieved of the boredom of shopping. In no rush to leave the shop now, the husband was thoroughly enjoying himself. With an occasional apology for being "not so good," the gentleman happily played on while a $650 necklace was being sold to his wife. The upright was about to pay for itself.

After his wife admiringly admonished him for filling our ears with a less-than perfect performance, appreciatively we praised him for having taken the "American tour" and hoped that we had contributed towards the idea that the United States—Florida in particular—was not just the land of cowboys, guns and robbers.

One Saturday morning a man walked in with his teen-age son. As they looked over our paintings, I recognized their conversation as Russian. (I had briefly studied Russian in college after World War II, speculating at the time that, if things were to turn out badly with the Soviets, as forecast, I might get a better "job" than one as an infantryman.) With the man and son, I was able to communicate enough to realize they were especially interested in one oil painting.

I wrote down my price on a piece of paper, over which they spoke a few words to each and headed for the door. It was then when the father noticed the upright; hesitating, he ran a finger over the keys. I mentioned Rachmaninoff, and in Russian, motioned for him to "Sit, please."

Excellent was the word for his playing, rendered with much gusto, although I did not recognize the music. After a few minutes, they thanked me and walked back to the painting, mumbling quietly to each other. Nodding their heads, they walked out.

I was mildly astonished the next morning when the Russian gent returned, bringing with him another man and woman. He asked to examine the painting, then the three of them went into a discussion. By their language, Flavia, standing nearby, detected some French, which she spoke fluently.

The rest was easy. The two women interpreted everything. The woman's husband, a Lithuanian, jotted down $1200 on a scrap of paper, the price the Russian would pay for the picture. But, in English, the deal still came down to "What's your best price?" as the Russian paid off in American dollars.

The minute they left, I sat down to the Hamilton upright (built by Baldwin) and played "Getting To Know You" from The King and I. An international affair, all the above was going on in a dusty antique shop off an Atlantic Ocean beach.

Every day thereafter, the upright was fingered by someone, if only for a few misguided notes. People the world over are drawn to a piano. There was no doubt that we at the shop had established a unique, informal relationship with those who come here to buy, sell or just browse.

I truthfully told a twelve-year old girl that her performance was by far the best treatment this upright had received from someone so young. She and her family (tourists all) escaping especially frigid Minnesota temperatures, were pleasantly surprised that a stranger would encourage her to "Sit down and practice, or play something."

Others, of those talented, were two young ladies. Vacationing from Canada, they clearly gave us, in their 30-minute concert, their renditions of Chopin, of Broadway melodies, and of modern Rock with professionalism. It was worth a price. So I gave them two antique pieces of silver plate that could be better identified with the application of a good silver polish and a measure of elbow grease. Dents and monograms were included.

For young children, the upright became a toy by which they could amuse themselves while their parents browsed.

And there were times when the music overflowing into the street attracted the unfortunate. One such unshaven, down-on-his-luck young man came in and pounded away at several melodies, obviously talented. He had been a musician with a band. After asking if I could "loan" him a few dollars, he departed. As in the opera Tosca, anything for art's sake.

By far, from most who are asked to "feel free to express your talents," comes the reply, "Oh! No! It's been years. I was a young girl" (or boy). Who knows how many youngsters had been encouraged or forced to take piano lessons, then given up, only to regret it years later. Yet these are the ones who commonly come into the shop, who enjoy the singing and the playing. Unexpectedly, they blend in with our business sales and purchases. After all, if we can't take the excessive commercialism out of times like Christmas, every year, we can do it daily in our shop, and make our work more fun while shopping here becomes a pleasure.

So it goes, to date, the upright remains a permanent fixture in our shop, to which we invite anyone desiring to express their talents. The upright's presence in the shop's relaxed, extraordinary atmosphere has resulted in business from sources as diverse as the antiques there and from individuals just as unique. Whether its Beethoven or Boogie flowing out in refrains, antique dealers might do well to have an upright in their shops. One that's not for sale!

EPILOGUE

When the time came to renew our three-year lease on the shop, I signed it promptly. Antique dealers don't retire! Our benefits come in the daily routine of frequent, pleasant surprises. For some of us, our pensions were sacrificed the day we disappointed our parents by abandoning the struggle and security of scholastic endeavors—had we the opportunity to begin with.

We have enrolled in a profession that is as honorable as its students make it. We enter a world of dusty, musty, but desirous objects, smiling at those who are scornful, happy with those who are pleased. We can strike out at nearly any age. Forty years in the business and still going strong. Like a battery-powered bunny, one challenge after another keeps us going.

On my annual fall visit to upstate New York, I like driving through residential neighborhoods. Where I see an old home in a quaint village and someone raking leaves, I have the irresistible urge to jump from my car and ask if they have any old jewelry or antiques to sell. Yes! It's the instinct of the house call addict.

Better to leave it to the younger generations. Keep the game going! One wonders if there will be any antiques left for future generations. Of course there will, but at what prices?

Things are changing in the business. The fat, excessive Eighties have given space to what I see as the Narrow Nineties. Did the arts and antiques have it good from 1980 to 1990? You bet! That's when the field really expanded. And in the early 1990's there was a tightening of the belt, as there was in most industries and businesses. The later half of the Nineties have shown still more interest in antiques universally.

The future is brilliant with innovations. But as the young dealer, who recently came into the shop, thought that a four foot long lady's gold Victorian watch chain was a belt of some kind, so, too, are we ignorant of the many objects featured in the Antiques and Collectibles Shows of the 1990's.

Like in the late Seventies, the surge of international dealers to our shores in search of antiques will undoubtedly continue. The most important single advancement in the antique business in the last several years has been the appearance of foreign dealers from all over the world, returning from here a lot of antiques nearer their place of origin. Having witnessed some of the artistic seduction of Europe by Americans after World War II, I found it amusing to watch the international dealers. By reverse circumstances, they not only are succeeding in hauling back a lot of antique treasures to various nations, but they have equaled and surpassed the American dealer in plain, down-to-earth haggling.

Around the globe from one country to another there's an unimaginable volume of antiques, whether available for purchasing or not, from which a portion will emerge daily, year after year. Antiques to adorn the human form or to enhance a dwelling or an edifice—structures from cottages to castles to cathedrals.

Antiques are passed on to new owners—purchased or inherited—some are out of sight for decades (stored, hoarded, stolen, forgotten). What's sold today will be tomorrow's treasure for a future generation. Value, beauty, rarity, pride of ownership and sharing with others, their appeal will always be the driving incentive for their acquisition.

There will always be someone to acquire an antique—at a show, shop, auction, flea market—scrutinizing it, wanting to possess it more each second and finally asking the dealer, "What's your best price?"

And, with the perpetuity of antiques, there will forever be the enthusiastic couple dashing into the antique shop or show. They burst with energy and desire to possess an object, but leave without buying anything, though faithfully promising to "bee-back." Another person to appear wherever antiques are exhibited and not to be upstaged, gleefully notes each object with pupils dilated to the size of silver dollars, who squeals with delight. "Eye-gott" the same . . . !" 'Till the end of time, will any antique dealer be spared those immortal words from the customer who exclaims: "Oh! My grandmother had one just like that?"

Not to be outdone, the Queen of all garage sales, Mourning Marie, has reportedly updated her image. With a shining new van and a designer's wardrobe of the day, she no longer needs the mask of somber and melancholy grief. With the latest in computerized gadgetry, she has a head start each morning, using the software and the hardware of the "Nifty Nineties" to maintain a complete file on every garage and estate sale in three counties—if not a direct hookup to the dailies' obituary columns.

She has my number, I'm sure.

Like so many of my customers, I've been hanging on to my personal antiques far too long. I have a well-founded suspicion that my fellow associates in the antique profession—even those just a couple of months younger than myself—cast their eyes upon me with thoughts of my demise: "How are you today, Henry?"

"Fine! Thank you!"

A year ago, we took a trip to the Grand Canyon and Las Vegas. While in that city, we visited Liberace's Museum. Among his fabulous collection of jewelry, of antique pianos and automobiles, there was a separate room for what the museum's brochure listed at his most "priceless treasure," the fabulous Louis XV desk that belonged to Tzar Nicholas II.

This desk was the same we saw and examined while visiting Mrs. Wilson's home that Christmas Day in the early Sixties, which resulted in one of the most monumental house calls a collector could ever make.

Even after his death and the auction of many of his antiques, apparently the estate has felt that the desk should not be sold, but kept for the pleasure of generations to enjoy.

As for my most prized possession, the "Tiffany necklace," now is probably the time for it to surface after thirty-five years of seclusion in my possession. An oft-forgotten wonderful acquisition, it has been both a pleasure and enigma to own. With the imprint in the original box: TIFFANY & CIE—36B15 Avenue De L'Opera—Paris, its place of sale is clearly defined. However, because of the small and thus-far indiscernible maker's marks, the artist is still a mystery. With a French hallmark, it is in the style of Rene Lalique—who lived "around the corner" of that address about that time. Of superb enameling and craftsmanship, it is the quintessential example of French ingenuity of the Art Nouveau period, and certainly of museum quality. Names being all important in determining the value of rare antique objects, ascertaining a price for the necklace has only led to further intrigue. Solving the puzzle is the present challenge.

Such is the lot of antique dealers and collectors. We deplore having to part with certain items, often setting aside objects that we say are "not for sale,"—to the annoyance of dealers and public, alike. Whether of immense or minimal value, there should always be something in every antique shop that is not held hostage to that indomitable, unavoidable question: "What's your best price?"

The End